DEATH AND AFTER-LIFE
IN THE THEOLOGIES OF KARL BARTH AND JOHN HICK

AMSTERDAM STUDIES
IN THEOLOGY

VOLUME V

KEITH RANDALL SCHMITT

DEATH AND AFTER-LIFE
IN THE THEOLOGIES OF KARL BARTH AND JOHN HICK
A Comparative Study

AMSTERDAM 1985

CIP-GEGEVENS KONINKLIJKE BIBLIOTHEEK, DEN HAAG

Schmitt, Keith Randall

Death and after-life in the theologies of Karl Barth and
John Hick : a comparative study / Keith Randall Schmitt.
— Amsterdam : Rodopi. — (Amsterdam studies in theology,
ISSN 0169-0272 ; vol. 5)
Met bibliogr., index. — Met samenvatting in het
Nederlands.
ISBN 90-6203-528-0
SISO 251.36 UDC 236
Trefw.: Barth, Karl / Hick, John / eschatologie.
©Editions Rodopi B.V., Amsterdam 1985
Printed in The Netherlands

TABLE OF CONTENTS

CHAPTER IV.   A COMPARISON AND CONTRAST OF BARTH AND HICK

CHAPTER I

INTRODUCTION

The Subject

During the Middle Ages death was often portrayed as the Grim Reaper. Indeed the Grim Reaper struck fear in the lives of all. People dreaded him and wondered who his next harvest might be.

Times have changed. The Grim Reaper no longer incites the fear which he once did--and with good reason! Tremendous advances have been accomplished by medical science in terms of life expectancy. During the Stone Age the average life expectancy was perhaps eighteen years, and, since death generally came through some human or animal enemy, death was rarely the result of natural causes.[1] At the time of Jesus Christ the average life expectancy was still only twenty years. By 1850 the average life expectancy had doubled to forty, and in 1965 it had reached seventy-five.[2] In Germany the average life expectancy between 1900 and 1970 has more than doubled from thirty-four to seventy--even allowing for the decimation of two world wars![3]

Because of the dramatic increase in life expectancy, particularly during the last century, modern man has been lulled into a benign neglect of the issues raised by death. In polite conversation one would not refer to topics related to death, much like the Victorian, nineteenth century refrained from matters of human sexuality. The impetus is coming now from several directions to reverse this benign neglect.

We note this impetus first in the fact that the Grim Reaper continues his harvest. The harvest may be delayed, but it is inevitable. Everyone faces the unavoidable fact that his life on earth will at some moment end or be terminated. This realization inevitably prompts reflection upon death and after-life.

Second we note that the behavioral sciences in particular have prompted additional reflection upon death and after-life. Elisabeth Kübler-Ross, a psychiatrist in Chicago writing of her experiences, first prompted attention to the "plight" of the

1

dying. Our benign neglect of death and those who are dying inflicted needless pain both upon the dying and upon our culture. Since her initial writings Kübler-Ross has focused attention more upon death and after-life than dying per se. Her work in this latter regard has found considerable support in the writings of Raymond Moody, a medical doctor who also holds a doctorate in philosophy. Both Kübler-Ross and Moody have reflected upon death and after-life utilizing non-Western traditions. Moody in particular makes considerable reference to the *Tibetan Book of the Dead*.[4] In any event the popularity of the work of Kübler-Ross and Moody prompts reflection upon death and after-life.

Third we note that the medical and legal professions have prompted reflection upon the phenomenon of death. Modern medicine has been able to prolong "life" and postpone death through the use of life-support systems. The medical profession is premised upon the tenet that death is accursed and/or to be avoided. But to many within and without the field of medicine the artificial prolongation of life seems worse than death. Medicine has therefore coerced the legal profession in particular to examine the issue of death.

Even apart from these more secular reasons for this study there is, fourth, the fact that our faith seeks for understanding. Death and after-life are matters of faith. How we interpret death and how we understand what transpires in death and after-life is a matter of no little concern, indeed a matter of the greatest concern. Our faith seeks to understand these matters, and therefore this provides a fourth impetus for our study.

We thus note that several forces join to prompt reflection upon death. Three questions continue to abound regarding death. *What is the cause and significance of death? What happens to the individual in death? What happens after life?* The questions are ancient, and though there has been a hiatus in concentration upon these questions, our day and age is being impelled and at points compelled to address these perennial questions.

The Response

It is the purpose of this study to examine the responses which Karl Barth and John Hick, two major theologians of the twentieth century, have made to these three enduring questions. Our primary concentration will be upon the theological issues involved, but we will not limit ourselves exclusively to these issues since our investigation has ramifications in other realms, and these other areas prompt our reflection.

Karl Barth is the first of the theologians to which we will direct our attention. When one contemplates twentieth-century theology one invariably will direct attention to Barth. In fact in any discussion of a theological issue in the twentieth century it is more difficult to defend omitting reference to Barth than it is to defend his inclusion, so extensive has been his influence. It seems natural, therefore, for us to study Barth in regard to our three ancient, yet modern questions. Yet it is not only because Barth is the leading theologian of the twentieth century that we cite him for our study. Barth has been referred to as neoorthodox, and our study of his writings regarding our three questions will demonstrate that Barth is orthodox yet not afraid to break with orthodox views where the Word of God directs him to. Barth has given innovative and perspicacious response to the three perennial questions which are the foci of our investigation, and that is the primary reason for our focus upon him.

Barth's life involved a circle of sorts in that he was born in Basle, Switzerland, in 1886, and it was there that he died in 1968. From Basle the family moved to Bern, where his father Fritz taught on the theological faculty of the university. Bern is also where Barth began his university training, then subsequently studying in Berlin, Tübingen, and Marburg. In 1909 Barth became an assistant pastor in Geneva, and two years later the pastor of the parish of Safenwil, where he remained for ten years. It was during his pastorate there that Barth wrote his commentary *The Epistle to the Romans*, the first edition appearing in 1919 and a second, fully revised edition in 1922. These works elevated Barth into prominence, and in 1921 he began teaching with the theological faculty at the University of Göttingen. In 1925 he moved to Münster and in 1930 to the University of Bonn. Barth lost his position at Bonn in 1935, due largely to his critique of national socialism. Thus it was that Barth returned to his hometown of Basle where he continued to teach until his retirement in 1962.

Due to the epic-making character of his commentary *The Epistle to the Romans*, in particular the second edition of 1922 which initiated a new stage in the history of theological investigation, it is appropriate to begin our examination of Barth's response to our three questions at that point. But the reason for our focus goes beyond the prominence of the work in general. As we will note, death plays a significant role in Barth's understanding and interpretation of this Pauline epistle. The notion of death recurs throughout the work and provides answers to our three questions or foci.

In 1923 Barth dedicated time to a study of 1 Corinthians with especial attention being focused upon chapter 15. This study was eventually published in English as *The Resurrection of the Dead*. We shall also accord it our attention for the subject at hand since any reflection upon 1 Corinthians 15 bearing the title *The Resurrection of the Dead* must have pertinence for our study.

In 1935 Barth had found himself in transition. As a result of his outspoken criticism of the German government, Barth was restricted from public speaking. Eventually he was dismissed from Bonn, and within three days he was invited to a special chair at the University of Basle. But prior to his formal dismissal from Bonn Barth was invited by the University of Utrecht in the Netherlands to deliver a series of lectures. This Barth did, and these lectures were published in the book *Credo*. They are of peculiar interest to our study not only because they present us with "the surprising interlude" but because they also evidence numerous points of agreement with both Barth's earlier and later writings in regard to our subject. They also enable us better to interpret the later writings of Barth.

It is in the *Church Dogmatics*, his magnum opus, that Barth provides the most explicit and detailed response to the questions we raise. Primarily it will be *Volume III/2*, which was published in 1945, which will draw our attention, though other volumes of the *Church Dogmatics* as well as the works *The Faith of the Church*, *Dogmatics in Outline*, and *The Humanity of God* will also receive attention at appropriate points. We will note in this particular section how Barth discusses man in the three dimensions of space and also in the fourth dimension of time. In conclusion to our study of Barth we will speculate upon the conclusions which Barth himself might have reached had he had opportunity to bring his *Church Dogmatics* to completion.

Furthermore we note that whenever an investigation is made in one field there are implications for others fields. Our study of Barth will focus upon the response he offers to these three ancient and basic questions. But there will be implication in other realms. Most especially there will be ramification for other questions which have been asked concerning the theology of Barth, though it must be borne in mind that such comments will be ancillary to our primary subject and furthermore must be viewed as tentative since our primary subject is a limited and specific field of study within the thought of Barth. With these qualifications in mind, however, we feel that reflections upon such secondary topics to our study will be of value and interest in gaining a better appreciation and understanding of Barth.

John Hick is the second theologian to which we will direct our attention. He is of much more recent vintage than Barth, having been born in 1922, the year in which Barth published his second edition of *The Epistle to the Romans*. Educated at Edinburgh, Oxford, and Cambridge Universities, Hick was ordained in the Presbyterian Church of England in 1953 and served as minister of the Belford Presbyterian Church in Northumberland from 1953 to 1956. From there he crossed the Atlantic to teach philosophy at Cornell University in New York from 1956 to 1959 and subsequently from 1959 to 1964 at Princeton Theological Seminary in New Jersey. He then returned to England and became a professor of theology at the University of Birmingham. Hick has characterized Birmingham as "a multiracial, multicultural, and multifaith city."[5] During his tenure in Birmingham Hick also spent three study leaves totaling nearly a year in Hindu India and Buddhist Sri Lanka. His exposure to other cultures, especially the East, has profoundly influenced Hick. Since 1979 Hick has been serving as Danforth Professor in the Department of

Religion at the Claremont Graduate School in California.

Hick exemplifies an Anglo-American, empirical heritage spiced with exposure to the East. It is this which makes an investigation of him regarding our three foci of such interest and merit. While others have speculated of it, in a critical manner Hick has fashioned a global eschatology. Hick contends that his conclusions are consistent with Christianity and the Eastern religious traditions, especially Hinduism and Buddhism. This, of course, agrees in part with the conclusions suggested by Raymond Moody. Hick accordingly exercises a strong appeal for those with empirical predilections as well as those who advocate a global, ecumenical, and/or interfaith theology. He is *a*, if not *the*, leader within this range of response to our three questions.

Three books will prove the primary sources of our discussion from Hick--*Faith and Knowledge*, the second edition of 1966; *Evil and the God of Love*, published in 1966; and *Death and Eternal Life*, Hick's magnum opus on the subject which was published in 1976. In addition we will cite various articles of Hick where these are pertinent and relevant. These will provide us with an illuminating, stimulating, and clear contrast to Barth.

Anyone vaguely familiar with the works of Barth and Hick will readily recognize the great disparity which distinguishes them. One might well accordingly ask what justifies a comparative study of two such different individuals. In fact there are several justifications for such an endeavor.

First it is this very disparity which provides reason for comparison. Differences can help to illuminate and clarify positions adopted. Thus the fact that Barth and Hick do differ provides rationale for a comparative study of these two men.

Furthermore both Barth and Hick invite and incite such a comparative study. Perhaps no theologian has been disinclined to comparison with others, but Barth and Hick clearly encourage such a venture. During the course of his career Barth had vigorous disputes with colleagues who both supported and challenged his views. Emil Brunner, for example, was early associated with Barth but later was in marked disagreement with him. After thirty years in which they avoided face-to-face encounter, Barth and Brunner again faced each other in what Barth referred to as a meeting of "the elephant and the whale,"[6] two great creatures from different realms. Barth encouraged reflection upon differences and similarities of view in his own day, even when the participants were from vastly different realms, and undoubtedly Barth would advocate the same today. Hick likewise encourages comparison of views. Indeed, as we will note, Hick regularly analyzes and compares traditions and views to ascertain the essential elements within them. At one point Hick even analyzes positions of Barth and attempts to utilize them in building up his own views. This fact further serves to justify this comparative study of Barth and Hick. To be sure both Barth and Hick encourage a comparative study such as ours.

A third reason why a comparative study of Barth and Hick is merited on this subject relates to the positions advocated by Barth and Hick in the line of the Christian tradition. Obviously over the centuries *anna Domini*, i.e. after the Lord, numerous responses have been made by Christian theologians to our three questions. Especially with regard to our second and third questions, i.e. What happens to the individual in death? and What happens after life?, there have been broadly speaking two responses, even within the Reformed tradition to which both Barth and Hick belong. On the one hand there is the Christian mortalist-psychopannychian response. This response holds that nothing of man continues to exist after life, though the psycho-pannychian view affirms resurrection while the Christian mortal-ist need not. We will note in our study that Barth is broadly representative of this response. In contrast Hick can be grouped with those who view death as a separation of body and soul. This is the more popular manner in which to view death, and it is generally associated with a resurrection which enhances and perfects life post-mortem. Because they are broadly representa-tive of these two responses to our latter two foci we deem it appropriate to compare Barth and Hick in our study.

The Format

For our study we will begin with Barth, investigating the cause and significance of death, what happens to the individual in death, and what transpires after life first in *The Epistle to the Romans*, then *The Resurrection of the Dead*, the *Credo*, and finally the *Church Dogmatics*. It cannot be doubted that Barth regarded his *Church Dogmatics* as the fruit of his labors, the best expression of his beliefs. Nonetheless we examine other writings of Barth because the subject of death and after-life is evident and even prevalent within them. This investigation will also enable us to illustrate both the continuity and discontinuity of Barth's thought regarding death and after-life. However though we will be noting some shifts of emphasis within Barth's theology, this we hope will not distract from the unity of his life work.

The thought of John Hick regarding death and after-life will follow next. Though we note here as well changes of emphasis and perhaps even changes of direction within the thought and works of Hick, we have in Hick just one prime work, i.e. the monograph *Death and Eternal Life*, which will enable us to treat Hick in briefer though no less complete fashion than we do Barth.

The concluding chapter of our study will compare and contrast Barth and Hick relative to each of our three basic ques-tions. Previous to this we will focus upon the methods of Barth and Hick, which will provide some clues and answers as to why and how Barth and Hick differ as they do. Each of these four topics will in turn be followed by "a personal perspective" in which we outline our own responses to these topics.

Footnotes

[1]Hans Küng, *Eternal Life? Life After Death as a Medical, Philosophical, and Theological Problem*, trans. Edward Quinn (Garden City: Doubleday and Company, Inc., 1984), p. 160.

[2]Robert Fulton, *Death and Identity* (New York: John Wiley & Sons, Inc., 1965), p. 106.

[3]J. E. Meyer, *Death and Neurosis*, trans. Margarete Nunberg (New York: International Universities Press, Inc., 1975), p. 119.

[4]Raymond A. Moody, Jr., *Life After Life* (New York: Bantam Books, 1975), pp. 119-122.

[5]John Hick, "Pluralism and the Reality of the Transcendent," *The Christian Century* Vol. 98, No. 2 (1981):45. This article is reprinted in James M. Wall, ed., *Theologians in Transition* (New York: Crossroad Publishing Company, 1981), p. 61.

[6]Eberhard Busch, *Karl Barth: His Life from Letters and Autogiographical Texts*, trans. John Bowden (London: SCM Press, Ltd., 1975), p. 449.

CHAPTER II

DEATH IN THE THEOLOGY OF KARL BARTH

Death in the Epistle to the Romans

INTRODUCTION

If you were seeking to learn a theologian's views of eschatology you would traditionally look to the concluding chapter of that particular theologians's Christian dogmatics where you would appropriately find a chapter on the last things. In his second edition of *Der Römerbrief*, translated into English as *The Epistle to the Romans*, Karl Barth warns against such a practice as being able "to lull us comfortably to sleep by adding at the conclusion of Christian Dogmatics a short and perfectly harmless chapter entitled--'Eschatology'."[1] Barth believed that eschatology ought to pervade Christianity. He in fact claimed: "If Christianity be not altogether thoroughgoing eschatology, there remains in it no relationship whatever with Christ."[2] In this vein it is noteworthy that these comments of Barth do not derive from a formal dogmatic study. Rather they appear in the course of his celebrated commentary upon the Apostle Paul's letter to the Romans. In this context and by this method Barth himself was able to avoid the pitfall of placing a chapter on eschatology as a final chapter of a dogmatic study.

This creates two problems for our current study. First any study of death and after-life in *The Epistle to the Romans* may be viewed as illegitimate since Barth deliberately avoided focusing upon death and after-life apart from the whole of Christianity. To write on this subject may be viewed as a failure to apprehend sympathetically what Barth was attempting to communicate in his famed second edition of *Romans*. Nevertheless with this sort of warning we do not feel it is inappropriate to investigate the three basic problems which are the foci of this study.

But as our second problem we are posed with the challenge of gleaning and organizing from Barth ideas which Barth does not make readily available for us in some concluding chapter. To accomplish this illegitimate task in such a way as not to distort Barth is a challenge, yet a challenge not without reward.

8

There is also a third problem inherent in a study of death and after-life in *Romans*. This commentary was absolutely revolutionary for its day. In the introduction to the first edition Barth notes: "The historical-critical method of Biblical investigation has its rightful place."[3] The historical-critical study of the Bible had been developed and propounded during the nineteenth century, and it had become the standard, accepted method of approach to Biblical research. Barth found this method to be grossly inadequate. In fact he comments: "were I driven to choose between it (the historical-critical method) and the venerable doctrine of Inspiration, I should without hesitation adopt the latter."[4] Barth notes that he is fortunate in not having to make such a choice, but the novel character of Barth's approach becomes clear in such a prospective choice. The character of *Romans* is thus decidedly different. Barth does not refer to matters of syntax, textual criticism, source strata, etc. Rather he attempts to identify himself with Paul, literally to become one with him: "till I know the author so well that I allow him to speak in my name and am even able to speak in his name myself."[5] With this method Barth believes that fortuitous, incidental, or merely historical conceptions will nearly be eliminated.[6] He does not expend time on the various interpretations of the text(s), but rather he is concerned to move directly toward explication and clarification of the essential meaning, truth, and implications of the text(s). Also in the years intervening the first and second editions of *Romans* Barth had become better acquainted with Plato and Kant through his brother Heinrich. He also culled from the writings of Kierkegaard and Dostoyevsky what he considered important for the interpretation of the New Testament.[7] The latter two in particular are the most frequently cited extra-Biblical sources in *Romans*. Admittedly influenced as he was by Kierkegaard and Dostoyevsky at this stage of his life, Barth writes with an existentialist ring in *The Epistle to the Romans*. It is this tone or ring which helped to promote the novel and distinctive sound of the commentary in its day.

For our study this creates a hermeneutical difficulty. In *Romans* Barth will often speak in antitheses, e.g. No and Yes are often coupled. As we examine death and after-life we must ascertain whether Barth is speaking literally, whether a figurative-metaphorical interpretation is intended, whether a combination of these two is prescribed, or whether even another interpretation is the appropriate and proper means for interpretation.

Thus we turn to our study of the meaning and significance of death, what happens to the individual in death, and what happens after life. We are aware of the challenges and difficulties, but we believe that the effort will not be without reward.

THE CAUSE AND SIGNIFICANCE OF DEATH

Orthodox teaching within the Roman Catholic, Lutheran, and Reformed traditions teaches that death is the result of sin. It suggests that there was a time when death was unknown to man, but when Adam sinned death was the result. Death is understood as a manifestation of the wrath and displeasure of God.

There are aspects of thought in *The Epistle to the Romans* which would agree with the orthodox description of the cause and significance of death. As Barth portrays it, in the Garden of Eden there was no division between God and man.

Originally, there was no separation. Man dwelt in the Garden of Eden, in which there were no absolute and relative, no 'Higher' and 'Lower', no 'There' and 'Here': such distinctions marked the Fall. The world was originally one with the Creator, and men were one with God.[8]

The world was originally holy. It was responsive to its Creator. There was peace. But sin disturbed the peace, and as a direct result death arose.

Through sin death. Death is the reverse side of sin. It entered into the world as a result of the original and invisible sin by which the Life, which is the relationship of men to God, was damaged. Sin is guilt; and the destiny of sin and guilt is death.[9]

Barth notes that we see all men sin and then die, and he believes that the then is really a "therefore," though the direct causal relation is invisible to us.[10] In Barth the teaching of orthodoxy is apparent. Death is envisioned as a negative phenomenon. It was not intended that man should die, but the sin of man changed that.

Barth further illustrates the negative character of death with an appeal to the work of Michelangelo in the Sistine Chapel.

Look how Michelangelo has depicted the 'Creation of Eve': in the fullness of her charm and beauty she rises slowly, posing herself in the fatal attitude of--worship. Notice the Creator's warning arm and careworn, saddened eyes, as He replies to Eve's gesture of adoration. She is manifestly behaving as she ought not.[11]

God does not, according to Barth, appreciate the worship of Eve as signified in His arm and eyes. Since orthodoxy does not envision the worship of Eve in the Garden as being less than perfect, the idea that Barth promotes here is novel.

Barth writes that the Fall is not simply the result of Adam's sin, but rather the transgression in Eden Barth presumes to be the first manifest operation of sin. He interprets the Fall in Eden in line with "the venerable Reformation doctrine

of 'Supralapsarianism.'"[12] Barth believes that predestination
unto rejection precedes the fall of Adam. Here again Barth is
in concert with Reformed and Lutheran orthodoxy, while Roman
Catholicism has maintained a more ambiguous stance at this
point. It would be incorrect to assume that Barth views the
Fall as being a historic event, however. "Primordial and non-
historical" are the words which Barth uses to describe it.
The Fall is non-historic; it refers "to that timeless age to
which all men belong."[13] Barth clarifies that only a parable
is able to communicate such truth.[14] Time as we know it is a
result of human separation from God, and similarly time will
cease whenever a person becomes united with God again.

One must accordingly question whether death is wholly
negative for Barth since death appears to be intended by God
according to the supralapsarian view. This might raise the
further question of the responsibility for the Fall, but that
is not a question Barth handles here. As we will note the
question of ultimate responsibility for sin becomes moot as
the condemnation of sin is but half of the story for Barth.

Barth noteworthily adds a dimension to the relation between
sin and death which distinguishes his position from orthodoxy.
Orthodoxy referred to this relationship in metaphysical terms
with the one being the occasion for the other. Barth would
add an existential relationship between the two whereby men
who live in sin and guilt live without sharing in life. They
may be thus defined by their unrelatedness, absoluteness, and
independence as being relative. For Barth it is thus inevitable
that death should clarify the relationship between God and man.[15]
The condemnation of men unto death constitutes both their curse
and destiny. Men must live their entire life under the threat
of death.[16] Here again we note an existential flavor being
brought to the fore, and it represents again a negative evaluation of death.

The use which Barth makes of Adam per se is less restricted
than orthodoxy where the primary reference was to a historic
figure Adam who was the first human being. Barth emphasizes
the typology of Adam in which all human beings are involved.
As men do what Adam did it becomes proper to call and define
them by the man in whose shadow they stand. Men who are invariably in Adam die, and that Barth views as a causal relationship.[17]

To this point we have noted the negative nature of death--
its being the result of sin and impacting negatively upon human
existence. Nevertheless, though Barth would never want to deny
this negative evaluation of death, he does not envision death
wholly in negative terms. Barth notes that "Death forms the
limit of our life and marks the boundary between us and God."[18]
Death clarifies for man who alone ultimately is God. Death
inhibits apotheosis, the deification of man. Man is not
infinite, and death serves to remind man of his finitude. In
death God directs His question to us, which can certainly be

experienced as negative, though Barth also understands it as
preparation for the divine answer to this question. Death is
the 'No' which is also and nevertheless His 'Yes.'[19] "God is
Alpha, and therefore Omega; He rejects, and therefore elects;
He condemns, and therefore is merciful. God conducts men down
into Hell, and there releases them."[20] God dissolves man in
order to establish him; He kills in order to give life.[21] This
dialectic relationship Barth refers to as "double predestination,"[22] a novel interpretation of this concept to be sure.
Nonetheless this illustrates a positive element which also
characterizes death for Barth.

This positive aspect is further illustrated by Barth when
he refers to death as a parable. He writes that faith "finds
in death the only parable of the Kingdom of God"[23] and again
"everything corruptible is only a parable."[24] Parables are
learning devices, and they teach in both a negative and a
positive sense. Negatively they direct one to a better situation or state of affairs. Such is indeed the case with the use
Barth makes of death. Death points to the inevitable end of
man's activities in separation from God. It thus gives a negative evaluation to man's current situation and state of affairs.
Yet Barth believes that this negative evaluation ought as well
to do service as a prelude to a more positive evaluation.
Hence we hear that God condemns in order that He might have
mercy. God says "No" as a necessary step toward saying "Yes,"
which is Barth's understanding of double predestination.

It is also interesting to notice that Barth believes that
man may come naturally to this point. This is particularly
remarkable in light of the reputation Barth has received as a
result of his later writings, especially *Church Dogmatics II/1*.
The supreme possibility which man is able to achieve outside
revelation and inside the realm of sin is the marking of death
as the distinction between God and man. Yet his possibility
is ironically paradoxical: "Now, that this supreme and urgent
necessity of our existence should be identical with that capacity
by which our direct union with God was destroyed, constitutes
the final paradox of the Fall."[25] The result of the Fall aids
man in learning something necessary. Perhaps Barth might be
interpreted here as advocating a "fall upwards" after the
manner of Paul Tillich, but Barth certainly does not indicate
that man is in any sense enhanced by the Fall. Rather the one
necessity equals the other capacity. And in any event it is
not at this point where men are supposed to remain. Men need
to see beyond this point.

Sooner or later all men must encounter the final barrier,
which Barth alludes to as "the Pain in our pains."[26] All of
life as we experience it contrasts with life in God and therefore bears the mark of death. It places before man the ultimate question which thence prepares us for His answer. The
recognition that we must die is forced upon us, and this
occasions for man an ambiguity. He may either attain wisdom
or remain a fool, and that in the most reprehensible sense of

the term.[27] Here again, besides the existential dimension,
we note the dialectic between death and life, condemnation and
forgiveness, No and Yes, etc., with the negative phenomenon
giving rise to the positive.

Still noteworthily it is by faith that men are enabled to
see beyond the No of death to the divine Yes. Human reason
may attain to the No, and even existentially yearn for the Yes,
but only faith is able to bring us to the divine Yes. Barth
hence deplores reason.

> It (faith) grips reason by the throat and strangles the
> beast. It effects what the whole world and all that is
> in it is impotent to do. But how can faith do this? By
> holding on to God's word and by accounting it right and
> true, however stupid and impossible it may appear.[28]

For Barth there are truths which reason is unable to attain
while faith is able to do so. Barth even suggests that faith
is "creative of divinity." This does not mean that faith can
"add to the eternal and divine Being; nevertheless, it creates
It in us."[29] Faith is able to perceive in death not simply
the negation of God, His No, but His affirmation or Yes. Faith
can also create the eternal and divine Being within us.

This raises two additional concerns. The first pertains
to the content of the divine affirmation, which we will note
below. The basis for that Yes needs to be noted, and it is
to that that we turn directly.

The doctrine of the manus triplex, the doctrine of Christ
as prophet, priest, and king, is criticized by Barth because
it obscures and weakens the New Testament concentration upon
the death of Christ. Barth does not believe that the death of
Jesus may be treated independently or even beside the death of
Christ as a second or third aspect of his life. To the contrary
Barth writes: "Everything shines in the light of His death,
and is illuminated by it."[30] Barth recognizes that the centrality
of Christ and the effect of His death upon the cross may not be
apparent to and acknowledged by everyone. There yet remain
questions whether the good wrought by death is in fact good and
whether the man on whose behalf death is dared, i.e. sinful
human beings, is good. There is also the question of why the
death of Jesus is hailed as being so significant. Other good
men have died and/or been killed and no atonement was effected.
No security is claimed for other individuals on the basis of
their deaths.

> But the death of Christ is concerned precisely with this
> benefit. It is a benefit which, 'rather than providing
> us with the knowledge of God--where indeed is such know-
> ledge?--provides us with the assurance that He knows us'
> (Overbeck).[31]

This truth is beyond reason. It comes to man by faith, and it is nonetheless true.

It also is apparent that Barth is speaking literally of death at this point. The death of Christ effects an objective atonement which enables man to be reconciled to God now. Coupled to the objective atonement, however, is the subjective appropriation of it in faith by men. When Barth refers to the latter it is built upon the former, i.e. the subjective pre-supposes the objective.

In conclusion we reiterate that the cause and significance of death in *The Epistle to the Romans* are primarily viewed as adverse matters. Barth is very conscious of death as KRISIS, judgment, the divine No, etc. He adjoins to this, however, the positive in terms of divine grace, the Yes, etc., even suggest-ing that the former is a necessary prelude to the latter. Death therefore has both negative and positive aspects within *Romans*. Barth also suggests that though some of these truths are evident to all, others derive from faith in the revelation of God. Finally we remark how Barth writes with an existential flavor and consciousness in this book, very much in contrast with the primary theological literature of his day. Though Barth demonstrates concern for the essence of death, he stresses the existential dimension and how this affects man. We have had to derive some of our conclusions from the existential termi-nology and ideas which Barth uses. This will be even more so the case in the subsequent section.

WHAT TRANSPIRES TO THE INDIVIDUAL IN DEATH

The primary idea and reality of death to which we refer in this study is physical death. We insert this reminder because much of what Barth writes in *Romans* concerning death carries figurative, metaphorical, and/or existential import. This might tend to confuse our subject, especially since we must examine these figurative, metaphorical, and existential phrases to ascertain whether they portend something concerning the essence of physical death. Indeed we believe that the existential statements of Barth with regard to death must bear witness to what Barth believes concerning the nature of death or else they would be inappropriate for the use Barth makes of them. It is the reality and nature of physical death which concerns us here.

Throughout Barth's *Romans* we are confronted with the notion that the eschatological moment is both No and Yes, dissolving and establishment, killing and giving life,[32] judgment and betterment, barrier and exit, end and beginning, sign of divine wrath and signal of His imminent salvation.[33] Barth writes:

The words *apart from* cover everything both before and after the 'Moment' when men stand before God and are moved by Him; for no comparison between the 'Moment' and works which are done either before or after is possible.[34]

The Being and Action of God in His realm are wholly different
from the being and action of men within their realm. Barth
refers to the line of death which separates these two realms.
But again the line of death is also the line of life, even as
the No is related to the divine Yes.[35] Because Barth believes
that this eschatological moment is a constantly renewed[36]
though irreversible event,[37] references to the moment of
KRISIS, our moment of decision, pervade this work. For example
Barth writes: "Rightly understood, there are no Christians:
there is only the eternal opportunity of becoming Christians"[38]
and "Confronted by Jesus, men must die, they must die daily."[39]
Whenever Barth refers to it, he does so in a sense of discontinuity. There is a radical break with the life which went
before. The new life in the Spirit is radically dissimilar
from what preceded it, so dissimilar in fact that the apparent
antonyms above serve as appropriate description. However it is
the same biological individual which continues from one to the
other and therefore lends credence to the notion of continuity
between the No and Yes, dissolving and establishment, etc.
Nonetheless it is the notion of discontinuity which is conveyed
with regard to death in *The Epistle to the Romans*. This is
most noticeable where Barth notes a contrast in the second
edition of this work as compared with the first edition.

> We must beware of all those attempts which have been made
> from Oetinger to Beck and from Rothe to Steiner--and also,
> though with some reserve, in the first edition of this book--
> to utilize the speculation of an observable and real Spirit-
> Body. . . By the knowledge of God this body of mine is
> defined as altogether mortal.[40]

Such statements prohibit the idea of some immortal aspect of
man surviving after life. Though Barth can write that "I am
the individual, soul and body, who stands in my place" and
thus seemingly be interpreted as envisioning man as a duality,
Barth appears to employ the phrase "soul and body" as reference
to the totality of the individual which is mortal.[41] He also
writes that "THIS mortal must put on immortality,"[42] again
suggesting that man in his totality is mortal and corruptible.
As will become even more apparent when we discuss Barth's
ideas of what happens after life, Barth does not envision a
segment or aspect of man which is immortal and therefore an
entity which continues between physical death and the resurrection. Death marks the end of man.

WHAT HAPPENS AFTER LIFE

Despite the finality of death Barth makes it plain in
several manners that physical death is not the final chapter
for man. Though death marks an end to physical life and though
Barth indicates that there is no aspect of man which is
immortal, he would not subscribe to the belief that nothing
happens to man after life. After life will come the resurrection. Barth does not describe the nature of "life" or "existence" between death and resurrection, and it would seem

therefore that Barth envisions no "life" during this period.
But he does believe that God will resurrect man. Three
considerations support this.

First Barth suggests that consciousness of death implies
the possibility of resurrection. He asks: "Is there any consciousness of the sentence of death hanging over human life
which is not an--incomprehensible!--awareness of the--impossi-
ble!--possibility of resurrection?"[43] This is actually the
two halves of the eschatological moment being fit together.
In the first half we hear the divine No and in the second the
divine Yes. This accordingly leads to the second consideration
which supports the belief that Barth does envision life after
death. Barth typically refers to death as God's No. There
would be no corresponding affirmative voice of God, His Yes,
if there were nothing more for man after life. Finally Barth
speaks of renewal being initiated in this life, but this
renewal is not brought to completion in this life. "But I,
the temporal and corporal man of this world, am not the new man.
My final possibility is to groan--and to await the promise."[44]
Barth notes with Paul that *Flesh and blood cannot inherit the
Kingdom of God.*"[45] There must therefore remain for Barth something after life since we are flesh and blood in this life.
Further parroting the words of the Apostle Paul, Barth writes:
*"This mortal must put on immortality and this corruptible must
put on incorruption."*[46] Man is not immortal or incorruptible
in this life, else he would not die. If the mortal is ever to
become immortal and the corruptible incorruptible, then it
must needs occur after life. Barth makes this more than clear
in the following:

> In this world, on this earth, and under this heaven, there
> is no redemption, no direct life. Redemption can be only
> through redemption! But redemption can only take place
> at the coming Day, when there shall be a new heaven and
> a new earth.[47]

The coming day which Barth envisions entails a radical and
qualitative change, a transformation from life as we experience
it here in this life.

Barth refers to this future day of transformation as the
"Futurum resurrectionis."[48] Though Barth has employed considerable terminology which has an existential character and thus
opened the possibility that resurrection might be understood
as complete during the course of this life, the word future in
description of resurrection eliminates the possibility that
resurrection might be complete during the course of this life,
though it does not preclude its use in reference to events in
this life. Barth stresses in a foremost manner that the future
resurrection is an act of God, not a human act or capacity.
The resurrection comes at the divine initiative and not by human
initiative.[49] Man does not in any sense direct the resurrection
but is rather himself directed. To clarify what he understands
by future resurrection Barth uses four different means.

The first means that Barth employs is the positive expression of conformity with Christ. The future resurrection is perceived as entailing true and positive conformity to Jesus.[50] Barth explicitly states that man in space and time as we know him is not the new man he is intended to be. For Barth complete adoption entails the redemption of the body with complete identification between Christ and man.[51]

But by far the most popular means for Barth to clarify the future resurrection is by means of negation and contrast with the present, and this we might expect from one who stresses the idea of discontinuity so much. Barth writes that not even the tiniest fragment of the Kingdom of God has come into being.[52] The Kingdom is not an evolution or development of something already existent in this world: "it is not a mere eruption, or extension, or unfolding, of that old 'creative evolution' of which we form a part, and shall remain a part, till our lives' end."[53] Rather Barth awaits "*a new heaven and a new earth*"[54] which will be radically and qualitatively different from the world we now know and experience. The world in which we live is in conflict with the world which God promises. While we are surrounded with mortality and corruption, God promises incorruption. While we are yet caught in sin, God pronounces man righteous.[55] Nevertheless though Barth is willing to concede that it is THIS mortal which shall become immortal, thus affirming a degree of continuity between this life and the resurrected life, on the whole it is discontinuity and contrast which prevails in his description, e.g. flesh and blood being unable to inherit the Kingdom. It is a vastly different realm which Barth envisions for the resurrection, so different that Barth employs antonyms in description of it.

The third means which Barth uses to clarify the future resurrection is indirect. We may infer that since we are to conform to Christ that we will be like him in his resurrection. Barth believes that Jesus underwent a bodily resurrection as well as a bodily crucifixion.[56] It therefore follows that men will also be resurrected bodily.

Furthermore Barth suggests that men shall "stand naked before God, and . . . in their nakedness be clothed upon with the righteousness of God."[57] Though the language is figurative, it connotes bodily resurrection in a form distinct from the present. It also indicates noteworthily that the new life will represent completion of what was initiated in this life. Barth also writes: "From this manifestation of redemption no hair of our head can be excluded."[58] If the resurrection and redemption will entail the hairs of our head it certainly must be bodily, even in a nonetheless transformed body.

The final means that Barth employs in clarification of the resurrection, though it is again figurative, points to a return to God. Man achieves the end for which he was intended and created. Barth almost makes it seem as if man returns whence he came, i.e. the Garden of Eden. But he writes:

> As the arrow, loosed from the box by the hand of the prac-
> tised archer, does not rest till it has reached the mark;
> so men pass from God to God. He is the mark for which
> they have been created; and they do not rest till they
> find their rest in Him.[59]

This quotation which Barth makes of Kierkegaard demonstrates
that the idea of the end as a recreation of the Garden of
Eden would be an inaccurate and insufficient statement of the
end. He writes: "The innocent and direct life of the garden
of Eden is not reproduced in the mission of the Son. That,
indeed, could not, and must not, be, for his mission took place
on account of sin."[60] Man is unable to return to the Garden of
Eden because sin has scarred the creation to such a great
extent. Furthermore a return to the Garden of Eden might allow
for another Fall with a subsequent history of salvation. The
end must be better than the beginning in order that this eventuality not be repeated. Barth hereby views time not in a
circular fashion but as linear. He does not envision time or
history as being repeated, no matter how lengthy the cycle
might be, but rather time is moving toward a τέλος, an end or
goal. That τέλος entails a direct life between God and man, a
union of God with man.

Despite these means of clarification of the resurrection,
however, much concerning the nature of the resurrection remains
open to question. Indeed this is precisely as it must be
according to Barth. Human language is simply inadequate to
describe this future reality. "The more coldly" resurrection
of the body is described, the better since putting it into
words at all will almost certainly obscure the truth of resurrection, much like smoke can hide things which we wish to see.[61]
Barth reiterates the qualitative difference between now and the
"new order upon a new earth and under a new heaven."[62] This new
order will be so vastly different from the present order that it
eludes expression, "for when expressed, it appears as though
it were a second or peculiar disposition of human affairs
capable of being compared with other dispositions."[63] Barth
thereby repeats the idea of discontinuity which is so prominent
within *The Epistle to the Romans*. Still Barth does not prohibit
attempts to describe the future resurrection, though he does
indicate that attempts at description are precisely that--
attempts--and therefore removed from the reality itself.

Barth also indicates that this day of resurrection is not
being delayed. He asks rhetorically, "Will there never be an
end of all our ceaseless talk about the delay of the Parousia?
How can the coming of that which doth not enter in ever be
delayed?"[64] Barth envisions the end as a boundary beyond which
we may pass into a new world, but it is a world where even 1900
years are of no consequence. Barth chides those who would
depress into a temporal reality what is capable only of description in parables.[65]

In conclusion to this section which details what happens after life we should focus upon the scope and extent of the resurrection. Barth believes that all will be resurrected by God. This conclusion we may glean from an interesting turn of phrase from Nietzche: "'Only where graves are, is there resurrection' (Nietzche); rather, wherever graves are, there is resurrection."[66] Wherever there is death there God initiates anew. God turns death into a new beginning for all in the resurrection.

The question of whether all will be saved, i.e. the issue of universalism, follows naturally upon the scope of the resurrection. On this question Barth definitely leans toward universalism, though he remains reluctant to specify quantities. Two types of sources lead us to this conclusion regarding Barth's position.

First we note that the reconciliation accomplished by Christ is universal. Barth does not hold to the teaching of limited atonement. "Those who do not see Christ according to the flesh and have no direct experience of Him are not less reconciled to God through Him than others are."[67] Barth cites the passage relating Christ's preaching to the imprisoned in 1 Peter 3:19 as demonstrating this universality. While man was weak and godless Christ accomplished a vicarious atonement on man's behalf. Barth is aware that the atonement is invisible, but that hardly makes it any less real.[68] Certainly from this we may conclude that the potential universal redemption of man is evident. Barth leans toward this belief by noting the universal reconciliation of Christ, but it is at this point a mere though real potential.

It is from the second type of source which we are led most readily to conclude that Barth believes in a universalistic redemption. This belief is clearly implied in the numerous examples of the divine dialectic which pervade *The Epistle to the Romans*. The following quotation is typical, and we shall cite other ideas which point to the same conclusion.

We are not saved by our knowledge of God. Our knowledge brings us under judgement. God is Alpha, and therefore Omega; He rejects, and therefore elects; He condemns, and therefore is merciful. God conducts men down into Hell, and there releases them.[69]

Barth envisions the divine No as the prelude to the divine Yes. Rejection is the shadow of election.[70] God moves from Esau to Jacob, from Pharaoh to Moses, from the vessel of wrath to the vessel of mercy.[71] The end and goal of hardening is the extension of salvation to the Gentiles. The exhausting of human possibility opens and in fact presupposes the possibility that God will intervene.[72] Barth is conscious of the fact that Elijah is informed by God that there are 7000 men upon whom God has mercy because they have not bowed down in worship to Baal.

Barth, however, does not understand the 7000 to be exclusive. It means rather that the mercy of God is infinite, extending to thousands. Barth does not believe that there is a calculable number of persons who enjoy and will enjoy the final, new life in Christ. Rather there is no limit to the grace and mercy of God. Clearly in all of these references Barth implies a move beyond universal atonement and reconciliation to universal redemption. All will be positively involved in the eschatological Kingdom.

We also recall the idea of double predestination as Barth understands it. All human beings are doubly predestined--to the divine No and the divine Yes. For Barth the doctrine of double predestination refers not to the quantitative limitation of God but rather to its qualitative definition.[73] It refers not to how much but simply to how. If all men are involved in this qualitative double predestination we clearly have a universalistic position suggested in Barth.

Yet a word of caution is in order at this point. It is apparent that Barth implies a universalistic stance, both in terms of atonement and eventual salvation in unity with Christ, but he makes it apparent that this represents merely a potential or possibility.

The faithful heathen, of whom we say that they call upon the Lord, do not compose a definite and analysable number of men. They are an eschatological quantity, embracing potentially the totality of psychologically analysable individuals, whether they belong to the Church or not.[74]

The word to underscore is *potentially*. Barth hesitates to move beyond potentiality to actuality, though reason would imply that he does view universalism as an actuality.

CONCLUSION

As we draw our "illegitimate task" to a conclusion it is worthwhile to reflect briefly in passing upon our conclusions regarding the three foci which have occupied our thoughts upon *The Epistle to the Romans*. We noted first in our discussion of the cause and significance of death that death is viewed primarily in negative terms, though Barth also accords death positive aspects. We noted points in which Barth was in agreement with orthodoxy, but he also demonstrated points where the beliefs of orthodoxy are modified. Barth's understanding of double predestination with death serving as the natural and necessary prelude to new life is one clear example of how Barth modifies orthodox belief. Second in our analysis of what transpires to the individual in death we noted that death is final. There is nothing of man which continues to exist after life. Man is mortal. Nevertheless we noted in our discussion of what happens after life that God resurrects man to a new life in which man is clothed in incorruption and immortality. Because of God man may look beyond death. We

noted as well that logically Barth is led to endorse universalism, but we also reminded ourselves that logic does not
control the teaching of Barth as much as faith.

In *The Epistle to the Romans* Barth gave people something
unanticipated and unexpected. We have in fact referred to
this study as an illegitimate task in that it may tend to
place eschatology once again as a study of the last things
which will be studied in dogmatics, rather like an addendum.
Nonetheless our task, as an attempt to apply what Barth would
suggest concerning our three topics, is hardly illegitimate.
It may be questioned whether we have anticipated all that Barth
might want to say on these matters at this stage in his career,
especially since much of the essence of death and after-life
must be gleaned from statements with an existential character.
Yet this is the task and responsibility of the theologian, and
it has proven here to be a task with considerable reward.

FOOTNOTES

[1]Karl Barth, *The Epistle to the Romans*, 6th ed., trans. Edwyn C. Hoskyns (London: Oxford University Press, 1933), p. 500.

[2]Ibid., p. 314.　　　　[3]Ibid., p. 1.

[4]Ibid.　　　　[5]Ibid., p. 8.

[6]Ibid.　　　　[7]Ibid., p. 4.

[8]Ibid., p. 247.　　　　[9]Ibid., pp. 169-170.

[10]Ibid., p. 172.　　　　[11]Ibid., p. 247.

[12]Ibid., p. 172.　　　　[13]Ibid., p. 249.

[14]cf. below p. 12.　　　　[15]Ibid., pp. 169-170.

[16]Ibid., p. 181.　　　　[17]Ibid., p. 172.

[18]Ibid., p. 168.　　　　[19]Ibid., p. 111.

[20]Ibid., p. 393.　　　　[21]Ibid., p. 61.

[22]Ibid., p. 250.　　　　[23]Ibid., p. 202.

[24]Ibid., p. 210.　　　　[25]Ibid., p. 251.

[26]Ibid., p. 301.　　　　[27]Ibid., p. 251.

[28]Ibid., p. 144.　　　　[29]Ibid., p. 143.

[30]Ibid., p. 159.　　　　[31]Ibid., p. 162.

[32]Ibid., p. 61.　　　　[33]Ibid., p. 169.

[34]Ibid., p. 111.　　　　[35]Ibid.

[36]Ibid., p. 321.　　　　[37]Ibid., p. 177.

[38]Ibid., p. 321.　　　　[39]Ibid., p. 108.

[40]Ibid., p. 289.　　　　[41]Ibid., p. 206.

[42]Ibid., p. 102.　　　　[43]Ibid., p. 383.

[44]Ibid., p. 312.　　　　[45]Ibid., p. 102.

[46]Ibid., p. 112.　　　　[47]Ibid., p. 169.

[48] Ibid., p. 196.

[49] Ibid., p. 102.

[50] Ibid., p. 196.

[51] Ibid., pp. 312-313.

[52] Ibid., p. 102.

[53] Ibid.

[54] Ibid.

[55] Ibid., p. 143.

[56] Ibid., p. 205.

[57] Ibid., p. 109.

[58] Ibid., p. 313.

[59] Ibid., p. 438.

[60] Ibid., p. 278.

[61] Ibid., p. 289.

[62] Ibid., p. 223.

[63] Ibid.

[64] Ibid., p. 500.

[65] Ibid.

[66] Ibid., p. 416.

[67] Ibid., p. 160.

[68] Ibid.

[69] Ibid., p. 393.

[70] Ibid., p. 401.

[71] Ibid., p. 359.

[72] Ibid., p. 414.

[73] Ibid., p. 346.

[74] Ibid., p. 384.

Death in The Resurrection of the Dead

INTRODUCTION

Barth completed work on the second edition of *The Epistle to the Romans* at the same time as he was completing his pastorate in Safenwil, Switzerland. Barth then temporarily departed Switzerland for Germany, and specifically for a new chair for Reformed theology at the University of Göttingen. His elevation to "proper academic theology"[1] marked a distinctive new phase in his life, a switch from a church to a lecture room. One might expect that Barth would become more structured in his approach. The fact that in the summer of 1923 Barth dedicated time to an interpretation of 1 Corinthians 15 might certainly seem to point in that direction. Theologians have tended to conclude their dogmatics with a study of the "last things," and Barth's concentration upon 1 Corinthians 15 might be indicative of a more structured and traditional approach. But as he had done in *Romans*, Barth remains "unorthodox" in the sense of not following tradition. We might also expect to hear again the existential character found in *Romans*, but this we do not find. In the published edition of his interpretation of 1 Corinthians, entitled *Die Auferstehung der Toten* and translated as *The Resurrection of the Dead*, Barth concludes that theology continues to be impossible to man. Barth writes:

> This chapter is admirably suited to clarify what Christianity as a whole involves, and to provoke a salutary shock at the fact that theology really signifies an enterprise which is impossible to man.[2]

After the various problems which the Apostle Paul addresses in the first fourteen chapters of 1 Corinthians, chapter 15 is not a collection of innocuous thoughts tacked on to the real concerns of Paul. Rather chapter 15 represents "the very peak and crown of this essentially critical and polemically negative Epistle."[3] Chapter 15 is a more positive statement of Pauline belief which is crucial and at the very center of the first letter to the Corinthians.

Barth is well aware of the misunderstanding to which 1 Corinthians 15 has been exposed.[4] This stems in part from the attempt by man to transform God from being the subject into an object. But for Barth "God always remains the *subject* in the relationship created by this testimony. He is not transformed into the object, into man's having the right to the last word."[5] God is the other who escapes and transcends human categories. God is in dialogue with man, and even as human beings remain impossible to characterize, so God cannot be characterized like an object. For Barth "the meaning of the goal to which the whole epistle is moving is the glory of God and really only the glory of God."[6] Hence whatever observations we will make from *The Resurrection of the Dead* for our particular study must be understood and interpreted in this light.

In *The Resurrection of the Dead* Barth deals with four
key topics which merit our consideration. We shall concern
ourselves in turn with revelation, eschatology, death, and
after-life, and to these we now direct attention.

REVELATION

The central issue of 1 Corinthians is exemplified already
in the very first verses of chapter 15 and becomes apparent in
Barth's discussion of vss. 3-7. Barth is well aware of the
diverse manners in which these verses have been interpreted,
but he is averse to following their patterns. Paul is not
attempting to provide us with a historical narrative here
Barth contends. There is no attempt made to detail the event(s)
of the resurrection. Likewise Paul is not presenting a proof
of the resurrection, as Barth indicates Lietzmann believes.
Investigations of the sources of these verses, the localities
and times of the various sources, or the lack of any mention
of the empty tomb is secondary and insignificant to Paul.[7]

Barth is emphatic that the facts which Paul enumerates
are ambiguous. What was seen was the tomb, the stone, the
linen, the handkerchief, etc. Barth makes the noteworthy
comment that these things represent "the last word that can
be said on the basis of historical observation."[8] He notes
that conclusions other than the resurrection of Jesus are
entirely possible. The body might have been stolen or Jesus
might only have appeared to be dead. The New Testament writers
remark that the empty tomb and the appearances of the Lord were
heavenly and different from our experience on earth. Barth in
fact chides Christian theology when it attempts to establish by
historical means just what the resurrection entailed. No man
has ever seen the resurrection as he may have witnessed other
historical facts. The resurrection lies beyond and outside human
experience.[9] To reduce the resurrection to the level of human
experience is to misunderstand it.

In order to overcome this misinterpretation Barth focuses
upon the verbs of 1 Corinthians 15:3-7, and there he notes that
the subject is Christ. It was not Peter, the twelve, the 500,
or Paul who saw Christ, but rather Christ who appeared to them;
Christ was seen *by* them. Peter and the others were passive, as
reflected in the verbs used. But Christ was active. Barth
suggests that if one were to attempt to get behind Paul to the
witness of the primitive Christian community one would encounter
there the same testimony to Christ as having appeared to others.[10]
There is no way to get beyond this appearance to some cold, hard
historical facts. Paul speaks from the resurrection appearance
of Christ, and it is ultimately this alone which serves as the
prime source of his teaching.[11] Paul reflects into and out of
this appearance event. It controls his thought. Paul thereby
demonstrates how one ought to think from the standpoint of
Christ, of revealed truth.[12]

The Corinthians by contrast viewed the resurrection as an
isolated and remote event with no fundamental and vital meaning
and significance for themselves. Whereas Paul was astounded
that those who had seen the Lord had died, or "fallen asleep"
as Paul expresses it, the Corinthians viewed the appearances
of the risen Lord like any other of the experiences of life
which are terminated at death. If this were the case then
Paul can ask why we should not eat, drink, and be merry (vs.
32). But though this is the understanding of the Corinthians,
it represents a misunderstanding to Paul. The resurrection of
Christ was not an isolated miracle. Paul argues with passion
in vss. 17-18 that the resurrection of Christ is the revelation
of the miracle that God worked on men. Hence if the resurrection of Jesus is an isolated event which will not be repeated
in the resurrection of others, "then even this miracle is not
true, then Christ is not risen, and those whom we now so amiably
call 'those that have fallen asleep' are perished."[13] Life and
death then become meaningless, and the notion of "falling
asleep" is purely euphemistic. But Paul is convinced that
Christ is not a singular event. He perceives in the resurrection
appearance of Jesus a key to the meaning of life, death, and
after-life. Paul perceives the resurrection of Jesus as a model.

The Corinthians were too inclined to follow human logic
and reflection, as is illustrated by their willingness to form
factions and parties. The main defect of the Corinthians con-
sisted "in the boldness, assurance, and enthusiasm with which
they believe, not in God, but in their own belief in God and in
particular leaders and heroes."[14] The Corinthians were confused
about Christian faith. They identified belief "with specific
human experiences, convictions, trends of thought and theories."[15]
Paul by contrast notes discontinuity here. Revelation must not
be viewed as an extension of our life here on earth and/or our
intellectual capacities. Revelation should not be understood as
a continuation of human experiences, even human "insights of a
higher and the highest kind."[16] Barth specifically levies
criticism at Friedrich Christoph Oetinger for perpetrating this
error.[17] Along this line Barth makes an astute observation,
which was borne out by the experience of the Apostle Paul as well:

> Truth is dead, or at least mortally ill, as soon as it
> receives a human name, or takes on human semblance, espe-
> cially in the form of a school, party, tendency or movement,
> which carries a label, and is distinguished from like
> movements by definite slogans and customs.[18]

The truth is to be identified with the revelation of God.
According to Barth Paul contends that revelation can "only be
proved by revelation itself."[19] Revelation for Barth continues
to be self-authenticating.

In this vein Barth relates the various attempts by liberals
and positivists to interpret the resurrection. The former relate
to visions, both objective and subjective, while the latter are

concerned for historical facts and sources. Though these might
suggest that the resurrection of Jesus is "marvelous beyond
comparison,"[20] even these for Barth remain inadequate to the
reality of resurrection. Barth believes that Paul is concerned
in 1 Corinthians to demonstrate the essential nature of revelation. He counters the Corinthians' depreciation of revelation by
two means. On the one hand he eliminates the ground upon which
they were taking their stand and on the other hand he surrounds
them on every side with the idea of revelation. Nothing but
revelation can stand as a basis for Christian belief according
to Paul.[21]

After the devaluation of human reason and logic in *The
Epistle to the Romans*, we would not expect Barth to commend
human rationality to man. In this Barth does not disappoint
us. Barth leaves us with no doubt that revelation is both the
starting point and focus for the thought of Paul in 1 Corinthians
and especially in chapter 15.

ESCHATOLOGY

When one compares *The Epistle to the Romans* with *The
Resurrection of the Dead* one notes a decreased emphasis upon
the eschatological moment and KRISIS which were so prominent
in the earlier work. It is noteworthy in fact that among the
misunderstandings which characterized the Corinthians Barth
cites the following:

> For the Kingdom of God does not fall outside the sphere
> of flesh and blood; to seek incorruption in corruption
> does not appear to them to be at all impossible; but they
> see in it the very Christian possibility "to be eternal in
> every moment" (verse 50).[22]

We cannot be surprised at the emphasis upon discontinuity
implicit within the first clauses, but the third and final
clause appears surprising. In *Romans* Barth had stressed the
inbreaking of the eschatological moment in the present, which
is very similar to what he criticizes here. Perhaps Barth,
noting this criticism by Paul of the Corinthians, applied it
to himself or at least his position in *Romans* and became less
inclined to speak any longer in such terms. It would however
be incorrect to suggest that Barth discontinues altogether
reference to the eschatological moment or KRISIS in the present.
A second explanation for this shift in Barth is possible. As
an outgrowth of his understanding of 1 Corinthians 15 Barth
diminished his stress upon the eschatological moment in favor
of the future when God's glory will be complete. Nonetheless
there is a third point of explanation which views this quotation
more in concert with *Romans*. The Corinthians viewed the Kingdom
of God as nothing spectacular. It was within the capacity of
human beings to attain. Barth, as he had in *Romans*, answers in
the negative. The eternal, God's Kingdom, breaks in from outside.
It is not a human disposition. This third understanding allows

Barth a consistent understanding between *Romans* and *The Resurrection of the Dead*, though there yet remains a diminished emphasis upon the vertical in favor of the horizontal.

In whatever manner we might come to interpret it, there is
a notable shift in emphasis in Barth from the vertical, existential dimension so prominent in *Romans* to the horizontal in *The
Resurrection of the Dead*. Barth notes that time is bounded by
eternity, both at the beginning and at the end. He writes:
"But as the word that first establishes and as the history of
the beginning it must be understood, as the word and history
of the origin of all time, of the whole of time."[23] Eternity
forms a boundary for the beginning of time; time indeed has a
beginning.

Likewise for Barth time has an end, and it was this end
or goal which was revealed in the resurrection of Christ. When
"God raised up Christ," as Paul notes in vs. 15, the "frontier
of history" became visible in history.[24] The utterly amazing
thing is that the boundary of time has been seen in time. Man
need no longer await a nebulous future, for Christ has revealed
that to man.

Barth dedicates considerable attention in *The Resurrection
of the Dead* to clarification of the relationship between time
and eternity, especially regarding the end or last things. On
the one hand Barth points up aspects of the end which illustrate
the discontinuous nature of the end with the present. Barth
speaks of the insurmountable wall which is placed in front of
man. The infinite series of time will come to a stop and become
a finite series in view of this wall.[25] Barth indicates that
the "last things" as they are referred to in the New Testament
and 1 Corinthians 15 in particular are not "final possibilities"
as men might imagine them to be. Even if men were to conceive
the last things as "preliminary stages to physical-metaphysical,
cosmic-metacosmic transformations and revolutions of an unpar-
alleled kind," even then man is unable to contemplate the reality
of the last things. Even if this picture is complemented with
images and materials taken from the Bible, even then the reality
will exceed our human capacities to conceive of them. As Barth
had noted in *The Epistle to the Romans*, everything transitory
is only a parable.[26] There is obviously for Barth a continuing
emphasis upon the notion of discontinuity between the present
world and the future realm.

Yet on the other hand Barth also speaks of elements between
the present and the future which will be continuous. We may
note three aspects which confirm this. First there must be a
degree of continuity if Christ has revealed the future already.
The future relates to the present as does Christ. Thus we may
expect that since Christ is common both to the present and the
future that there will be some continuity. Second Barth speaks
of "the absorption of all this and that, all here and there,
all once and now into the solemn peace of the One."[27] Time and
history and this world will not disappear at their end, but

rather they will be absorbed into God's eternity. But if all that we know and experience is not going to be destroyed or annihilated, then one must suspect that there will be a degree of continuity, however limited, between now and eternity. Third we note several references in Barth clarifying that eschatology is properly not the study of *last* things, as if there is nothing further or additional. Eschatology refers not so much to final things but to the end of things as we know and experience them. Barth is troubled by the conception prevailing in "ordinary dogma" where, after all other pertinent issues have been exhausted, the attempt is made to say "something about death, the beyond and world perfection."[28] Reminiscent again of *Romans* Barth writes: "we have to do here with the doctrine of the 'End,' which is at the same time the beginning, of the last things, which are, at the same time, the first."[29] It is apparent that Barth must allow for some continuity else he could not speak of the last things also serving as the first things.

In *The Resurrection of the Dead* Barth teeters between continuity and discontinuity with regard to the "last things." On the one hand Barth seeks to avoid any notion of the end of history as a termination of history. Time is limited by eternity.[30] But eternity merely marks the end of time. It does not terminate it. Barth clearly wants to avoid the temptation to confuse the end of history with the termination of history--no matter how impressive and wonderful such a termination might seem! Barth on the other hand seeks to stay clear of the other temptation which he suggests is the confusion of eternity and the end of history with the annihilation of history. This world is not to be destroyed or obliterated. That, as was noted above in our second point, would be contrary to the idea of absorption.

It is apparent, therefore, that Barth is aware of numerous pitfalls to which the topic of eschatology is susceptible unless it is thoroughly explained and clarified. Barth clarifies that casual reflection upon eschatology as typically done in dogmatic studies fails to perceive eschatology as the study of the end. Focusing upon the final events of history or last things, eschatology as typically done fails to do justice to the end or goal of all things in and from which they derive their meaning. It is the absolute transcendance of God in and from eternity which accords significance to the events within history.[31] Hence Barth in expounding Paul believes that time will not continue *ad infinitum*. Time will be absorbed into eternity at a particular place and moment. Thus though we may speak of an end to time, we may not understand this to mean that nothing continues.

DEATH

The subject of death is the third topic which will concern us from *The Resurrection of the Dead*. We shall focus upon three topics--the negative nature of death, the relationship of sin and death, and positive aspects of death.

The Apostle Paul could share language with the Corinthians, but he had a vastly different understanding of the words involved. Paul and the Corinthians could both refer to death as "falling asleep." The Corinthians perceived in this, however, something natural for which this beautiful and edifying description had been found. Paul's reaction is quite the opposite.

> He cannot acquiesce in the fact of dying. Neither the idea of Providence, nor that of natural order, nor that of an immortal soul, can appease him respecting the gulf between death and life.[32]

Paul will not euphemize death. Though some might appeal to Philippians 1:21ff. to substantiate just such a claim, Barth believes the context of Philippians prohibits such an understanding. Barth suggests that the expression "the nuissance of dying" may not be altogether unbefitting of Paul.[33] Yet even the notion of death as a nuisance may be too mild since Paul views death as the enemy, indeed the last enemy. Death represents everything in the world which is contrary to God. The Corinthians were adept at accommodating themselves to this world. Their beliefs could be understood as a form of naturalism. They believed that Christ had already accomplished all that he could and/or would. The work of Christ was already concluded and was in itself satisfying.[34] Barth suggests that this Corinthian view, since it is a form of Christian monism with the Kingdom of God already being established, is nothing other than "a pious godlessness."[35] The Corinthians expected nothing new in the world. Paul by contrast could not view the world as it is either as complete or natural. This constituted the great divide between Paul and the Corinthians. Paul could not conclude a peace treaty with "a spiritual-religious-moral Kingdom of God" on this earth while the enemy was still active. Death was not natural. Paul was emphatic that flesh and blood cannot inherit the Kingdom of God while the Corinthians believed that if man had not already inherited it he most certainly would by nature in the future. Paul could not concur. Paul was further frustrated by the fact that the Corinthians had forgotten, betrayed, and/or disregarded the comprehensive and interpenetrating power of Christ in the world even today.[36] Again Paul affirms that Christ is not only an event of the past. Christ is a force in the present and the future.

In summary the Corinthians were in Paul's opinion too oriented to this world and much too inclined to accept things as they are. Paul in contrast envisioned death neither as natural nor the world as he knew it corresponding to the Kingdom of God. There was a cosmic difference between the two. Paul had caught a glimpse of the frontier of this world and was attempting to direct the Corinthians to that frontier.

The negative condition of death can also be seen in a second aspect of the thought of Paul which draws Barth's attention. Paul suggests that the Corinthians lack a profound appreciation (perhaps better *de*preciation) of sin. Here again

the Corinthians were accommodating themselves to this world and
not expecting significant changes. Barth intimates that because
the Corinthians did not perceive the negative nature of death
they were unable to connect death and sin in their minds. The
Corinthians were timid with regard to sin. Barth writes:

> Sin is too serious a matter to be overcome by religious
> protestations and enthusiasms. It is a dominion over man,
> not merely a moral defect that attaches to him. It is
> given with his existence as a child of Adam, and is only to
> be overcome with his existence.[37]

The Corinthians did not seem much concerned with sin. They did
not perceive it as rebellion against God nor as a dominion which
continues to exercise an adverse influence over man. Sin and
death were treated in a similar fashion by the Corinthians
whereby both became innocuous. Though Paul treats sin and death
together, he does so because he perceives in sin the sting of
death which prohibits man from attaining the fulfillment which
God in Christ has revealed. Sin and death must both be overcome
in the resurrection.

Thus we note that due to their acceptance of the present
state of affairs the Corinthians were complacent with the present
things which God had revealed to Paul to be both contrary to His
will and grossly inadequate.

The third topic concerning death which we wish to highlight from *The Resurrection of the Dead* is the positive aspects
of death. There are two, but both are rather what might be
termed inadvertently positive. Barth notes that because the
Corinthians did not view death as the enemy, they failed to
see death as the decisive question which confronts man and
also the place where the decisive answer can be noted. This,
however, is inadvertently positive because, though we can
perceive death in this fashion, the Corinthians did not.[38]
Second Barth notes that the recollection of death is so urgent
and disturbing because it bears "the tidings of the resurrection
behind it."[39] Death can make us aware of the fulfillment which
lies behind it but which remains not yet ours due to sin though
undeniably ours in the future. This again, however, is only an
inadvertent though positive aspect of death because the
Corinthians failed to grasp it. In both of these positive
aspects of death there is a degree of what man and the Corinthians especially ought to perceive in death by nature. Though
this was missed by the Corinthians, it is something which we may
sense, though one might question whether Barth assumes that this
is revealed to all men.

In conclusion we reiterate that Barth understands death
to have very little positive significance in *The Resurrection
of the Dead*. Death is a negative phenomenon, is closely related
to sin, and is only inadvertently positive in nature.

AFTER-LIFE

Resurrection and Revelation

Revelation is the source of what Paul writes in 1 Corinthians 15. As we noted above Barth criticizes those who have
attempted to discover in this chapter a historic account of the
resurrection. Barth views this as a misunderstanding of Paul,
who is attempting to focus attention upon revelation as the
source of their faith and not some ambiguous historical fact(s).
Curiously and ironically the nature of the resurrection of
Jesus Christ was not at dispute between Paul and the Corinthians,
though it is disputed by modern theologians whom Barth critiques.
The Corinthians somehow were able to believe in the miracle of
the resurrection of Christ,[40] and they did not contend over this.
But they regarded the resurrection of Jesus Christ as an isolated
event of history, a point which Paul along with Barth, as noted
above, will contest.

It is worthwhile, nonetheless, to note what Barth does
believe concerning the tomb, even though Barth is indifferent
as to whether the tomb was open or closed. Barth in concert
with Paul and the Corinthians certainly believes that the tomb
was empty. "The tomb is doubtless empty, under every conceivable
circumstance empty! 'He is not here!'"[41] Since the tomb was
empty, then one may conclude that the resurrection must have been
bodily. In fact neither Paul nor his detractors anywhere doubt
in chapter 15 that the resurrection entailed the body.[42]

Nonetheless Paul and the Corinthians certainly were not
in complete agreement--else there would have been no need for
this letter. Barth summarizes the basic problem: "The error
of the Corinthians may be understood in this wise: they com-
prehended what had happened in Christ in the world as something
finished and satisfying in itself."[43] The Corinthians agreed
that Christ was unique, but they failed to note in Christ any
revelation and relevance for themselves.

There are several ways in which Paul corrects this Corinthian misunderstanding. First Paul corrects the Corinthian view-
point in reference to the ideas of Philo. Philo had spoken of a
first or heavenly Adam and then a second or earthly Adam, this
being based in the creation accounts of Genesis. The first
Adam for Philo was heavenly and more glorious than the second
Adam, but for Paul precisely the reverse is true. Paul did not
wish it to appear as if the reality of the new man lay behind
man in a lost paradise, as it does for Philo and Platonic ideals
in general. For Paul the second Adam, who is Christ, is future,
and he is coming to us. Paul does not lay upon the Corinthians
the hopeless task of going to heaven; rather he introduces the
idea that Christ, who is before us, is coming to us. Barth also
chides the Corinthians in the following:

How dreadful, if we have to tell ourselves, that it is
already given for us, and that the scanty thing we are

now and have is already the life of the new man, so that
we should already have our reward there![44]

Barth obviously envisions a future with Christ which will be a
notable improvement upon the present. It is also clear from
this that Barth thinks from Christ to others, something the
Corinthians were failing to do. For Paul Christ was exemplary.
He was the model--and certainly not for Paul just a model in
the past but one for the present and from the future.

Paul also develops a second line of reasoning which
attracts the attention of Barth. The concept of the firstfruits
from the Old Testament proves helpful for Paul in clarifying
this issue. The firstfruits was the portion of the harvest
which God claimed for Himself to symbolize that the entire harvest belonged to Him. Paul utilizes this concept in a fruitful
manner in demonstration of the fact that Christ represents the
firstfruits of those resurrected from the dead. He thereby
expresses that all the dead belong to God. "That is our hope"[45]
writes Barth in commenting upon Paul. The resurrection is the
divine horizon for our existence also. What transpired in Christ
will therefore be repeated.

Ultimately, however, when Paul is pushed to reveal his
source of authority and the basis of his ideas of the first and
second Adam and the firstfruits he will promote revelation and
the "appeared" of the first verses of chapter 15. It is upon
the basis of this revelation that Paul is able to employ human
metaphors and analogies which clarify the content of this revelation. But revelation is primary for Paul, and by extension
for Barth.

The Corinthians nevertheless had a problem noting any
relevance for themselves in the revelation appearances of
Christ. For Paul revelation ipso facto had relevance to everyone. Once therefore Paul was certain that Christ was the
revelation of God it was only a matter of applying that revelation in and to the lives of others. Barth puts it this way:

> If we see God at work there, then what is true there is
> also serious for us here and now, then our life, too, it
> goes without saying, is placed in the light which proceeds
> from that horizon of all that we call life.[46]

Revelation forms a backdrop which influences the way everyone
perceives the world and his relationship(s) in it. Barth writes:

> we are living the life limited by that horizon, we are living
> in time for eternity, we are living in the hope of the
> resurrection, it is that which cannot be denied, if Christ's
> resurrection is to be understood, not as miracle or myth or
> psychic experience (which all come to the same thing), but
> as God's revelation.[47]

But the Corinthians could render quite another interpretation
of both revelation and the resurrection. They understood that
the appearance of Christ to Paul could be a miracle, a myth, or
an inward experience. It was like any other event in life
which is given to explanation as this or that. But according
to this scheme "'Christ is risen' then means, fundamentally, as
much and as little as 'Christ is not risen.'"[48] The Corinthians
were leveling all experiences to a common denominator in order
that the extraordinary was interpreted as being ordinary.

Christ according to the understanding of Paul is the end
who is simultaneously the beginning, and it is the "not yet"
which separates man from that moment. Barth is certain that
the end is coming. The question of when is the principal one
left open for Barth. During time the not yet remains in conflict with the penultimate powers. In the end there will be
perfection. Now Barth offers several means of clarifying the
nature of the end, this perfection. Principally he clarifies
via negativa,[49] i.e. by negation, but Barth notes several
positive statements in Paul as well. He concurs with Paul
that corruption cannot inherit incorruption.[50] Barth also
emphasizes the contrast of the resurrection to human experiences
of life and death with the suggestion that "Life and death rather
approximate, faced with the reality of the resurrection."[51]

As a final negative fashion of clarifying the nature of the
end Barth remarks how loath he is to clarify the resurrection by
means of natural theology, as he notes some theologians have
done. Friedrich Christoph Oetinger in particular is cited by
Barth. Barth agrees with Oetinger as well as his pupil Bengel
and the younger J. T. Beck that Paul speaks of the resurrection
"in a 'real' and not an 'ideal' sense."[52] But Barth laments
when Oetinger then proceeds on the basis of vss. 35-49 of 1 Corinthians 15 "to develop a whole natural philosophy of the resur-
recting power of God, which as imperishable seed, as the impel-
ling vital essence, slumbers in every thing, while all else is
husk."[53] Furthermore Oetinger attempts to test this claim by
means of a chemical experiment with oil of balsam. Barth
considers this an example of interpreting the truth of the
resurrection via the positive or in analogy to known human
data, albeit in the form of a higher natural process. What
Barth perceives in the resurrection cannot be interpreted or
understood by analogy to experimental reality. Barth does not
focus here upon the "'internal processes' of nature which
aroused such a burning interest in the eighteenth century, but
the origin of 'nature,' its creation and redemption. . ."[54]
The latter lies on quite another plane from the former, and the
one may not be used, certainly not uncautiously or indiscreetly,
to clarify the other.

Nevertheless Barth does not leave us devoid of any possibility for detailing in a positive fashion the nature of resurrection. Barth poses a question for himself and then offers an
answer which is apologetic in tone. "What kind of a life is that

of which, by its definition, we can have no conception? How are
we able to affirm the truth of this life? The answer which Paul
gives is very exactly articulated."[55] Barth notes three
responses of Paul in 1 Corinthians 15. First he presents what
he terms the general answer. This is the analogy to plants
that between the seed sown and the plant is death (cf. vs.
36).[56] There is a continuity between the seed and the plant
even though death intervenes. What was seed can become plant
without ceasing to be the same. Barth accordingly asks:

> Where was the body of the plant before, and where is the
> body of the corn after? Answer: in the middle, in the
> utterly inconceivable critical point between the before
> and after lies a creation, more strictly speaking: a new
> creation, for something does not come out of nothing here,
> but, equally strange, out of Something comes something
> different.[57]

Barth refers to this metaphor as *"the change in the appearance
of the something in the order of time."*[58] This remains an
enigma, "as little to be understood as the present between the
past and the future, from which standpoint alone are both, as
such, to be understood."[59] There is a subject which persists,
though it assumes different forms through time.

Second Paul points out that in nature the same being can be
successively and simultaneously in varying shapes amd forms.
Paul gives three examples--flesh, bodies, and glory and then
notes these in men, beasts, birds, and fish; heavenly and earthly;
and heavenly and earthly again of the sun, moon, and stars all
respectively. It is possible to see infinite variations of the
same entities and qualities.[60] Barth notes that the subject
remains while the predicate or forms differ.

The third response which Barth notes in Paul concerns the
double analogy of vss. 42-44a. In nature predicates may change
while subjects persist. This is also true of the resurrection,
though Barth is explicit that this in no way represents a
natural process. Barth notes:

> nothing *is*, and nothing can *be*, proved in relation to the
> resurrection. What is rather shown purely hypothetically
> is that which the resurrection is, *if* there be a resurrec-
> tion, so that such questions as the doubters are accustomed
> to ask may no longer be raised.[61]

Analogies and the conclusions which are drawn from them derive
not from something being sought but from something already
found. Barth writes: "Nature can only offer analogies,
similes; the rational contemplation of nature can only make
room for the truth of the Resurrection."[62] The truth of
revelation is independent of rational truths, though the latter
can be of assistance in preparing for the possibility of the
former.

Though the Corinthians held that "there was a continued existence after death in a somehow conceivable beyond,"[63] the contrast which Paul envisions between now and after-life transcends human language while the contrast between the present natural body and the future resurrection body bursts the limits of biological demonstration. Hence, though Barth offers positive analogies and metaphors for the truth he recognizes, it is principally via negativa that the truths of the resurrection are imparted.

Body and Soul

As we noted in description of death, death is the death of the body. But the Corinthians believed that at the least the soul of a man continued to exist after life. Barth contends in contradistinction that the soul is known only in relation to the body. This the Corinthians ignored, concealed, and evaded as much as possible, but Paul rips this veil. Human beings know only the natural body which is corruptible, dishonorable, and weak "together with the soul, or, at least, without the soul altering in any way the character of that which makes it a human body."[64] Furthermore Barth argues that the idea of the immortality of the soul is disputed by what Paul says in 1 Corinthians 15, specifically in vss. 35-44. This is not to say that Barth believes that the idea of the immortality of the soul is not plausible. Barth in fact recognizes its plausibility; he even recognizes that it may be "asserted, if not perhaps demonstrated, without disturbing the picture of world uniformity."[65] There is much to say and argue for the immortality of the soul, but Barth opts to hope and believe in the scandal and irrationality of the resurrection, which he suggests may even be viewed as "religious materialism."[66] This is because Barth advocates the resurrection of the body,

> This same body that we plainly see dying and perishing, the assertion, therefore, not of a duality of life here and life to come, but of an identity of the two, not given now, not to be directly ascertained, but only to be hoped for, only to be believed in.[67]

Barth believes that an attempt to be God's without the body is rebellion against God's will and a secret denial of God. "We are waiting for our *Body's* redemption"[68] he writes. Furthermore Barth states that it is not the soul which continues unto the resurrection but the body. "The persisting subject is rather just the body. It is 'natural' body this side, 'spiritual' body beyond the resurrection."[69] The resurrection for Barth will involve the repredication of the body. The soul, as predicate, must give way to something else.[70] Barth refers to the body in relationship to a non-bodily entity, which though Barth does not specify, we might describe as soul. This non-bodily does "determine" the body. It exercises an influence upon it. The non-bodily remains a vague and indefinite term for Barth, while the body is unambiguous. The resurrection

represents a change effected noteworthily by the Spirit of God.[71]
It is not an aspect of man which effects the resurrection but
rather God who becomes involved to bring it about.

Three Symptoms

Barth notes that verse 52 mentions briefly three remarkable
symptoms of the "dawning crisis" of the resurrection when the
dead and living will put on incorruption and immortality. First
it will occur "literally 'in a moment,' therefore not even in a
fraction of time, else it could not happen at any rate to all
races simultaneously, but in the present."[72] Second the phrase
"in the twinkling of an eye" bespeaks the suddenness of the
approaching crisis. It will not be preceded by gradual or
catastrophical developments.[73] The third phrase is "at the
sound of the last trump." The trumpet, being the sign of
command, "is the decisive sign of this crisis."[74] Thus the
resurrection will occur instantaneously if not more quickly and
at the command or initiative of God. It certainly is beyond the
comprehension and ability of man.

Christian Monism and Universalism

Though Barth notes that Christian monism is untenable in
this life,[75] ultimately Barth believes that the resurrection
will be a type of Christian monism. "That God is all in all,
is not true, but must become true. Christian monism is not a
knowledge that is presently possible, but a coming knowledge."[76]
God being all and in all is in the background and on the horizon
of every human event and decision. Barth thus understands the
end, as he does the entire purpose of this Corinthian correspondence, to be the glory of God.

Implicit within this is the idea that the resurrection
will be universal. Though Barth writes that perfection will
entail the resurrection of his own,[77] still if God is to be
all in all, then all must be resurrected. Barth says as much
in comments upon the first and second Adam. "'In Adam all
die,' is the account of every human life ruled off; 'in Christ
shall all be made alive.'"[78] Barth focuses upon the antithesis
between the present and the future. While the former describes
our present condition the latter is our hope. Furthermore
Barth notes that the all which comes after "in Christ" is
intended in a representative and not an exclusive fashion.
"The resurrection, like death, concerns *all*."[79] It will be
universal. This, too, undoubtedly for Barth will enhance the
glory of God.

FOOTNOTES

[1]Eberhard Busch, *Karl Barth: His Life from Letters and Autobiographical Texts*, 2d. ed., trans. John Bowden (London: SCM Press, Ltd., 1976), p. 123.

[2]Karl Barth, *The Resurrection of the Dead*, trans. H. J. Stenning (New York: Fleming H. Revell Company, 1933), p. 111.

[3]Ibid., p. 101.

[4]Ibid., p. 110.

[5]Ibid., p. 16.

[6]Ibid., p. 37.

[7]Ibid., p. 131.

[8]Ibid., p. 136.

[9]Ibid., pp. 137-138.

[10]Ibid., p. 139.

[11]Ibid., p. 151.

[12]Ibid., p. 184.

[13]Ibid., p. 145.

[14]Ibid., p. 15.

[15]Ibid.

[16]Ibid., p. 140.

[17]Ibid., p. 183.

[18]Ibid., p. 146.

[19]Ibid., p. 140.

[20]Ibid., p. 138.

[21]Ibid., pp. 143, 148-149.

[22]Ibid., p. 116.

[23]Ibid., p. 106.

[24]Ibid., p. 134.

[25]Ibid., p. 105.

[26]Ibid., p. 103.

[27]Ibid., p. 105.

[28]Ibid., p. 107.

[29]Ibid.

[30]Ibid., p. 106.

[31]Ibid., pp. 105-106.

[32]Ibid., p. 144.

[33]Ibid.

[34]Ibid., p. 168.

[35]Ibid., p. 169.

[36]Ibid.

[37]Ibid., p. 158.

[38]Ibid., p. 116.

[39]Ibid., p. 109.

[40]Ibid., p. 143.

[41]Ibid., p. 138.

[42]Ibid., p. 116.

[43]Ibid., p. 168.

[44]Ibid., p. 200.

[45]Ibid., p. 165.

[46] Ibid., p. 151.   [47] Ibid., pp. 151-152.

[48] Ibid., p. 154.   [49] Ibid., p. 85.

[50] Ibid., p. 207.   [51] Ibid.

[52] Ibid., p. 183.   [53] Ibid.

[54] Ibid., pp. 183-184.   [55] Ibid., p. 185.

[56] Ibid.   [57] Ibid., p. 188.

[58] Ibid., p. 187.   [59] Ibid., p. 188.

[60] Ibid., p. 189.   [61] Ibid., p. 186.

[62] Ibid., p. 195.   [63] Ibid., p. 116.

[64] Ibid., pp. 195-196.   [65] Ibid., p. 117.

[66] Ibid.   [67] Ibid.

[68] Ibid., p. 197.   [69] Ibid., pp. 191-192.

[70] Ibid., p. 196.   [71] Ibid.

[72] Ibid., p. 208.   [73] Ibid.

[74] Ibid.   [75] Ibid., pp. 116-117.

[76] Ibid., p. 170.   [77] Ibid., p. 164.

[78] Ibid., p. 166.   [79] Ibid.

Death in the Credo

AN INTERLUDE OR AN OVERTURE?

Barth's fascination with Wolfgang Amadeus Mozart is well-known. He cites Mozart in *The Epistle to the Romans*[1] and dedicates several pages of *Church Dogmatics III/3* to him.[2] His study he considered to be one of the few among theologians where pictures of Mozart and Calvin could be seen on the same level.[3] Because of his love for Mozart and his music it does not seem inappropriate for our investigation of Barth in the *Credo* to utilize some musical terms to describe some of the phenomena we will encounter. We will note themes which resonate with what Barth had written previously as well as what Barth will write later in his career. We will also hear a note of dissonance with former and future writings which will prompt us to ask whether this is not an interlude, indeed a surprising interlude. The notion of an overture may also be appropriate to the themes which appear in the *Credo*, especially when viewed as an overture to Barth's magnum opus, the *Church Dogmatics*.

The *Credo* actually stems from a period of turmoil in the life of Barth. In 1934 Barth had been removed from his position at the University of Bonn. On March 1 of 1935 he was served a total ban from speaking in public in Germany. Hence the opportunity for Barth to lecture outside Germany in the Netherlands was a welcome one, though Barth found that his Dutch audience was doing theology "in a leisurely way."[4] All tolled Barth delivered sixteen lectures under the title "The Main Problems of Dogmatics, on the basis of the Apostles' Creed" between February 8 and April 6 of 1935. These form the basis of the work *Credo*, to which we now direct our attention.

THE PROCEDURE

In our study of the *Credo* we will not organize our thoughts according to the three questions which represent the three foci of our investigation. Instead we will first take note of various points which continue along the lines which Barth has advocated in *The Epistle to the Romans* and *The Resurrection of the Dead* before we proceed to examine one point which seemingly departs from both the previous and subsequent writings of Barth.

NOTES OF RESONANCE

Between the writings of the earlier Barth and the *Credo* there are a number of similar themes and ideas. We shall detail eight here.

First there is a note of resonance or a point of continuity which characterizes the thought of Barth at this point concerning the qualitative difference between time and eternity. Barth writes that "over against human history and society, time and world, there is a totally different future existence of man."[5]

Resurrection of the body and the life everlasting clearly
signify an existence different from life in this world. At
the same time Barth cautions that because we do our thinking
in the concepts of the world and time we know, we "have not
the slightest idea what we are saying when we talk either
positively or negatively about the time of that God with Whom
we shall live in unbroken peace in eternal life."[6] Resurrection
and eternal life are without parallel in and to this world.
Note as well that when Barth portrays the future in terms of
unbroken peace that this is reminiscent of *Romans* when he wrote
that there was no separation between man and God in the Garden
of Eden.[7] Nonetheless Barth employs several Pauline terms
from 1 Corinthians 15 and 2 Corinthians 5 to describe the future
existence: incorruption, power, honor, redemption, and peace.[8]
Such words of description, however, remain ultimately outside
of human experience and illustrate the qualitative difference
between time and eternity.

Despite the qualitative difference which Barth continues
to note, however, he reduces the radical difference between
time and eternity. Whereas he had spoken of the difference
between time and eternity as a border, he now terms it a "frontier."[9] While we may see over a frontier, the image of a
border and death as omega and the divine No discourage such a
view. Thus though we note that Barth continues to stress the
distinction between time and eternity, the stress is less pronounced than formerly.

We also note that time as we know and experience it is
granted to humankind by God as an opportunity for repentance.
Barth, however, would not wish this to be understood as simply
a time of remorse for sin. "The present is the *regnum gratiae*,
between the Ascension and the Second Coming."[10] This time,
our time, is a time of divine grace to which we are called to
respond to Christ. We are called to celebrate the work of
Christ and joyfully to anticipate His final coming.

Furthermore Barth notes that eschatology plays a rather
insignificant role in the theology of the Reformers. That he
suggests derives from the centrality of forgiveness of sins
to their message. The Reformers stressed so much the forgiveness
of sins that anything that could be said concerning resurrection
and eternal life could be understood as already stated under
the forgiveness of sins.[11] Similarly Barth views the end time
of redemption as an unveiling of that which we already know.
In the context of the Apostles' Creed he puts it this way:
"This last word of the Credo is concerned with the enforcing,
emphasising and unfolding of truth already perceived and
known."[12] There is a continuity here between the present and
the future. Eschatology can only display and develop the hope
which is already before us.[13] Barth thus extrapolates from
the past and present in portraying the future. The future
will not be so radically different, therefore, as previously
supposed by Barth. There is a degree of continuity though the
emphasis still falls upon discontinuity.

Second in the *Credo* we note a heightened emphasis upon the Christ and His centrality, an emphasis which is more in the character of the *Church Dogmatics* as compared with *Romans* and *The Resurrection of the Dead*. Barth suggests that Christian eschatology concerns not some*thing* but some*one*. Christians expect the coming of the Lord. Christ Himself forms the frontier of time.[14] "Our sole future is that He will come, just as our sole present is that He has come. . . Christ is our hope."[15] "He awakens the dead; He gives eternal life; He is the Redeemer."[16] There is a specific personality associated with the end of time, and it is the person of Christ. Barth does not talk about the end of time so much as the final revelation of Christ.

> The Second Coming of Christ is the restoration, but at the same time the universal and final revelation, of the direct presence of Jesus Christ as "God-man" as that was the content of the forty days after Easter.[17]

As a corollary to this we note that the heightened emphasis upon Christ includes stress upon our unity with Christ. Barth suggests that there exists the "highest degree of *unity* between Jesus Christ and His own, a unity that in itself is in its *substance* unsurpassable. Even in the present there is no defect in this unity."[18] The reconciliation of God and man was accomplished in the death of Christ. Only its disclosure and the final redemption of man remain to be accomplished.

The unity of man with Christ brings us to a third note of resonance within the theology of Barth. This is the notion that death is unnatural. Though the New Testament speaks of death as "falling asleep," this is not conceived as something natural but rather as very astonishing.[19] The miracles of the New Testament are, as Barth notes, directed against the power of death. Hence one would not expect death to continue to reign. Yet for Barth the unnaturalness of death stems primarily from our unity with Christ. Death interrupts and disturbs that substantial unity. Such is the unity between man and Christ that Barth notes solemnly with the Apostle Paul that "If the dead rise not, then is *not* Christ raised."[20] Man and Christ may not be divided and/or dissociated. Nevertheless our human unity with Christ "cries out for a change, for resurrection."[21] Death may be unnatural but some form of transition is required if we are ever to be free of this fight with the body of "flesh" of this world. We thus hear again the themes of discontinuity amidst continuity and vice versa.

A fourth note of resonance is evident here as well. In *Romans* Barth referred to the fact that human consciousness of the sentence of death also brings with it an incomprehensible awareness of resurrection.[22] This is echoed in *Credo* when Barth speaks of our unity with Christ which "cries out for a change, for resurrection."[23] It appears that we have here an echo of the existentialism prevalent in *Romans*. Our awareness

of the sentence of death hanging over human life impels us to
believe that death cannot be the final terminus for man.

Resurrection is the fifth topic which we hear resonating
between the previous writings of Barth and the *Credo*. Barth
speaks of resurrection as an answer to our existential questions
and also clarifies the nature of the resurrection in positive
and negative terms. As noted above our unity with Christ *cries
out* for a change from its present imperfect condition. We have
also cited above the words of Paul which describe the future
existence. Barth understands resurrection as an answer to the
existential question: "Who shall separate us from the love of
Christ?"[24] While current life, as Barth notes, provides an
ample number of responses to this question, resurrection represents the divine response. Negatively Barth notes that man in
the resurrection will become neither a god nor an angel. It
signifies that human carnal existence and "our heaven and earth
as theatre of *revolt*"[25] will be dissolved and changed. Positively
resurrection signifies that man will become incorrupt, powerful,
and honorable, and that he will be initiated into a realm of
peace with God.[26] Barth also speaks of resurrection as a transformation, a transformation from our present form of unity with
Christ into the new form of unity which Scripture refers to as
eternal life. Resurrection is the "carrying out of the accomplished reconciliation of man in his future redemption."[27] It
confirms that Easter and the forty days were not a chance miracle
but the sign of the end, aim, and meaning of all history.[28]
Hence again in the *Credo* we hear notes of continuity conjoined
with notes of discontinuity.

The subject of eternal life, the sixth topic which we must
address, follows upon our fifth topic of resurrection. Resurrection is not the end toward which man proceeds. Rather
resurrection is the means that God chooses to issue men into
eternal life. Though we must remember that Barth writes in
the *Credo* that we humans lack the slightest idea of what eternal
life will be like, nevertheless Barth does offer, as he had
previously, clarification of eternal life in both negative and
positive senses.

Negatively Barth offers four points of clarification.
First eternal life is not a super-temporal realm; neither is
it timelessness nor infinite time. Eternal life does not
according to Barth stand outside time. Second eternal life
does not mean a life in a carefully and boldly conceived perfection. It is thus curious whether Barth leaves open the
possibility that sin may coexist with and/or within man in
eternity, and perhaps this is a primitive form of the idea of
eternalizing which we meet in the *Church Dogmatics*. Third
eternity does not mean that this life that we now have is annihilated and replaced by another, even an eternal world. Eternity
must therefore for Barth relate to this world. The precise relationship to this world is not detailed for us, however. Fourth
eternity of our life does not mean that our life becomes identified with the life of God. Eternal life is related to God but

not identical with Him. Barth does not envision our being
absorbed into God and disappearing. Though related to God
resurrected man will be characterized by self-autonomy, though
Barth leaves open the possibility that man may be like the
image on a movie or a film, i.e. readily available to God but
not really "live."[29]

Positively Barth understands eternal life from Scripture
as this life which we have now in this world, but a life which
has become new by means of its relation to God. "Contact with
God" or at least being attuned to God thus determines whether
or not one enjoys eternal life. Eternal life can thus be
experienced already in this earthly life. Eternity invades
the realm of time. Here again we note an increased emphasis
upon continuity in Barth, especially in contrast with *Romans*.
While in *Romans* the eternal can be visualized as breaking into
time from above, in *Credo* the horizontal dimension of time gains
recognition. Eternal life can continue through time in this
life and of course beyond the resurrection. Since the future
does parallel to a degree the present, the likelihood of man's
becoming merely an image is diminished while the possibility of
some form of self-autonomy is enhanced.

Barth also reviews in passing former theological descriptions of eternal life. The beatific vision in which man
contemplates God as He is is one traditional image of eternal
life which Barth notes. A second description is being in a
loving relationship with God as God Himself wishes to be loved.
The Reformation fathers stressed as well that in the consumma-
tion of God's dealings with man that man will be giving glory
to God. Barth endorses each of these descriptions and further
suggests that supertemporaneousness, timelessness, or infinite
time might be ascribed to eternal life. Nevertheless such
attributes Barth allows only under the qualification that we
"have not the slightest idea what we are saying when we talk
either positively or negatively about the time of that God with
whom we shall live in unbroken peace in eternal life."[30]
Barth accordingly encourages that in order to avoid unnecessary
pains we ought simply hold to the decisive feature of eternal
life: "it is eternal in its being lived in the unveiled light
of God and in so far participating in God's own life."[31] Though
the glory of God may be veiled from us now, we nonetheless may
enjoy eternal life already in this life if we turn toward and
remain attuned to Him. For Barth eternal life is preeminently
a quality of life rather than quantity of life, though quality
and quantity should not be viewed for Barth as mutually exclusive.

Apocatastasis is the eighth subject in which there is
resonance between the earlier Barth and the *Credo*. As Barth
demonstrated some ambivalence in this regard previously, so we
note in the *Credo*. Barth suggests that none of the best theological camouflage and entrenchments will hinder God from judging
man. "Not all the orthodox, not all the pietists, not even
all the followers of Kohlbrügge will enter heaven!"[32] God will

not judge necessarily as men expect. Not even those who praise
"grace, the whole grace and nothing but grace"[33] can count on
being justified. These statements clearly demonstrate Barth's
reluctance to endorse and affirm apocatastasis. Nevertheless
Barth seems inclined toward this very position. We noted
previously that Barth extrapolates from the past and present
into the future. He expects that the eschaton will unveil
what we already know. Since Barth believes that the reconciliation of God and man was accomplished in the death of Christ,
it seems reasonable that Barth would expect the final redemption
to involve all men. Barth demonstrates a clear tendency in this
regard when he writes:

> For Jesus Christ really comes from heaven as He Who sits
> at the right hand of God, therefore as the Risen One,
> therefore as the Revealer of the reconciliation accomplished
> in Him, therefore as He Who has accomplished this reconcili-
> ation, and therefore in fact as the Judge Who anticipated
> the judgment for us and through Whose punishment we are
> righteous.[34]

Barth would not have man discount that universal reconciliation
and its corresponding universal redemption in favor of a human
figure of a judge.[35] Also returning to a previous thought,
being "in Christ" is understood as a substantive unity which
reckons men as belonging to God and therewith implying the
doctrine of apocatastasis.[36] Nevertheless Barth will not allow
logical arguments to dictate his thought or the thoughts of
God, but rather he disannuls logic in favor of credo, the presupposition of every creed.[37] Though logic might suggest an
idea, Barth holds that faith is the better and preferred guide.

We have thus heard eight notes of resonance between Barth's
earlier work and the *Credo*. There is considerable resonance and
continuity evident between the *Credo* and Barth's prior works.
Nevertheless there remains for us to examine an apparent note of
disharmony.

A SURPRISING INTERLUDE?

In the *Credo* Barth uses a peculiar phrase, peculiar at
least in terms of what we would expect Barth to write and at
odds with what he will express in the *Church Dogmatics*. The
phrase in question is "death as separation of the immortal
soul from the mortal body." It occurs twice in the *Credo* and
we shall cite both instances:

> Death as separation of the immortal soul from the mortal
> body confirms the fact that we *still* exist in a state of
> ambiguity as children of Adam and as children of God, as
> righteous and as sinners, in the time of Pontius Pilate and
> in the time of grace.[38]
> Resurrection of the flesh does not mean that the man ceases
> to be a man in order to become a god or angel, but that he

may, according to I Cor. xv. 42f., be a man in *incorruption*, *power* and *honour*, *redeemed* from that contradiction and so *redeemed* from the separation of body and soul by which this contradiction is sealed, and so in the totality of his human existence *awakened* from the dead.[39]

We have noted previously in *Romans* and *The Resurrection of the Dead* that Barth did not believe in an immortal aspect of man continuing to exist after life. The closest Barth comes to such a position is in reference to repredication of the body in resurrection. There Barth spoke of the body in relation to the non-bodily.[40] Though this non-bodily aspect sounds almost like the idea of soul, Barth in the same work clearly disputes the immortality of the soul.[41] This is to be distinguished from what Barth expresses in *Credo*. Since Barth will strongly deny immortality to man or even an aspect of man in the *Church Dogmatics*, his remarks in *Credo* are puzzling and difficult to clarify, though we shall posit several possible explanations.

Eberhard Busch in his biography of Barth provides one possible manner in which to understand how Barth may have come to alter his views regarding the immortality of the soul. Busch notes that Karl Barth's youngest brother Heinrich was a scholar of Plato. Through Heinrich Karl faced "the wisdom of Plato."[42] In fact according to Busch his brother Heinrich

> had a fruitful influence on Karl's thinking with the concept of 'the wisdom of death' and, like Emil Brunner, stimulated him to a combination of a theological approach and Plato's philosophy of origins.[43]

In this light it might be possible to appreciate Barth's altering his views concerning the immortality of the soul under the sway of his brother Heinrich. Nevertheless the period Busch mentions for this influence of his brother is the year 1920[44] when Barth was completing the second edition of *The Epistle to the Romans* and well before *The Resurrection of the Dead*, works in which immortality of the soul is denied. Even if the period of his brother's influence and Karl Barth's use of Marburg, neo-Kantian terminology is extended to the years 1919 to 1924, as Hendrikus Berkhof advocates in an article detailing three hermeneutical problems of the early Barth, we are still a decade before the appearance of the *Credo*.[45] Certainly from his brother Heinrich Karl Barth would have learned of the subtle variations associated with the use of the word "soul" and should have avoided any careless or casual usage of the term. But this only serves to render his description of death as separation of body and soul in the *Credo* more enigmatic.

Examining the context in the *Credo* leads to no definite resolution of the peculiarity either. In this particular context Barth is speaking of our real unity with Christ which is initiated in this life. Nevertheless due to sin this unity with Christ is veiled and to that extent gives way to uncertainty. Death in particular clarifies that we live in ambiguity as offspring of Adam and of God. If Barth is employing the words "immortal soul" to describe the relationship which exists between God and those who turn toward Him we can see how death tragically interrupts that relationship of eternal life, this supposing of course that there is no life per se immediately subsequent to death. Eternal life, though describing basically a quality of life, would hence possess as well for Barth a quantitative dimension which death interrupts by separating the body from the soul. However there seems to be no explicit justification for such an interpretation, though it is not inconsistent with what Barth writes.

A similar explanation suggests that the separation of body and soul is a sign of our ambiguity. The immortal soul would thus be a symbol for the new man in Christ which is already present and which will be unveiled in the resurrection.[46] This new man continues to be related to God after life, but it is accomplished without the body, and hence death is the separation of the immortal soul from the body.

There is also the possibility that the soul as the focus of personality in man becomes eternalized with God, a notion we will note more extensively in the *Church Dogmatics*. Being eternalised could be accomplished without a body and therefore could clarify Barth's unexpected terminology. But though it is again a plausible explanation of the terminology, this interpretation lacks support from the *Credo* itself.

There is the further possibility that Barth is citing the position of the Corinthian opponents of Paul. Hence death as separation of body and soul would not indicate a position that Barth is advocating but rather one which he along with Paul contradicts.[47] Such an explanation is possible, but again explicit justification for it in the *Credo* appears lacking.

Death as separation of the immortal soul and body thus remains an enigmatic phrase in the *Credo*. The phrase is simply surprising in terms of what preceded it and what will follow. One might describe it as the introduction of a new, brief theme into a symphony which is never heard again, a surprising interlude if you will. It does seem peculiar that Barth would make use of such terminology in an ambiguous, unclarified fashion, especially in light of his familiarity with the work of his brother Heinrich in this realm. Yet he did use it, and if we are forced to choose between the various options outlined above we would opt for one which understands the soul as the focus of our relationship to God, a relationship which is without end.

CONCLUSION

Our discussion of the *Credo* and the positions which Barth advocates relative to our three questions must remain incomplete at this point. We have noted numerous points where Barth advocates positions which either agree with and/or only slightly modify what Barth has written previously, but we must continue our investigation into the *Church Dogmatics* to ascertain whether this continues. We must also defend the possibility that "death as separation of the immortal soul and body" is inconsistent with what Barth will write in the *Church Dogmatics*. Finally we will want to note whether the *Credo* represents an interlude or an overture and how this might affect our interpretation of death and after-life in the *Church Dogmatics*.

Nevertheless before turning to the *Church Dogmatics* we will highlight our discoveries from the *Credo*, and we shall do so by focusing upon our three questions. Concerning the cause and significance of death we find some modification of his previous position. Because he stresses more of the horizontal nature of history and because he emphasizes our unity with Christ death does not appear so much of a negative phenomenon. Nonetheless death disrupts our unity with Christ and must be therefore a negative matter. Barth does not directly address the question of the origin of death, as he had previously and will do in the *Church Dogmatics*. We might speculate that this derives from Barth's heightened emphasis upon Christ with a corresponding and implicit decline in concentration upon the cause of death. Barth rather points to and celebrates the hope which Christ has precipitated.

Concerning what transpires to the individual in death we receive ambivalent signals. This stems from the fact that Barth does not develop an anthropology per se in the *Credo*. But Barth does refer to death as the separation of the body and immortal soul, an idea we have tried to interpret in terms consistent with earlier and later writings of Barth, but an idea which remains a surprising interlude all the same. On the other hand we note that the separation of the body and immortal soul suggests an interim period between death and the resurrection. Barth gives no firm indication as to the nature of this period, but since death interrupts the relationship between God and man we may suspect that nothing transpires in the interim as far as man is concerned. Ordinarily one would expect something to transpire to the soul while it is apart from the body, but Barth mentions nothing in this regard.

We learn nothing in terms of anthropology from the description Barth offers of what transpires after life either. The resurrection and eternal life are viewed much the same as before in Barth's writings--a transformation though seemingly less radical. Because Barth uses the word transformation to describe resurrection rather than rejoining of body and soul we suspect that the immortal soul must represent in some sense our relationship to God rather than an aspect or segment of man. In the *Credo* Barth seems more inclined toward apocatastasis, setting up little obstacle to such a conclusion. Nevertheless apocatastasis for us as well as Barth still remains subsumed not to logic, etc. but to *credo*.

FOOTNOTES

[1] Karl Barth, *The Epistle to the Romans*, 6th ed., trans. Edwyn C. Hoskyns (London: Oxford University Press, 1933), p. 500.

[2] Karl Barth, *Church Dogmatics III/3*, trans. G. W. Bromiley and R. J. Ehrlich (Edinburgh: T. & T. Clark, 1960), pp. 297-299.

[3] Eberhard Busch, *Karl Barth: His Life from Letters and Autobiographical Texts*, 2d ed., trans. John Bowden (London: SCM Press, Ltd., 1976), pp. 410, 419.

[4] Ibid., p. 260.

[5] Karl Barth, *Credo*, trans. Robert McAfee Brown (New York: Charles Scribner's Sons, 1962), p. 161.

[6] Ibid., p. 171.

[7] Barth, *Romans*, p. 247.

[8] Barth, *Credo*, p. 169.   [9] Ibid., p. 10.

[10] Ibid., p. 164.   [11] Ibid., p. 163.

[12] Ibid., p. 162.   [13] Ibid.

[14] Ibid., pp. 120-121.   [15] Ibid., p. 120.

[16] Ibid., p. 166.   [17] Ibid., p. 121.

[18] Ibid., p. 164.   [19] Ibid., p. 167.

[20] Ibid.   [21] Ibid., p. 165.

[22] Barth, *Romans*, p. 383.

[23] Barth, *Credo*, p. 165.   [24] Ibid., p. 169.

[25] Ibid.   [26] Ibid.

[27] Ibid., p. 166.   [28] Ibid.

[29] Ibid., p. 170.   [30] Ibid., p. 171.

[31] Ibid.   [32] Ibid., p. 125.

[33] Ibid.   [34] Ibid., pp. 123-124.

[35] Ibid., p. 124.   [36] Ibid., p. 171.

[37]Ibid.   [38]Ibid., p. 168.

[39]Ibid., p. 169.   [40]Barth, *Romans*, p. 191.

[41]Ibid., p. 196.   [42]Busch, *Barth*, p. 116.

[43]Ibid.   [44]Ibid.

[45]Hendrikus Berkhof, "Drie Problemen bij de Interpretatie van de jonge Barth," *Nederlands Theologisch Tijdschrift* 34 (1980):294-306.

[46]Hendrikus Berkhof, personal letter (Leiden, Netherlands: December 29, 1983).

[47]H. J. Adriaanse, personal letter (The Hague, Netherlands: December 26, 1983).

Death in The Church Dogmatics

INTRODUCTION

In the year 1932 *Volume I/1* of Barth's *Church Dogmatics* was published. It was the first of four volumes comprised in turn of thirteen individual books or parts which consumed Barth's attention for more than three and a half decades. Though with the publication of *Volume IV/4 (fragment)* in 1968 the *Church Dogmatics* extended to 9185 pages, nine times as long as John Calvin's *Institutes of the Christian Religion* and almost twice as long as the *Summa* of Thomas Aquinas, it remained an *opus imperfectum*,[1] an incomplete work. Nevertheless the *Church Dogmatics* is the most outstanding theological work to be written in generations, and it marks Barth as one of the premier theologians of all time. For our study the *Church Dogmatics*, Barth's magnum opus, provides a rich resource of materials and ideas. It is the apex of our investigation of Barth's understanding of death and after-life.

THE METHOD OF THE CHURCH DOGMATICS

The *Church Dogmatics* differs from the previous works of Barth which we have examined in that the *Church Dogmatics* was organized and structured by Barth himself. In the previous works Barth had been commenting upon a structure provided by someone else, i.e. the Apostle Paul in his letters to the Romans and Corinthians as well as the Apostles' Creed. In the *Church Dogmatics* Barth established his own method for presenting the Christian faith or, as Barth would prefer to say, the dealings of God with man and man with God in the Old and New Testaments and the history of the Church. The manner in which Barth accomplished this consequently provides an added dimension to our study of the *Church Dogmatics* as compared to the earlier studies in which we examined Barth's understanding of another's structure and ideas. We gain a better perspective on the thanatology and eschatology per se of Barth in relation to the whole of his theology in the *Dogmatics*.

We will also note that a number of concepts and ideas which were evident in previous writings of Barth recur. Yet these ideas are more fully developed, thereby enabling us to gain a more complete understanding of ideas and notions which appeared previously.

In our study we note again that Barth assumes a position(s) which is not orthodox, though terming it unorthodox does not befit the position(s) either. Barth has accordingly been termed neoorthodox, thereby signifying a tension between Barth and orthodoxy while demonstrating a continuity with that very orthodoxy. The neoorthodox nature of Barth in the *Church Dogmatics* is apparent in its very structure. We noted in our discussion of *The Epistle to the Romans* that Barth felt it inappropriate to place a study of death and/or after-life as a short and harmless

concluding chapter to dogmatics. Then it was that Barth wrote
that theology must be thoroughgoing eschatology. In his own
Dogmatics Barth followed his own prescription from *Romans* and
did not write a short and harmless concluding chapter concerning
death and/or after-life. There is an obvious irony in that
statement, of course, in that Barth never completed his *Church
Dogmatics*. Perhaps if Barth had been able to complete his
magnum opus the harmless sort of comments that he had chided in
Romans might have been included there, though that seems unlikely.
Nevertheless it is definitely true that Barth did not place his
thought concerning the cause and significance of death or what
transpires to the individual in death at that point. Even his
thoughts concerning what happens to man after life are evident
well before the proposed concluding volume, though in imperfect
form. Two reasons give rise to this determination. First
despite its thirteen extant volumes and even though an *opus
imperfectum*, the *Church Dogmatics* demonstrates a compact and
integrated quality. There is a marked unity to the *Church
Dogmatics*. Whereas some theologians are able to write on individual topics with little relation to other subjects and topics
this is definitely not the case with Barth. Whereas some theologians compose units of theology, Barth's *Dogmatics* demonstrates
more a unity of the whole. In *Church Dogmatics I/2* Barth notes
that in a Church dogmatics the position usually occupied by an
arbitrarily chosen basic view belongs properly to the Word of
God rather than to any conception of that Word.[2] It is the
center of dogmatics even as a circle has a precise center.[3]
"But the Word of God may not be replaced even vicariously by any
basic interpretation of the 'essence of Christianity', however
pregnant, deep and well founded."[4] This marks a profound change
of approach than had been customary in dogmatics for centuries,
indeed basically since the Apologists of the second century.
It was the intent of the Apologists and the majority of their
successors to relate their faith to the thoughts and experiences
of people in their day. Accordingly they would claim some view-
point of the day as a common basis upon which to argue for their
beliefs. Notably the Reformers saw negligible value in such an
enterprise, though Protestant Scholasticism soon introduced the
same precedure.[5] Barth rather believes that the center and
foundation of Christian dogmatics must be the Word of God. From
this center the content of the Word of God is unfolded and presented in both obedience and daring. It must be obedient in
being inspired by the Word of God alone, while it must yet be
daring in that every attempt at dogmatics involves responsible
human decisions. Dogmatics dare not claim for itself the
absolute necessity and binding force of the Word of God alone,
while it must yet be daring in that every attempt at dogmatics
involves responsible human decisions. Dogmatics dare not claim
for itself the absolute necessity and binding force of the Word
of God because it reflects human choice.[6] But Barth would not
have the Church neglect its teaching responsibility because "The
one Church is both the hearing and the teaching Church. It can
never be the one without the other."[7]

Reminding ourselves that method signifies the path or way followed, it is with the critical background outlined above that Barth proceeds to outline his own particular dogmatic method. In concluding *Church Dogmatics I/2* he accomplishes an outline of this method *via negativa*, by noting four different centers which have been promoted for dogmatics--the Word of atonement, the doctrine of God itself or the doctrine of His kingdom and lordship, God as creator, and God as redeemer--each of which in turn Barth rejects as inadequate to the task. He then suggests that rather than subordinating or superordinating these four centers one to another that they should instead be coordinated as a result of their common origin and end in the Word of God.[8] The Word of God serves as the center from which each of these four subjects or topics diverge. But at their center, which like the center of a circle is invisible, they are one.[9] There exists a parallel here between dogmatics and the existence of the Trinity,[10] which according to Barth entails the three divine modes of being existing as the Triunity.[11] The centers are intimately intertwined and yet distinct. This Barth holds does not reflect any imperfection in human thinking but instead follows the process of revelation as it has taken place.[12] Barth accordingly follows classical tradition and the natural pragmatic order of revelation and organizes his *Church Dogmatics* into four basic sections--the doctrine of God, the doctrine of creation, the doctrine of atonement or reconciliation, and finally the doctrine of redemption.

Each of these four doctrines is in turn concerned with several key issues. The doctrine of God revolves around four issues--the knowledge of God, the form of expression which this knowledge may take, the unfolding of God's fundamental attitude towards man, and the ethical claims which derive from these three issues. The doctrine of creation revolves around three concerns--first God's being and activity with respect to His creature and His creation; second man relative to his insight as God's creature, his destiny as the focal point of creation, and the lost righteousness consequent upon his own decision; and third the absolute claim of God the creator upon His creation. Though Barth does not consider the doctrine of atonement or reconciliation the systematic center of theology (that being the Word of God), the doctrine of atonement is the actual center of dogmatics and Church proclamation. It concerns four basic issues. The first is the divine-human covenant which God ratifies and confirms. The second issue of atonement is the objective fact of reconciliation in the mediator Jesus Christ, and the third concerns man's subjective appropriation of that atonement. The fourth issue of atonement for Barth is again theological ethics, this time reflecting upon man's response to the judgment and grace of God. Finally the doctrine of redemption is the fourth and last section of dogmatics for Barth, and it involves three issues. First comes the life of man in his hope resulting from the objective content of faith, i.e. Jesus Christ. Second appears the content of this faith as it relates to the promise and its future realization. And third comes the ethical claim of God

upon man in this eschatological context.[13] This in capsule form
is the briefest of outlines of what Barth intended to treat in
his *Church Dogmatics* if he would have been given the opportunity.

It is evident from this outline that Barth intended to
deal with what happens to man after life as part of the doctrine
of redemption, the projected fifth volume, under the topic of
the content of faith as it relates to the promise and the future.
Barth could be expected to describe the nature of after-life,
but this Barth was unable to accomplish. *Volume V* was never
written. Nevertheless we are not bereft of response in the
Church Dogmatics to our three primary questions. This again
results from the compact nature of the *Dogmatics*. One doctrine
is intertwined with another; each doctrine examines the Word of
God from a particular perspective or angle. The four doctrines
which Barth treats are not separate and isolated units. Therefore it is not unusual to learn something with regard to our
three questions outside Barth's projected fifth volume of his
Church Dogmatics.

THE THREE QUESTIONS IN THE CHURCH DOGMATICS

Certainly it is not simply a "harmless final chapter on
eschatology" which is the concern of this study. Barth did not
relegate his thoughts concerning death to the proposed fifth
volume. Rather, as is not uncommon amongst theologians, the
section which details man treats issues which are especially
pertinent to our first two questions.

Still even here there is a markedly new aspect to the
theology of Barth. Barth can remark that there is a prototype
of the distorted and caricatured time in which man now lives.
The time of sinful man is the counterpart of this time. Barth
writes that

> our lost time could not be at all without that first and
> genuine time, just as man could not have been lost had he
> not first been created in that first time with a true and
> proper nature which he afterwards lost.[14]

This seems consistent with the precepts and teachings of orthodoxy, according to which Adam and Eve were created, placed in the
Garden, but then they elected for disobedience and the Fall was
the most unfortunate consequence.

Yet there is a difference with Barth. Barth believes that
there is as well a second counterpart, which is of far greater
importance. This time is the time of grace, the time in which
the covenant of grace takes place. When man sinned after the
time of creation God initiated simultaneously this time of grace.
The time of sinful man was also the pre-time of fulfilled time
in Jesus Christ. Thus Barth can write: "From the beginning his
(man's) lost time was surrounded and enclosed by the time of the
divine covenant of grace directly continuing the time of

creation."[15] It would be tempting to conclude that the time of
creation is nothing more than the time of grace. After all the
two times are identical in nature. Yet Barth prefers to draw a
distinction between the two for two reasons. First during the
lost time the time of grace has an opponent which the time of
creation lacked, and second the time of creation is commencing
time which the time of grace is not.[16]

Furthermore, and this is essential to an understanding of
his theology, Barth questions whether the time of grace can
properly be called the counterpart of the time of creation.
Rather Barth believes that the time of grace is the true prototype of all time.

Real time, in this case, is primarily the lifetime of Jesus
Christ, the turning point, the transition, the decision
which were accomplished in His death and resurrection. . .
It was in correspondence with this real time, and as the
necessary and adequate form of this event, that time was
originally created--in and with creation and at the same
time as the form of the history of creation itself.[17]

Thus we note in Barth three time periods--the time of creation,
the time of the Fall and sin, and finally the time of grace.
But it is the time of grace which dominates each of the periods.
It reflects backwards over the two other periods and casts them
in a more favorable light. The time of sin and grace certainly
overlap and the time of creation reflects the time of grace,
which represents the focus of creation. We thus note here in
Barth another example of the compact and integrated character
of his theology which we noted above.

Barth argues in a similar fashion in two other contexts,
and it is worthwhile to note them as well for they offer additional clarification of the neoorthodox character of his thought
as well as justifying our focus and method for this section of
our study.

First Barth believes that from all eternity God has existed
as Father, Son, and Holy Spirit. God exists as three persons,
but since Barth desires to distinguish the idea of person from
personality and thus from tritheism he employs the term "mode of
being." Thus God reveals Himself in three modes of being. God
is a triunity. Hence God is one. But within Himself God exists
as three modes of being. It was and is the case that God had
complete and perfect fellowship within Himself. The Father and
Son were in communion one with the other through the operation
of the Holy Spirit. God was sufficient unto Himself. But of
His love and mercy God decided in complete freedom that he
wished to establish a covenant relationship with an entity *ad
extra*;[18] God elected to establish a relationship outside Himself.
And the relationship which was thus effected paralleled the bond
between the Father and the Son. "The eternal fellowship between
Father and Son, or between God and His Word, thus finds a correspondence in the very different but not dissimilar fellowship

between God and His creature."[19] God did not wish to remain by
Himself. Therefore from eternity He decided to create outside
Himself an entity with which He could have fellowship. Before
time, since time was yet to be created, God created the universe,
with no external presupposition, as an expression of His freedom
and purpose. Barth is clear that though the covenant of grace
may be actualised after the creation, in fact the creation presupposes the covenant.

> It would be truer to say that creation follows the covenant
> of grace since it is its indispensable basis and presupposi-
> tion. As God's first work, it is in the nature of a pattern
> or veil of the second, and therefore in outline already the
> form of the second. Creation sets the stage for the story
> of the covenant of grace.[20]

Creation as Barth understands it makes the work of God possible.
Creation is the necessary environment for God to work in; it
provides the foundation and stage for His work and activity.[21]

As a result of his exegesis of Genesis 1:1-2:4a Barth
describes the creation as the external basis of the covenant.
Creation enables God to establish covenant with the creature.
Barth notes this particularly in the fact that the first
creation narrative suggests that the creation was not complete
until the seventh, sabbath day was complete. Accordingly man
can only be described as "the crown of creation" with some reser-
vation.[22] Man, both male and female, is thus created and intended
for covenant fellowship with God. Thus the goal toward which God
is working in creation is already evident for Barth with the
creation of the universe and time. Creation is the stage for
covenant, and creation therefore cannot be properly understood
apart from grace.[23] In the creation accounts, then, we note
that creation is the external basis of covenant. Creation
enables God to effect covenant with an entity, man, *ad extra*.

The other context in which Barth argues for the priority
of Christ even with regard to creation is the review which Barth
offers of the Adam-Christ typology of the Apostle Paul, which
might better be termed for Barth the Christ-Adam parallel.[24] In
his brief study *Christ and Adam: Man and Humanity in Romans 5*
Barth points out that the traditional, orthodox understanding of
the Adam-Christ typology places too much emphasis upon Adam.
Adam is but τύποσ τοῦ μέλλοντοσ (the type of the one who is
coming).[25] Adam therefore anticipates Christ. Barth also notes
the πολλῶ μᾶλλον (how much more) of Paul in Romans 5:9-10 and
15-17.[26] Clearly the Christ is superior to Adam and dominates
the parallel. Furthermore Barth suggests that the only way to
Adam from Christ is via the cross, and it is upon that basis
that the two sides become related.[27] The significant point for
our study is that Christ is the focus for Barth. One does not
and in fact cannot gain an understanding of human nature from
Adam. Such an understanding may be derived only from Christ.

Man's nature in Adam is not, as is usually assumed, his true
and original nature; it is only truly human at all in so far
as it reflects and corresponds to essential human nature as
it is found in Christ. True human nature, therefore, can
only be understood by Christians who look to Christ to
discover the essential nature of man.[28]

Christ is the sole and exclusive key to human nature for Barth.
In *Church Dogmatics IV/1*, Barth indicates that there never was a
golden age in the Garden of Eden. Such a golden age never
existed, and there is no point searching for it.[29] Though Barth
acknowledges that the Biblical tradition intended that Adam
should be the first parent of humankind, the Biblical tradition
is much more interested in what Adam did.[30] It is the action of
Adam which attracts attention, and in Adam all of humankind can
perceive their corrupt nature, though again only by way of
reflection from Christ. Barth terms the narrative of the creation
and Adam with the Fall as saga.[31] For Barth this signifies that
the early chapters of Genesis, which have received a great deal
of theological reflection over the centuries, are non-historical
and pre-historical. Saga entails historical truth as *Geschichte*
but not in a form accessible to *Historie* with its modern,
historical techniques of investigation.[32] In these points we
hear echoes of what Barth had earlier written in *Romans*, but
with considerable clarification, as befits the more systematic
character of the *Dogmatics*. Barth had in *Romans* used such terms
as primordial and nonhistorical in description of Adam and the
Garden of Eden. The later writing of Barth in the *Dogmatics* is
consistent with the earlier writing of Barth concerning this
point, though other interpretations of *Romans* might be possible
due to the unclarified nature of the terms Barth then employed.
We can also note here the neoorthodox character of Barth's
thought. What Barth writes concerning the centrality of Christ
is certainly orthodox, but Barth heightens the emphasis placed
upon Christ and relegates Adam to a non*historisch* though
geschichtlich saga.

At this juncture we would do well to note in addition that
Barth views the resurrection of Jesus Christ simultaneously as
what we might term the fulfillment of Old Testament expectations
and as the completion of creation. The former is the traditional,
orthodox manner for understanding the work of Christ. Barth will
imply concurrence with this when he writes that creation was
completed with the seventh, sabbath day of rest.[33] On the other
hand Barth will indicate that creation becomes complete with the
resurrection of Christ. In him is revealed the end for which
God created the world. Barth will not contest facts as set
forth by the nontheological sciences such as psychology, physiol-
ogy, and biology, but he will offer a different interpretation
and understanding of those facts.[34] Thus Barth holds that the
resurrection manifests the covenant between God and man. In him
appears the fullness of time. But most especially Barth, in
concert with Paul in the New Testament, reflects that Christ is
the πρωτότωκοσ πάσησ κτίσεωσ (first-born of all creation).[35]

We perceive in Christ the fullest revelation of God's intent for
man. Adam failed to become God's covenant partner through his
sin and disobedience while Christ through his obedience became
all that God intended for man in creation and therefore the
first-born of all creation. Because of this we can expect that
Barth will focus upon Christ in expounding his understanding of
man. In a manner of speaking we can also say that Barth follows
the traditional approach of theology at this point for he
derives his anthropology from the first man. But for Barth,
noteworthily, the first man is Jesus Christ and not a prehistoric
Adam.

OUR METHOD

Hence as we focus our attention upon the response Barth
offers to our three questions in his *Church Dogmatics* we are
drawn in particular to two sections of *Church Dogmatics III/2*,
which of course belongs within Barth's *Doctrine of Creation*.
This entire volume, the tenth chapter of the *Church Dogmatics*,
is entitled "The Creature." Of this chapter sections 46 and 47
are those which are our primary concern in outlining the position
of Barth regarding the death and after-life of man. The former
of these treats man in the three dimensions of space and the
latter treats of man in the fourth dimension of time. From what
we have noted above we would expect Barth to focus upon the
particular man Jesus Christ because he reveals the true nature
of man.[36] This expectation will not be disappointed. For our
study we will examine these sections in reverse order because
our first topic of consideration, the cause and significance of
death, is related more in Barth's discussion of man in the fourth
dimension while the second topic of what transpires to the
individual in death is related more in Barth's discussion of
three-dimensional man. What happens to the individual after
life, our third topic of consideration, is an issue which will
require of us some extrapolation from the extant writings of
Barth. While we regret the fact that the *Church Dogmatics* is an
opus imperfectum, we nonetheless believe that Barth provides us
with sufficient indication in his extant volumes to infer the
nature of after-life. Certainly in sections 46 and 47 Barth has
provided us with a detailed and stimulating response to the
first two issues of our consideration.

MAN IN THE FOURTH DIMENSION

Man is more than three-dimensional; he is characterized
by a fourth dimension, the dimension of time. Thus in section
47, which is the final section of his tenth chapter, Barth
reflects upon man in his time.

As a basis for his covenant relationship with man, God
provides man with time. Time is the *conditio sine qua non* for
life. If he is to fulfill his being and nature as three-dimensional man, man cannot do without the fourth dimension of time.[37]
Noteworthily Barth distinguishes time with its succession of past,

present, and future from eternity with its simultaneity of past, present, and future. Thereby he clarifies that time is not a god and that time and eternity are not antithetical.

> Time is the form of the created world by which the world
> is ordained to be the field for the acts of God and for
> the corresponding reactions of His creatures, or, in more
> general terms, the creaturely life.[38]

Time is subservient to God; it enables man to establish relationship with God and his fellowman. Life without time would be as meaningless as life without space.

In this section of the *Dogmatics* Barth reflects upon the following subjects: Jesus as Lord of time, man in time, time from within, time from without, the beginning of man in time, the end of man in time, and death and the second death. In the first section we will note that time is subservient to Christ since Christ fulfilled time. Christ is its very basis; indeed as Barth expresses it Christ is the internal basis of time. Because Christ is Lord of time, including the future of man, even after-life must focus as well upon Christ. In the second section, man in time, the time of Jesus is contrasted with the time of man. In Jesus man may see himself as he was intended by God. This, however, points up the judgment of God upon man for living in contradiction to his nature. In the third section Barth argues that the dimension of time is not a curse, as some philosophical and religious traditions have argued. Time is a dimension God willed for man, and it is bounded by eternity, which is a dimension of God. In the section dealing with time from within Barth contends that God is the guarantor of man's past and future. God grants man time as it is needed to realize His ends and purposes for man. Initially Barth writes that life demands permanency in the section relating time from without. But then Barth develops six reasons why man is better off being bounded with a beginning and end. In the next section it is the beginning of man in time which draws the attention of Barth, for Barth sees a clear parallel between the beginning and ending boundaries of life. This leads naturally to the subject of the end of man in time. Here Barth notes that there are aspects of death which make it clearly evil. Nevertheless Barth argues that this evil is not intrinsic but extrinsic. Finally in the section we have entitled death and the second death we note that Barth shows the accursed but yet natural aspect of death. Death is part of the order that God created.

This is a most important section for coming to an understanding of the cause and significance of death in Barth. We will note that death does carry evil associations, but death can through Christ become once again natural as God intended it to be.

Jesus as Lord of Time

In the first subsection of his inquiry into man in his time Barth argues that Jesus is the Lord of time

because He has revealed Himself as such, because in the resurrection His appearance has proved to be that of the eternal
God. Otherwise we have no grounds for making this claim, and
it is better not to pretend that we have.[39]

Barth, as he had done previously, bases himself in revelation
with revelation again forming the basis and backdrop of his
thought. There is no appeal to reason or natural theology in
Barth, but rather he disdains these. The resurrection appearance
is again the pivotal point for Barth, as in his study of 1 Corinthians 15.

Barth contends that in the forty days that Jesus was with
the apostolic community after His resurrection that "in this
time the *man* Jesus was manifested among them in the mode of
God."[40] The forty days is important to Barth because the revelation of God in Christ was then complete. The disciples recognized that this Jesus brings with him the πλήρωμα τοῦ χρόνου
(fullness of time). In the forty days after His resurrection
the apostles came to realize that in His life all time--past,
present, and future--had been fulfilled. Its raison d'etre had
been revealed. Further in Ephesians 1:10 one reads:
ανακεφαλαιώσθαι τὰ πάντα εν τῷ Χριστῷ (all things are summed up
in Christ).[41] Christ is the meaning of history. There is nothing
more to expect beyond Christ. Everything reaches its head and
goal in him. Barth writes: "The fact that in His life all time
comes to fruition means that all time before it moved towards it
and all time after it moves away from it."[42] The only reason
for men to be granted time prior to Christ was to await Him, and
the only reason for time after Christ is to orient our lives
around this unique, once-for-all event.[43] The New Testament
writers extend the yesterday of Jesus all the way back beyond
the reach of historians to the primal time and even suggest that
He was the basis of creation,[44] indeed the internal basis of
creation as Barth expresses it. And on the other hand the
apostolic community anticipated a better future, but nevertheless
"a future which sets a term to the whole time process, and in its
perfection includes and surpasses absolutely all the contents of
time."[45] Noteworthily it was not the amelioration of present
conditions or an ideal state which was anticipated but rather the
coming of the Lord--Maranatha.[46] There was no notion of innate
and implicit progress. Rather there was the belief that Christ
would return and draw all things unto Himself. "Strictly speaking, there are no 'last things,' i.e. no abstract and autonomous
last things apart from and alongside Him, the Last One."[47] Jesus
is thus envisioned as the Lord of the future as well as the past
and present. He is Lord of time. Man cannot envision the
future, then, anymore than the past or present, apart from Christ.

Man in Time

In the second subsection in which he deals with man in his
time Barth begins by noting that though Jesus is the Lord of time,
one cannot expect to say the same of all men in their time. Man

is certainly not the Lord of time, nor does he fulfill his time. This leads Barth to conclude: "Our anthropology can and must be based on Christology, but it cannot be deduced from it directly. What is predicated of the being of the man Jesus in time is true because this man is also God."[48] But His time is unique, and it occurred once for all (ἅπαξ and εφάπαξ). It is readily apparent that the time of man contrasts with the time of Jesus. The past no longer belongs to man,[49] the future does not yet belong to him, and the present is a transition from future to past which also lies outside his control. Time is a riddle to man;[50] it is enigmatic.[51] Barth is not content simply to contrast the time of Jesus and man, for Jesus is also man and therefore like man. Nevertheless the contrast between Jesus and other men remains and "does not seem to be one which is original or natural."[52] Barth thus concludes that the contrast between the time of Jesus and man points to the judgment of God upon man. Man in his time is *sinful* man. Man has time in contradiction to his God-given nature. He lives in rebellion against God, and he has lost the quality of time for which God created him.[53] But God in Christ has effectively intervened and made it impossible for man to be content with his abnormal time.[54] The eternal God became temporal among man.

> Yet He does this in a manner appropriate to Himself. He is temporal in unity and correspondence with His eternity. But what can this mean but that He is temporal in a way which corresponds to man as His creature, in the original and natural form of the being of man in time before it was perverted and corrupted.[55]

Barth believes that it is on account of Jesus and the manner in which he fulfilled time that God does not turn away from man but rather toward him and even judges man according to His judgment upon Jesus.[56] Hence in Jesus man may see himself as God intended him in creation.[57] This clarifies further why Barth orients anthropology around Christology. In Christ we perceive what God wants to see and what He wants man to be.

Time as the Form of Man's Existence

The first proposition which Barth draws from his Christological focus at this point is that time is of the essence of man. Time is real. "Time is not, therefore, the abyss of our non-being, however perverted and corrupt we may be in it. We have time. . . Time is. It is the form of man's existence, the form of our existence."[58] Though this may only be definitely stated of man, because man lives in relation to the rest of the universe it may be concluded that time is the form of existence of everything created. Indeed particularly the first biblical narrative of creation implies that time was created with the universe as the form of its existence.[59] God created time and took time, seven days, to complete His creation. Barth notes that unlike any other religious tradition and even more any philosophy, the God of the Bible reveals Himself in history.[60] He becomes involved in history. Parallel to His creating man as soul of his body, which we will note subsequently, God gives man time.[61] "Time was in fact willed and created in order that there might take place His dealings in the covenant with man, which finds its counterpart in the relationship between man and his fellows."[62] Time is the fourth and necessary dimension for life. But noteworthily Barth continues:

> As our existence is not an end in itself, neither is time as its form. It is our time and we have it only to the extent that we belong to God, i.e. to the God who turned to us even in His eternity.[63]

The time which we have now is a time for repentance, to set ourselves in a right, covenant relationship with God.

At this juncture Barth interjects the following point of clarification:

> Time is not eternity. Eternity itself is not timeless. It is simultaneity and coinherence of past, present and future. Thus eternity is the dimension of God's own life, the life in which He is self-positing, self-existent and self-suffi-cient as Father, Son and Holy Ghost. It is this in contrast to time as the dimension of our life--the dimension in which past, present and future follow in succession.[64]

In contrast with time eternity is not created since it is the dimension of God, who is self-existent. Time, however, is willed and created by God. It exists *ad extra* to God, even as the creation exists outside God. Eternity thus forms a boundary for time, but the relationship appears to be not antithetical but one of completion, perfection, and fulfillment. In fact, as we will note below, God also lives in time. Time as the fourth dimension of man which was created by God is good and in no sense accursed.

Time from Within

Barth then examines the significance of the relationship of God to man in the present, the past, and in the future.

To man it is the presence of God which fills the present.[65] The present is the offer, summons, and invitation of God to be with Him,[66] "to receive or act, to speak or be silent, to say Yes or No."[67]

With regard to the past Barth asks what guarantee there is in the present that someone is really the same as the one who has been. Though Barth prefers a third alternative, he notes that this question has illicited two common responses--memory and oblivion. Memory proves insufficient, however. "Our reconstruc-tion of the past and the past itself are poles apart. The actual past never returns, however vivid and accurate the reconstruc-tion."[68] The response of oblivion turns in a wholly different

direction. Recognizing that he is incapable of remembering the
past, man reacts by "retreating" into the present or future.[69]
Barth suggests a third response--God guarantees man's past.

> If our whole time is the gift of God, then God also pledges
> to maintain its reality as a whole. . . The passing of our
> time would only mean destruction if we had to be men without
> God, outside the covenant He has established with us.[70]

The time of man thus exists before God and is as real now as it
ever was.[71] Indeed this is what must be expected of the One for
whom the past, present, and future are simultaneous and coinher-
ent. And because God has our past before Him, man is freed from
any positive or negative paralysis with relation to the past.[72]
It is the loving and forgiving God who guarantees our past. Thus
man is enabled to forget, particularly that of his past which
stands under the judgment of God. Yet man need not forget in
order to live; if so man would be paralyzed for he would have no
history.[73] Man requires time, even time past, to exist. The
past provides a basis for action in the present and the future.

With regard to the future Barth asks what guarantee we have
now that we will be or that we will be the same person only a
stage further along. Barth again notes two responses, both of
which end in a cul-de-sac, before he presents a third alternative.
The first is the unreflective way in which man assumes the future
will always be there. Man lives in dreams, and the dreams then
become his reality. But in reality it is impossible to be
careless and unreflective.[74] Second man can reflect upon his
future in time. But here he notes that he is actually unable
to control the future. In fact the future seizes him and over-
powers him. His reflection thus leads him to a pessimism regarding the future. Barth again believes that a third alternative
solves this dilemma. He believes that the will and action of
God are the meaning and ground of the future. Hence strictly
speaking it is God who will be, and man will be only insofar as
God creates, delivers, and sustains him.[75] Furthermore Barth
contends that since it is God who guarantees the future of man,
the end of man will not be terror nor can it terrify. Its end
will be the goal which God has set man. God has already arranged
the future; man in the present must step into that future to look
for this arrangement of God.[76] Since the future is already
arranged one might suppose that Barth would advocate an unreflective approach to the future. Barth nonetheless counters: "That
He constantly gives us life, and the time needed for it, means that
we are again and again, and in the end conclusively, challenged to
gratitude towards Him and responsibility before Him."[77] Barth
thus attempts to bring together both the reflective and unreflective attitudes.

> Indeed, if our knowledge of the God who is over and with us
> banishes all false fears of the future, enabling us to live
> unreflectively, the very same knowledge evokes and inspires
> the necessary and serious fear of God Himself.[78]

We conclude by noting that time from within points up the fact that God is the basis and guarantee of the past, present, and future. Man has time only from God. Time is one dimension of the external basis of covenant, a dimension God must maintain for covenant relationship outside of Himself.

Furthermore, though the immediate relevance of this topic for our subject may not be apparent, it will become more apparent as we examine our third topic of what happens after life.

Time from Without

After his examination of time from within as given and guaranteed by God, Barth turns to consider time from the outside, time as the totality of moments succeeding each other. God gives time to man, and man has time as he needs it for life. But the space of time is not unlimited; it has a beginning and end which are visible from outside. Man lives within a certain span with a particular beginning and end. This raises the question whether human life requires merely this limited space for its development. "Human life demands permanency, or rather duration. Human life would always like to regard itself as an unfathomable, inexhaustible reality. . . Human life protests against this 'only.'"[79] Barth believes this protest against his limitation to be natural for man. In fact as a result of the Fall some persons may resignedly accept their limitation as no threat. "Resignation of this kind is incompatible with the fact that life is created by God. It is an acceptance of sin and its consequent punishment as though they were our original and authentic destiny."[80] But Barth agrees that life is an unfathomable and inexhaustible reality. This is true vertically in his relationship to God and also horizontally in his relationship to other men. This prompts the seemingly rhetorical question: "What but an unlimited, permanent duration can be adequate for the fulfilment of this determination?"[81] Noteworthily, however, Barth cautions against man's demanding that duration is due him by right in virtue of his determination. Such a demand would be folly and presumption.[82] But to fulfill his determination man may expect to have time. To clarify this Barth makes six points.

First Barth remarks that God also lives in time.

But His time is eternity, which has no fixed span, no margins, no other measure but Himself. Eternity is not time without beginning or end. . . To identify with time without beginning and end would be to contribute to it an idealised form of creaturely existence.[83]

God in His eternity is beginning, middle, and end in fullness and simultaneity. Eternity is not timelessness. Thus God cannot be apart from time.[84] Eternity belongs to God. By contrast man has time as past, present, and future. But time is fitting for man.

The proper dimension for the life of the creature which is
not self-grounded or self-creative, welling up from within
itself, but has its basis in the life of God is the time in
which beginning and end are distinct, and therefore constitute
its boundaries.[85]

Human life as created by God has boundaries, as is indicated by
certain biblical passages, e.g. Psalm 90:5, 9; Isaiah 40:6;
Psalm 102:12; Job 14:2; Psalm 93:4; and James 4:14. We infer
that there is a naturalness both to the beginning and ending
boundaries of man's time.

Second Barth questions whether limitless duration would
truly serve the end of man. Such could only be the case if infinite
time could guarantee the determination and perfection for which
man aspires. Barth notes that it is legitimate to want much
time rather than little time in order to fulfill his destiny;
numerous scriptural passages point in this direction, e.g.
Deuteronomy 4:40, 25:15; Psalms 55:23 and 102:23-24; Ecclesiastes
11:7f.; Psalm 21:4; 1 Kings 1:31; and Genesis 5:4f. Psalm 63:3
suggests further that the loving kindness of God, His חסד, is
better than life. Time is not the best thing that God accords
man, though a certain amount of time is necessary for human
fulfillment. "And an infinite measure of human life can only
mean an infinite number of opportunities."[86] Quantity of time
need not signify fulfillment of human determination.

Third Barth actively believes that man would be worse off
in unrestricted time. Man would be perpetually on the way and
never attain the goal. As a result Barth raises the rhetorical
question: "Could there be any better picture of life in hell
than enduring life in enduring time?"[87] If man lives in unrest
he will aspire to realize his goal, to seek the peace of a
permanent life under God and with other men. Endless life
would prohibt man from ever attaining the goal.

Fourth Barth examines man in his time not abstractly and
generally, which leads to no solution, but from the specific
point of the relationship of God and man. Barth notes that for
this relationship to exist man must be "a concrete subject to
whom God can be an equally concrete Counterpart and Neighbor,
with whom He can enjoy communication and intercourse."[88] A being
in unending time would be centrifugal, however, and thus incapable
of being a concrete subject. God thus cares for man by giving him
an allotted span instead of unending time. It is to human
benefit that God gives man a limited space of time. Barth
continues by noting quickly that centrifugal existence or infinitely enduring time is to be distinguished from the time of God.
God exists as Lord of time, as past, present, and future simultaneously. He is not timeless and is hence Himself a concrete
Subject.[89]

Fifth Barth notes that man's desire for fulfillment may
find satisfaction only in God--not in a particular length of
time, even if it be unlimited. "It is in Him, who has determined

and limited us in this way, that we have the duration and perfection for which we rightly crave."[90] When man casts his lot with God the fact that human time is allotted appears quite in order.[91]

Sixth Barth claims that the limitation of time prevents apotheosis. During life it is possible that the utter dependence of humans upon God may be veiled from them. Such unawareness is impossible at two points--birth and death. Barth contends that man is either confronted here by nothingness or "exclusively, unequivocally, fundamentally and definitively by the gracious God. . ."[92] This is of course a position Barth has made in his previous writings.

Thus the fact that our time is allotted, and allotted by God, "simply means the proximity of His free grace in this clarity."[93] Though man must then perceive that of himself he is incapable of extending time, he is therein directed to the free grace of God. The principal, particular point in this section detailing "time from without" which we need to draw attention to for our study is the positive and natural aspects of death which Barth elaborates. Death for Barth clearly is not viewed as an unmitigated evil and/or curse.

The Beginning of Man in Time

Barth has just drawn attention to the fact that at birth and death man cannot escape becoming aware of his utter dependence upon God. Barth believes that both the beginning and end points of life confront man with the same problem, the border of non-being which precedes and succeeds man in his time, and it is this similarity between birth and death which makes it relevant to our study. Barth recognizes that the beginning of man in his time is often ignored in discussions because the urgency of the question posed by the beginning of life is in indirect proportion to the question concerning the end point as time passes. Barth believes that

consciously or unconsciously, we carry and bring with us from our beginning a lurking terror which in virtue of the irreversible direction of our life and our time takes the opposite form of fear of our end, but which in both its latent and patent form is essentially one and the same fear of the term set to our life, of the allotment of a fixed span for our time.[94]

For Barth the beginning of man creates for man as much difficulty as does the end. He notes that the older theology created difficulties with regard to the soul and its origin with its doctrines of traducianism and creationism. Barth acknowledges that both of these doctrines possess theological justification in their rejection of the Gnostic conception of emanationism, but neither really touches upon the heart of the problem. Both blur the distinction between the divine and human being,[95] and neither confronts man with the fact that there was a time when he was not. Barth believes that the "non-being from which the individual and the

race come is the non-being to which we also move."[96] This
represents a crucial point for Barth, as will again become
evident when we treat our third question or focus. Barth
believes that there exists a parallel between the state or
condition of man before and after life. He perceives man's
interest and concern to know as much as possible about the past,
to know the history which antedates each and every man, and
understands this as a manifestation of the incessant human urge

> to carve out for himself living space and therefore time at
> the point where he has not. . . He cannot accept the fact
> that he comes from non-being. Therefore he fills the gap by
> plunging into it with his historical investigations and
> discoveries.[97]

Thus, though man may appear more interested in his approaching
end point than his point of origin, Barth contends that he may
have much more interest in his point of origin than initially
appears evident. Man's search for identity in the past parallels
his search for identity in the future and after-life.

With this beginning and end as boundaries man is graciously
reminded that he derives from God. Barth then passes on to make
a significant point when he notes: "We certainly come from non-
being, but we do not come from nothing."[98] God is not nothing,
and it is from the being, speaking, and action of this eternal
God that man derives. Barth clarifies this in an exegetical
study:

> According to the Old Testament revelation, when the Israelite
> contemplates the beginning of his individual existence he is
> confronted with God Himself and with the history of the
> people of which he is a member. His thinking is indeed
> "historical," but under a particular token.[99]

For the Israelite God is not primarily a metaphysical first
principle or idea. He is first and foremost the refuge of Israel,
the Founder and Guarantor of the covenant relationship, and only
secondarily is He any type of metaphysical entity.[100] Thus when
the Israelite contemplated the past and his fathers and fore-
fathers, he invariably encountered the electing God and secondly
the creating God who was the source and spring of his life. As
there was a time when God as the source of the covenant raised
up Israel from non-being, so God continued in the present as
creator to raise up individual Israelites from non-being. Barth
notes the same principle active in the New Testament. Here the
fountain or source from which the New Testament community sprung
was the death and resurrection of Jesus. From non-being, though
certainly not nothing, God founded a new Israel.

> The establishment of the Church, upon which the individual
> Christian looks back as the origin and beginning of his own
> existence, is certainly the work of the same gracious and
> faithful God with whom the Israelite in earlier days sought,
> found and possessed his refuge.[101]

The establishment of Israel now finds its parallel in the
Christian Church, though something greater than Israel has
appeared here. The Church in turn can but mediate to others
the beginning of Christian life for individuals.

> And so the Church, whose life is sustained by the Gospel
> story and the apostolic message, can only mediate this
> beginning, testifying to the individual Christian that this
> beginning, Jesus Christ, is the beginning of his life too.[102]

According to Barth Jesus Christ, the goal and end of the history
of Israel, has become the *prius* for every human life.[103] This
becomes manifest in Christian baptism, for in baptism men are
made aware that they "come directly from Christ, from His birth,
His baptism in the Jordan, His crucifixion and resurrection."[104]

In this section it thus becomes clear that Barth parallels
the beginning and end of man and finds this analogous to Israel
and the Church. For Barth man clearly derives from God.

The End of Man in Time

In the final subsection of section 47 Barth focuses upon
the ending time of man. "Life desires life; it hungers and
thirsts for it; it strives and calls for further life. Life is
terrified at every limitation of life."[105] Man lives in the
shadow of his approaching end. His existence as such invariably
forces him to contemplate his non-existence. Barth notes that
Deuteronomy 30:19 suggests that there are certain connections
between blessing and life, cursing and death. Nevertheless
Barth observes that it is not here clarified whether death is an
intrinsic evil, and thus he makes further inquiry.

In the Old Testament to be dead means that one is not able
to live any longer. There is no continuation of life in time,
though the Old Testament never questions the possibility that the
dead can reappear.

> But in no sense does this imply that they are still alive or
> continue to live. In no sense does it alter the fact that
> the essential thing about life, i.e., the capacity for move-
> ment and action, and the possibility of entering into fellow-
> ship with the living, has ceased.[106]

In death one does not see God for it is in the world of the living
that God speaks to and deals with His people.[107] There is no
fellowship in which the dead can actively participate either with
others who are dead or with the living. "The dead exist in a
state of utter weakness and helplessness. They are, so to speak,
always dying (Is. 14^{10}). That is what is meant when the dead are
called *rephaim* (without power)."[108] The fact that one is dead
signifies that the power of the spirit of God which made man man,
or, as Barth expresses it, constituted man as soul of a body, has
been withdrawn. "What the living person had and was is not gone;
death has brought it to extinction."[109] Death brings the fear

that one will suffer misfortune, decay, poverty, and deprivation.
The reality and nature of death are further clarified by particular cosmological and topographical notions. Death is related
to the wilderness, to Egypt and Babylon. It removes man from
the places of worship. The realm of the dead is Sheol, a place
somewhere in the depths of the underworld.[110] The ocean represents
another localisation of death, here the element of chaos being
evident along with fathomless depths and muddy slime.[111]

Furthermore the Old Testament conception of death envisions
death as possessing its own dynamic according to which it can
invade the realm of life. In fact, though a person still be
alive, the onslaught of tribulations and approaching death sometimes results in characterizing an individual as already dead.[112]
Though he does not offer passages to substantiate it, Barth
claims that the New Testament conception of the nature and reality
of death is the same as that of the Old. From this description
Barth concludes that it is readily evident that death, the end
of man in time, can in no way be conducive to the well-being of
man.[113] Death again is a negative phenomenon.

Barth nevertheless continues to ask how one can understand
the finitude of time and death as its terminal point as divinely
created and hence part of the good nature of man. Barth believes
that above and beyond what may belong to the nature of finite man
there may be something abnormal about death which is inappropriate and contradictory to God's positive will for man, though it
may still serve the divine will. Barth is led to this thought
as he reflects upon the nature of birth. The fact that at a
particular moment every person emerged from non-being to being
is not intrinsically negative and/or evil. The very opposite is
indeed the case. Man's coming from God is positive. Yet if the
end of man in death is wholly negative, then one would be forced
to conclude that birth would also be negative. If one passes
not only into non-being but the negation of being, then one
would need to conclude that man has emerged from negation as
well.[114] Barth rejects these conclusions and seeks what may be
abnormal in death.

Barth notes very quickly that the actual existence of man
between his beginning and end points is hardly lived at all in
the manner which God intends. Man lives in guilt. And he bears
this guilt to his death, to that moment like birth when God is
unveiled to man. Thus Barth concludes: "Death, as it actually
encounters us men, is the sign of God's judgment on us. We
cannot say less than this, but of course we must not try to say
more either."[115] Noteworthily Barth refers to death as the sign
of divine judgment. Death need not represent the fulfillment of
human rejection or a plunge into negation and outer darkness.
"For there is a possibility of our being spared this death because
Another has suffered it in His death for us. The New Testament
assumes that this is in fact the case."[116] However death as it
actually encounters man is generally the sign of judgment. For
as it encounters man death meets sinful and guilty man. Barth
suggests that under the circumstances man "can hope for nothing

better than to be hewn down and cast into the fire."[117]   Death
as it is actually experienced by man is not an inherent part of
human nature as God created it.   It is negative and evil.   It is
an evil which signifies the judgment of God and is not thus a
fate but an ordinance proceeding from God and therefore to be
accepted.[118]   It is not something to be domesticated or termed
"brother," "friend," or even "deliverer."[119]

According to the Old Testament death epitomizes that which
is contrary to nature, for man's being constituted soul of a
body is natural.   There are in the Old Testament only rare
instances where the interconnection of sin, guilt, and death is
asserted.   Only in the threat uttered in the Garden of Eden in
Genesis 2:17 and its confirmation in Genesis 3:19 and 6:3 is
this relationship directly stated.   The New Testament displays
a considerable contrast at this point.   For Barth it is particularly the death of Jesus which reveals the character of death.
"For He suffered death as the judgment of God.   It would be out
of place to say here that He did so as the sign of God's judgment."[120]   In the crucifixion and death of Jesus the New Testament
writers perceive three decisions openly declared and given
universal validity.   First death exceeds, overshadows, and
fundamentally calls in question all human greatness and grandeur.
Not even the Messiah, the Son of God incarnate, escaped death.
The power of death over man is universal.   This impels Barth to
note: "Deliverance from death cannot be deliverance from before
it but only deliverance from out of it."[121]   Second Barth notes
the New Testament decision that the death to which all persons
move implies the threat of eternal corruption and punishment.
In the death of Jesus the man who is wholly and unreservedly for
God has God against him.   Jesus was made a curse and sin on
behalf of man so that man need not experience eternal death.
Barth notes that the New Testament conceptions of hell accordingly
become more vivid and represent punishment of a very positive
kind.[122]   Third the New Testament concludes that death is the
appropriate reward for life as actually lived.   No code of law
can reveal this.

> The crucifixion of Jesus Christ is the revelation of what it
> cost to restore the right of God and man which man had
> disrupted. . . It shows how great was the remissness, and
> what was its inevitable consequence.[123]

Because the New Testament sees man from the standpoint of his
being helped, it is able to speak of guilt and punishment so
radically.   Man's already being helped also accounts for the
missionary emphasis of the early Church.[124]

On the basis of Jesus the New Testament evidences the alien
nature of death, but Barth does not leave the matter there.   It
is not death itself which makes death so awesome but rather God
Himself.   In death man confronts God, the God who is angry with
man and punishes man in death.   This makes death dreadful.   But
Barth draws a distinction; death is not a second god beside God.
God has appointed death to its office and function.   Therefore

in death, and even in hell as Barth writes, man is not separated
from God. Man remains in His hands.[125] And this God noteworthily is the gracious God. He is the God who is for man and
has acted on his behalf. Barth draws the following paradoxes:

> Man cannot stand up to His wrath because it is the wrath
> of His love. The reason why His curse falls so hard upon
> us is that it is surrounded by the rainbow of His covenant.
> It is the dark side of the blessing with which He has
> blessed us and wills to bless us. Those whom He loves He
> chastens.[126]

Because it is God whom one must fear in death and not death
itself it is possible to find comfort in death.[127] In Jesus God
has already placed death behind and beneath us.[128] This is
ratified and confirmed in baptism.[129] Barth contends that
though death is the frontier of man, death itself has its own
frontier in God. Thus even as man suffers death it is already
behind him.[130]

In this section Barth has drawn attention to that which is
involved in death which gives it a negative and dread character.
Sin has interfered with God's covenant with man, and thus death
brings man before the wrath of God's love.

Death and the Second Death

Barth recognizes that he still has left unanswered the
question of whether death represents simply a curse, i.e. an
alien and inimical threat to human nature, or whether death is
a blessing, something which might be termed natural to man.

In order to respond to this question Barth again focuses
upon Christ. And here he notes that the death which he died
was an alien burden. "As a man like ourselves, He had not
deserved this end. His human life was not one of negation.
It was not, therefore, subject to death as the seal of its
negation."[131] Yet Jesus died. Thereby, as was noted above,
Jesus took upon Himself the judgment of God in death and freed
man from it. The death of Jesus therefore signifies release
from death as a curse. "The end of Jesus Christ has made our
end simply the *sign* of God's judgment."[132] We can perceive in
death the wrath of God, but it is wrath which has been placated.
Therefore one can conclude that human finitude in time need not
imply that man stands under the curse of God. Rather the death
of man limits man and sets man on the same ground as Jesus.
Thus it is that Jesus is able to take man as a whole and redeem
him. Barth therefore concludes:

> Finitude, then, is not intrinsically negative and evil.
> There is no reason why it should not be an anthropological
> necessity, a determination of true and natural man, that we
> shall one day have to die, and therefore merely have been.
> It belongs to the revelation of His glory in us, to the
> final proclamation of our justification in the judgment,

to the removal of the overhanging sign of divine judgment,
to the settled and incontestable factuality of our participation in God's eternal life, that one day we should merely
and definitely have been.[133]

This point finds echo in *Church Dogmatics III/3*:

And certainly it is not a curse but a blessing that there are
these limits to humanity and creation, and that in some cases
they are notoriously narrow limits, of which the brevity of
human life is only a single if rather drastic example.[134]

By means of his focus upon Christ Barth thus arrives at three
notable conclusions. First death and human finitude are not
intrinsically evil or accursed. If death were evil in itself
then it would have been impotent against Christ, since he was
without sin. Second the negative aspect of death which accrues
to it because of human sin has become impotent on account of the
crucifixion and death of Christ. Christ bore the curse of sin
in death himself and neutralized it. Third, though the curse is
without power, death continues as the sign of God's judgment.
We can perceive in death the extreme displeasure of God with sin,
indeed its repudiation, but this no longer pushes God to reject
man, this on account of the death of Christ.

Barth believes that the biblical description of the δεύτεροσ
θάνατοσ (second death) confirms this understanding. In Revelation
20:14 this second death is cast into the lake of fire. Barth
interprets this second death as the death of the ungodly, death
resulting from rebellion against God. In this sense death is
unnatural. It is this second death which Jesus bore on behalf of
man, and that death therefore does not any longer plague humankind.
But Barth notes that if there is a second death, and this an
unnatural death, there must also be a first death, and this a
natural death. Two notions coupled together lead Barth to this
conclusion. First Jesus died when he was not under bondage to
sin and the second death. Second man continues to die despite
the reconciling death of Jesus. Barth is thus led to envision
death as natural.

Another form of death is actually to be seen in the Bible.
In the biblical presentation, it is not the case that the
unnatural aspect of death has simply crowded out or veiled
the naturalness of man's end in itself and as such. There
is no compelling necessity why death should be for man an
unqualified evil.[135]

There are a number of Old Testament passages in which death is not
accepted in morose resignation, e.g. Psalm 90:12, 1 Kings 2:2, 6;
Isaiah 14:18; and Genesis 25:8, 35:29, and 46:30. Simeon in
Luke 2:29 echoes this Old Testament attitude as well. When life
has run its course it is fitting and proper that one should die.
Death nonetheless always retains an awful character. But the
enmity and menace of death can be absent.[136] In certain

instances death can be the transition of an individual from existence into non-existence where he enjoys eternal confrontation and supremely positive coexistence with God. And in certain passages it is openly stated that it is to man's best will and improvement that he is mortal. The removal from the Garden of Eden was occasioned lest man eat of the tree of life and live forever. It was to protect man from immortality that man was compelled to leave the Garden.[137] Barth cites Moses, Enoch, and Elijah as particular Old Testament figures whose ends are distinctively set apart from any debt to evil. And noteworthily it was God who initiated and was responsible for the removal of these individuals from the realm of the living.[138] Their death represents the good creation of God and not chaos.[139] Barth believes that death in the New Testament is also viewed as natural. By His death Jesus removed the curse of the second death. Thus the New Testament writers generally characterize death in which the second death is absent as "falling asleep" (cf. John 11:11, 1 Corinthians 15:6, and Acts 7:60). Though the expression may be deliberately mild and even euphemistic, it conveys a merited feeling of peace. Barth feels that it expresses the freedom of faith and love present in the New Testament community.[140]

Finally we note with Barth that despite the fact that death no longer is characterized by the curse or second death and that the New Testament admonishes persons not to love this life or seek to save it, the New Testament at the same time does not advocate one to seek death or martyrdom. In Philippians 1 Paul hopes to be with Christ when he dies and actually refers to after-life as "gain" and "better." Nevertheless Barth notes:

> He does not rejoice in the prospect of being freed from His service, of having his time behind him. On the contrary, the definitive prospect in which he rejoices is for him an authorisation and command to serve God in his allocated span with all the preliminary joy without which his joy in his end and new beginning with Him would be purely imaginary.[141]

As Barth had noted that חסד (God's loving-kindness) is better than life, and therefore life itself is not the ultimate value, so serving God in our allotted span with its preliminary joy is better than seeking death or martyrdom.

CONCLUSION

The cause and significance of death has again been our first focus as we examined at this stage the writings of Karl Barth in the *Church Dogmatics*. The cause of death is uniformly seen to be God in the *Church Dogmatics*. God is the Creator, and He is ultimately in control of His creation. He determines both the beginning and the end of human life. Thus death would appear to have a positive or natural significance, and this is indeed what we have noted in Barth. Death is the natural termination of life. Barth offers at one point six reasons why the condition

of man is improved by having a terminal point in time. Nevertheless Barth also notes that sin has entered the world, thereby
coloring and distorting death. There are now aspects of death
which are accursed. Yet even these negative elements are
eliminated through the work of Christ. Through His death, where
He took upon Himself the curse of death to which we would otherwise succumb, Christ effected the eradication and neutralizing
of the curse. Death therefore becomes again natural, again in
the created order for which God intended it.

THREE-DIMENSIONAL MAN

The fact that man has been granted the fourth dimension
of time clearly suggests that there are three other dimensions
to man. And indeed as created by God man has been granted the
three dimensions which constitute man as man in the length,
breadth, and depth of creation. Traditionally the constitution
of man in the dimensions of space has provided a basis for understanding what happens to man in death and particularly what
happens to the body. It is precisely because an understanding
of the constitution of man provides us with a basis for understanding the dissolution or death of man that this section
becomes pertinent to our study.

In this section we will treat the following subjects in
detailing the position of Barth relative to our second question
of what transpires to the individual in death: Jesus as one
whole man, spirit, the inner structure of human creatureliness,
monism, soul and body in their particularity, and the inner
order of the creature. Given the centrality which Barth accords
to Jesus Christ it is to be expected that Barth would focus
initially upon Christ. In Christ we again note man as God
intended him to be, and for Barth that is as one whole man, not
a composite of a distinct body and soul. In the section concerning spirit note is taken of the spirit as the divine principle
of animation for man. Man lives as he has spirit, else he dies.
Three subjects are treated in "the inner structure of human
creatureliness." These relate the inner unity, differentiation,
and order of man's structure. Barth also addresses materialistic
and spiritualistic monism as two mistaken notions of the structure
of man. In concluding this section we will note that Barth treats
soul and body in their particularity and order. Our conclusion
concerning three-dimensional man will then draw particular
attention to the relevance of this section in determining the
response Barth would offer to our second question of what transpires to the individual in death.

Jesus as One Whole Man

In section 46 Barth deals with one aspect of the way man
has been created by God, i.e. as soul and body. By way of clarification Barth indicates that there are several other pairs of
words which express the same idea: man as spirit and substantial
organism, as rational and sensuous, inner and outer, invisible
and visible, inapprehensible and apprehensible, intelligible and

empirical, and even heavenly and earthly.[142] Barth, however,
notes the paucity of reference to any of these pairs in the New
Testament with regard to Jesus. "The differentiation in the
constitution of man which they suggest has in His case only a
provisional and relative and not an ultimate and absolute meaning."[143] In Jesus one cannot distinguish between inner and
outer, etc. for what in Him is inner and not simultaneously
outer? Jesus is not presented as a union of two parts or
substances. Rather he is one whole man, an embodied soul and a
besouled body. The New Testament designates Jesus as εαυτόσ
(himself), sometimes as ψυχὴ αυτοῦ (his soul), and sometimes as
σῶμα αυτοῦ (his body). The three designations are interchange-
able, though the particular uses are not unpremeditated.[144]
Jesus is a whole unit. Despite this wholeness, however, the New
Testament does not distinguish the soul and body of Jesus and
place them in a particular order. The life of Jesus is determined from within so that one may speak of a dominating moment
and a dominated moment.[145] Though it is the soul of Jesus which
commands and controls while the body obeys and is controlled, the
relationship presupposed is not one of original separation nor
even the most hidden conflict.[146] "There is super- and subordi-
nation, but it is an order of peace in which both moments, each
in its own place and function, have equal share in the dignity
of the whole. . ."[147] For Barth soul and body are differentiated,
but they are not related antithetically, as they most certainly
are in Platonism. Barth also notes a third element which is
present in Jesus--the Holy Spirit. In Genesis 2:7 God breathes
into the nostrils of man, imparts some of His own life, and thus
makes a living being. Barth interprets this passage Messianic-
ally, suggesting that only in one man is the Spirit said to reside.
Other men may partake temporarily of the Spirit, but only on Jesus
as soul of a body does it rest throughout his life.[148] We hear
here an echo of thoughts expressed by Barth concerning the first
and second Adam in *The Resurrection of the Dead*.

Any attempt to understand man apart from God is shunned by
Barth.

We cannot try to understand man even hypothetically without
God in order to find out whether the last word in the matter
is an open question or a statement borrowed from theology,
or perhaps atheistic dogma.[149]

It is God, the God whom the man Jesus called His Father and whose
Son He called Himself,[150] who grounds and maintains the constitution of man,[151] and this He does by means of His Spirit. Like
Jesus, man as constituted by God is soul of his *body*. This
signifies that man occupies space; he belongs to the visible,
outward, earthly world of bodies.[152] Man is an organic, material
body. Furthermore man is *soul* of his body. Man is soul in that
he is the life which is essentially necessary for his body. This
does not mean, however, that life can be divorced from the physical body. The soul is "neither before nor beside nor after his
material body. He is the life of his physical body, not a life
in itself, and not a life hovering freely over his body or

dwelling in it only incidentally."[153] In this there is a notable contrast with the traditional understanding of man as being constituted of body and soul in which there is clear distinction. For Barth neither soul nor body would be itself without the other. The two aspects are intertwined and intermingled.

In Jesus, then, we note man in three dimensions as God intended him to be.

Spirit

Man nonetheless would never be soul of a body without a third element which derives from God. This is the spirit. Man is as he has spirit.[154] The spirit does not belong to man, and thus it is not some third thing alongside body and soul. Man is not a trichotomy.[155] "Yet it is soul and body as spirit comes to it, as it receives and has spirit, as spirit has it and will not leave it, but grounds, determines and limits it."[156] Spirit is the principle of animation which constitutes man soul of a body. It gives soul and body life. Being from God spirit is immortal.[157] It does not die with the body. Spirit in fact in its presence and absence determines whether or not there is life.[158] Barth understands the activity of spirit as the animation of a soul of a body in line with the general activity of Spirit, i.e. the operation of God upon His creation and especially upon man.

> This is what is meant when Scripture says of man that he has spirit or the Spirit, or that he has done this or that in the Spirit or through the Spirit, or has said or done or suffered from the Spirit. This never signifies a capacity or ability of his own nature, but always one originally foreign to his nature which has come to it from God and has thus been specially imparted to it in a special movement of God towards him. . . The Spirit, in so far as He not only comes but proceeds from God Himself, is identical with God.[159]

Spirit is never of the essence of man. Rather it comes from without and thereby signifies the relationship which God shares with man. Hence the life of man itself is based internally upon covenant relationship.[160] Barth uses the analogy of a circle and its center to clarify the relationship of Spirit to the soul of a body. "The Spirit is in man and belongs to him as the mathematical centre is in and belongs to the circle."[161] One cannot have a circle without a center, though the center is not part of the circle.[162] Furthermore in its relationship to man the Spirit is in immediate and direct relationship to the soul and mediate and indirect relationship to the body. "The soul is *a priori* the element in which the turning of God to man and the fellowship of man with God in some way takes place. The same is to be said of the body but only *a posteriori*."[163] On this basis Barth concludes that the soul is the life of the body.[164] According to Barth man is not distinguished from the other animals by his *possession* of the Spirit since Spirit is the sine qua non also for a beast being the soul of its body.

what distinguishes man from beast is the special movement and purpose with which God through the Spirit gives life; and, connected with this, the special spirituality of his life, which is determined by the fact that God has not only made him in his constitution as soul of his body, but destined him in this constitution for that position of a partner of the grace of His covenant. We know nothing of such a double determination in respect of the beasts.[165]

In short both man and beast live by the Spirit as soul of a body, but only man can be baptized.[166] Barth also refers to a more extensive and intensive presence of the Spirit in man. In the Bible the Spirit is granted to living individuals, e.g. Moses, David, Elijah, and Ezekiel. And in the New Testament this gift becomes communal, though here particular individuals may exceed the common standard. It is also noteworthy that the Spirit may be withdrawn.[167] God is under no obligation to maintain the spirit in man. When He takes away His Spirit man must return to the earth from which he was taken and die.[168]

The Inner Structure of Human Creatureliness

With these basic insights Barth moves on to discuss the inner structure of human creatureliness. There is one aspect of man which predominates over the other. As Barth elaborates this issue he subdivides the discussion into the three questions of the inner unity, the inner differentiation, and the inner order of the creature.[169]

The first of these three questions concerns the soul and body in their interconnection. Here Barth describes the unity of man. Barth refers to man as an event,[170] though there remains in him a relative antithesis of two moments.[171] He notes that the antithesis between soul and body does not parallel that of God and man. In fact Barth writes:

The thought of man in his differentiation as soul and body really having to repeat the differentiation between God and the creature is not only an arrogant but a terrifying thought. It would mean--and here perhaps we can first see why it is forbidden--that in every minute of his existence and being man himself must undertake to bridge the chasm which God Himself bridged by calling the creation out of nothing into a reality distinct from Himself.[172]

Man himself would become *creator ex nihilo* with the soul as absolute lord and creator of the body. Accordingly death in this conception would represent

the final and conclusive result of the delusion in which man wants to be both creator and creature. In death as the unnatural division of soul and body this sin is paid for. But death, too, makes it clear that this undertaking is a delusion and nothing else.[173]

In death the soul would become bodiless and therefore impotent while the organic body would merge into the material world. In death man would become "the spent body of a spent soul."[174]

Barth believes that it would be easier if one could speak of man without the differentiation of soul and body, or first speak of soul and then body, or speak of soul and body in symmetrical relation. But to follow any of these alternatives would mean that we do not have man as such in view.[175] Thus Barth advocates a type of empiricism. Soul does not exist apart from the body. Nor is the soul spirit. Spirit can exist apart from matter, but soul cannot.[176] As understood by Barth soul refers to the capacity of man to perceive himself as a specific subject[177] or to be conscious of himself.[178] However the soul never accomplishes this apart from its body. The body is the object which replies to the soul as subject. The material body is "a spatio-material system of relations."[179] Barth noteworthily distinguishes between the material body and organic body. As material body an entity is not "besouled and filled and controlled by independent life."[180] The German language bears this distinction in the words Körper and Leib, which have no parallel in Greek, Latin, French, or English.[181] Barth carefully points out that the soul is not an independent entity. As a material body is only the possibility of an organic body, so the soul is merely the possibility of a soul without a body.[182] The Old Testament נפש (soul) and the New Testament ψυχή (soul) both refer to the life of the body. Though neither term is exhausted by this particular usage, this usage characterizes all of the others as well. According to Barth certainly the Greek conception of soul as imperishable, immortal, higher, and even at times pre-existent substance as contrasted with the lower, mortal body is unbiblical.[183] Barth recognizes that this abstractly dualistic view, which is often termed the Greek view, "unfortunately must also be described as the traditional Christian view."[184] According to this view man is composed of two substances, body and soul, which are connected and even essentially and necessarily united, though the former is material, spatial, dissoluble, and mortal and the latter spiritual, non-spatial, indissoluble, and immortal. Barth notes that this Greek view taught by the fathers, schoolmen, and orthodox theologians of older Protestantism is still normative for Roman Catholicism. Its central affirmation is that the human, rational soul is immortal by nature and not by the grace of God.[185] In death the body and soul merely separate and go their separate ways. Barth believes it was disastrous that this understanding held sway for so long.[186] It overestimates the soul of man while providing an almost entirely negative estimation of the body.[187]

Monism

Despite his disparagement of the dualistic, Greek view, Barth is equally disparaging of two forms of abstract monism which have been set over against the Greek view. The first of these is monistic materialism.

On this view, the real is only what is corporeal, spatial,
physical and material. What cannot be brought under this
denominator is either mere appearance, imagination, illusion,
an irrelevant by-product or "epiphenomenon" of corporeal
causes and conditions, or, more mildly conceived and
expressed, its subjectively conditioned and necessary
phenomenal form.[188]

Barth believes that materialistic monism rests primarily on a
certain type of honesty and sobriety and secondarily upon scientific considerations. In fact the biblical conception of man
and especially the New Testament idea of resurrection impel one
to think along the lines of materialistic monism. Nonetheless
Barth believes that materialistic monism does not allow one to
see real man. Man is more than the body and its functions; he
is the subject which gives life to the material body.

Interestingly Barth suggests that the Reformation failed to
see the error of its dualistic perspective as "a just consequence
of the fact that the Reformation had too little time or understanding for biblical eschatology, and therefore saw no occasion to
undertake a revision of the traditional anthropology."[189] In
Credo Barth had made a similar point, attributing the lack of
biblical eschatology to the centrality that forgiveness of sins
played in the theology of that era. Barth makes the same observation now in the *Church Dogmatics* but does not offer explanation.
He also cites the Italian philosopher Pietro Pomponazzo who in
1516, i.e. the era of the outbreak of the Protestant Reformation,
challenged the Greek, dualistic conception with a monistic
materialism, though unsuccessfully. Barth also observes that the
materialism of the middle and later nineteenth century can only
in a qualified sense be said to derive from modern natural
science.[190]

The step from affirming that human consciousness is a function
of the brain to affirming that it is *only* a function of the
brain, from stating that the soul is materially conditioned
to stating that it is materially *constituted*, and therefore
to materialistic monism, was and still is a μετάβασισ εισ
άλλο γένοσ, which, when it is to be carried out, requires
another justification than natural science can provide.[191]

Barth notes a reticence on the part of a number of scientists in
this era against making such a leap. Nevertheless there is a
materialism which makes such a leap, not on the basis of true
science but a comprehensive world view. At the beginning of the
nineteenth century Idealists still envisioned the victory of
spirit over matter. However the many physical inventions and
their ramifications and establishment proved the Idealists incorrect. Man basically thought materialistically by the time that
Karl Marx and his historical materialism appeared.[192] Barth
nevertheless does not make a strong attack upon Marxism at this
juncture. Rather he chides the Church for its failure to follow
the teaching of Scripture in this regard. Furthermore as long as

it fails to revise its basic, dualistic anthropology it will not be in a position to confront the Marxist view of the world.[193]

The second type of monism which Barth combats is spiritual-istic. According to this view only soul exists. "Corporeality is only the garment, appearance, expression and symbol of the real, the form which its externality takes. Everything is real, as I am, only in so far as it is spiritual."[194] The material, corporeal world is merely the external basis of covenant, while the non-spatial, non-sensible, and immaterial is real. Barth notes that this makes of all science, including the natural sciences a form of psychology. The body is envisioned as the psychological shadow of the spiritual reality.[195] Barth under-stands spiritual monism as historically necessary in reaction to monistic materialism and abstract dualism. And though monistic spiritualism would solve many difficulties, Barth nevertheless cannot accept it because it is "too good to be true."[196] Man is not only soul; he is also body. He is both subject and object simultaneously. Yet he is this as a unity of person effected by the Spirit. In concluding this section Barth notes that human speech may be wiser in this regard than is human thought.

It is a remarkable thing that, in our use of the decisively important personal pronouns, we do not even remotely imagine that our expressions refer to the existence and nature of two substances or merely to one or other of them.[197]

Thus Barth can advocate that at this point man simply follow the wisdom of his speech.

Soul and Body in Their Particularity

Barth next moves on to consider soul and body in their particularity. This section is not developed from abstract consideration and assessment of man nor upon the basis of scientific and cultural studies. Rather he starts from a theological orientation; he considers man in his relation to God. As created man is "capable of meeting God, of being a person for and in relation to Him, and of being one as God is one."[198] After noting once again that it is his ability to stand in relation to God which distinguishes man from the animals, Barth examines the nature of the divine-human relationship. Man is the subject of his own decision, and he is aware that he does this. Man posits himself as a center in relation to his environ-ment and to God. In this manner man is *soul* of his body. The center also has a periphery, and together with the center it meets and stands before God. In the divine-human relationship, the body does not stand alone. In fact the body must and can only follow the soul. Barth does not understand man as a unity of two substances but as two moments, one an animating factor and the other the animated.[199] Barth utilizes the notion of percep-tion into awareness and thought, suggesting that awareness is primarily a bodily activity and thought of the soul. Yet the body is not aware of itself. This requires the soul. In terms of biblical thought it is as he is soul that man stands before God,

and it is to the soul of man that God wills to be present.[200]
On the other hand the soul does not think without the body.[201]
Furthermore it is in relation and correspondence to what he
perceives of God that man can be active. God wishes not only a
fellowship of knowledge but a fellowship of action,[202] and this
is the activity of the body. Barth also offers the example of
desiring and willing to demonstrate the particularity of soul
and body. The body desires, but the soul is capable of ignoring
and disavowing the desires of the body.[203] Its will need not be
directed by desires.

The Inner Order of the Creature

        In the final part of this section Barth describes the inner
order of the creature. As soul and body man is related in a
meaningful order. He follows a *ratio* or λόγοσ (word, reason,
logic) as Latin and Greek express it.[204] Man is addressed by
God as rational being. For Barth this prompts three points.
First God addresses man as soul, and soul in turn addresses its
body in a similar ruling manner.[205] Second man cannot understand
himself merely as a sensing and desiring subject. He is organic
body which, from the perspective of the body, is subject and must
serve. Third as established by God man cannot understand himself
as duel "but only as a single subject, as soul identical with his
body and as body identical with his soul."[206] In conclusion
Barth refers to two views of nontheological science as to the
relation of soul and body. The first is the theory of psycho-
physical parallelism. Under this teaching soul and body are
mutually independent with mutual correspondence. Barth reacts:
"With its mere positing of an X it fails to answer the question
concerning the one who exists in these two series or sides."[207]
The other view of the relation of soul and body is psycho-physical
alternation. This theory also assumes two series or sides to
human existence which causally determine and influence one
another. This theory, however, emphasizes the disparateness of
the two series and fails to clarify the nature of the unity.[208]
Attempts to combine these two views of parallelism also fail
because they continue to assume two series or sides instead of
two moments of the one human activity.[209] Barth concludes that
nontheological anthropology leads invariably to contradiction(s)
and fasities of one sort or another. And the real basis of this
contradition is the incorrect starting point--man in isolation
and apart from his relationship to God. Despite his difference
of approach from that of nontheological science, Barth does not
believe that one can close off from the facts as established by
these disciplines.

        We do not really question the data of the outer aspect of
        human reality, but we regret that they are not seen together
        in a very different way and applied as contributions to an
        anthropology based on the inner aspect of this reality. Thus
        we do not dissociate ourselves from the facts brought to
        light by modern science, but only from the one-sided and the
        mediating interpretations which it has hitherto given them.[210]

Barth would simply prefer to provide a better interpretation of the data, one in which the soul dominates the body which serves and one which has a conscious theological basis. Barth firmly believes that this will do better justice to the facts.

Furthermore though he recognizes that a true anthropology cannot be found in the Bible, Barth believes that the biblical writers knew well what they talked about with regard to man and that they demonstrate substantial unanimity in this regard. In terms of general historical characterization, man is represented unabashedly as primitive man.

> This representation knows the double-sidedness of the being of man. It knows what we have called the two moments of the human life-act. It reckons with both. But it knows of no division between them. It knows of no bodiless soul and soulless body. It knows only of the one whole man seen from both sides.[211]

Both soul and body in interrelationship are necessary to a Christian anthropology. Barth is also little disturbed by the fact that this might be termed primitive man.

> From our whole consideration of the matter, it appears that the supposed "primitives" are in this matter more sophisticated than the sophisticated whose approach has so successfully superseded their own in the civilised west and cultures influenced by it.[212]

We recall that Barth has since *Romans* questioned the conclusions of reason and has instead given preference and priority to revelation. In this section again Barth has followed this course. He does not deny the new data which the sophisticated instruments and procedures of modern science discover, but he opts for a better interpretation of the data, one which allows for the revealed truths of God as recorded in the Bible by so-called primitive men.

CONCLUSION

The paragraph heading provided by Barth for section 46 of the *Church Dogmatics*, which we have just reviewed, reads:

> Through the Spirit of God, man is the subject, form and life of a substantial organism, the soul of his body--wholly and simultaneously both, in ineffaceable difference, inseperable unity, and indestructible order.[213]

Our review has noted how man is thus constituted in the three dimensions of space. However what transpires to the individual in death has been mentioned only in passing. For Barth when God withdraws His Spirit man will no longer be the soul of a body and man will cease to be. Man will return to the earth from whence he came.[214] Death therefore for the individual represents the withdrawal of the Spirit by God.

The withdrawal of the Spirit terminates life. Throughout section 46 Barth has emphasized that man exists as soul of a body and body of a soul as long as there is Spirit. The soul does not exist apart from the body and vice versa. Whereas we have dedicated substantial consideration to this basic notion because it demonstrates clearly that man is a whole, Barth himself has been criticized for providing too little consideration, especially with regard to the Greek, abstract dualistic approach.[215] Barth is explicit in distinguishing his position from the dualistic and monistic understandings. There is an order to the creature which Barth notes, an order which exists as long as man is granted Spirit by God. Death is final because there can be no life without Spirit.

In this section Barth also indicates that if there is to be any life after death for man that it can occur only with "a new sending forth" of the Spirit. That this will occur, however, Barth does not indicate since such an indication might interfere with the divine freedom.[216] Thus there is a real finality to death for Barth. Nothing of man continues to exist after life. Man disintegrates as body of a soul and soul of a body and is no more.

Death thus represents for the individual the withdrawal of the Spirit with which God had endowed him, and the Spirit returns to God from whence it came. Whether man has any life post mortem will be the focus of our next section, but already from this section we note the several restrictions and limitations which any notion of life post mortem will encounter.

MAN POST MORTEM

Our third question of "what happens after life?" is easily the most difficult to answer of the three questions which we are posing to the *Church Dogmatics*. This results as we have noted previously from the incomplete nature of the *Dogmatics*. Barth had been intending to deal with the issue of our third focus in the fifth volume, the *Doctrine of Redemption*, which never appeared. Unlike our former two questions, then, we cannot focus our attention upon a single primary section of the *Church Dogmatics*. Rather we must glean response from other sections of the *Dogmatics*. Because of the method followed by Barth in the *Church Dogmatics* this is neither as difficult nor prohibitive as might normally be expected. We recall the compact and integrated character of the *Dogmatics* with its center in the Word of God. Because the doctrines of God, creation, reconciliation, and redemption are coordinated and intertwined we are able to surmise the basic tenets of the response Barth might offer to our third question. Our situation is not unlike that which we encountered with regard to *The Epistle to the Romans* in which it was necessary to glean and organize ideas which Barth, in part by intent and and design, did not make readily available to us. We thus recognize again the tenuous nature of our conclusions. Nonetheless here, even less than in *Romans*, do we feel that such a venture is unwarranted or "illegitimate." Barth did address the topics of

concern in this our third focus in various sections of the
Church Dogmatics. Moreover we will not limit our attention to
the *Church Dogmatics* at this point. Though Barth restricted his
outside involvements in order to concentrate upon the writing of
his *Church Dogmatics*, he did nonetheless produce several writings
during the era of the *Dogmatics* which give response to our third
question. *The Faith of the Church*, *Dogmatics in Outline*, *The
Heidelberg Catechism for Today*, and *The Humanity of God* of 1940,
1947, 1948, and 1956 respectively will each be cited in appropriate contexts as we seek to elaborate what Barth envisioned for
man post mortem.

Two topics will receive our consideration as we respond
to this third question or focus--the interim state and life post
mortem. The latter in turn will consist of sections treating
the return of Christ; the end of time; eternalising, unveiling,
and completion; apocatastasis; and the nature of eternal life:
three options. To these we turn directly.

The Interim State

Barth expends little time upon a description of the nature
of man between the time of his death and the termination of the
fourth dimension of time, the period often referred to as the
interim state. Barth seemingly wanted to affirm two notions on
this point. First he wanted to establish that man is mortal
and that nothing of him continues during the interim state.
Second he writes that Christ intervenes on behalf of man at
once at death.

First we note that from our review of man in the three
dimensions of space and the fourth dimension of time it seems
impossible that anything happens to man during this interim
state. Man is soul of a body and body of a soul as long as he
has spirit. But according to Barth there is no such thing as a
soulless body or a bodiless soul. We know nothing of life
without the three dimensions, except of course for God Himself,
their Creator. Likewise we know nothing of life apart from the
spirit. Furthermore in his 1948 study of the Heidelberg Catechism Barth refers to "the hope for a 'higher life' or the
dreadful idea that we must begin all over again and go back to
school (a heavenly school or a school of angels, perhaps!)."[217]
Hence we conclude that there is no life per se for man in the
interim between death and the end of time. Man simply ceases to
exist. Whereas some philosophies and theologies have conceived
of an immortality which is inherent in man, usually in his soul,
Barth clearly rejects such a notion. Barth does refer to the
spirit which returns to God from whence it derived as determining
the moment of our death. But the spirit for Barth is an impersonal life force and not anything resembling the immortal soul
which has typically been used in description of an immortal
aspect of man.

There is a finality to death which Barth unreservedly
affirms, and by clear implication there is no life for man in

the interim state. Man has no spirit to enliven him and can
therefore have no life. Man simply moves into the realm of non-
being. Man does not become nothing, but he has no life or spirit.

Second we find in Barth a trend suggesting that man is not
totally lifeless during the interim. Barth notes that the New
Testament community did not raise the question as to what
happened to man during the interim.

They simply held fast to the confession: "I am the resurrection and the life," and in the light of this hope they
came to see in the visible process of dying the last conclusive symptom of a life surrounded by the peace of God.[218]

The New Testament referred to those who had died as having
"fallen asleep." With the victory of Christ over the second
death death had been naturalized and the analogy of sleep, though
euphemistic, was deemed appropriate. For the New Testament
Christians Christ Himself was envisioned as intervening "at
once and absolutely on the far side of this event."[219] This
might appear to indicate that death would be gain or an improvement upon our life in this world, but Barth envisions things
less optimistically.[220] Barth believes that man will become
conscious of his sin and exposed for what he was and is.

The problem for us arises in that his conviction implies
an ongoing function of soul, which our first alternative clearly
discounts. It appears difficult to synthesize these two alternative views of the interim state, but they are not necessarily
antithetical either. Being convicted of our sin and need of
divine grace does not constitute a total life, certainly not a
full life in covenant relationship with God. There is certainly
the question, as we will note below, of whether there is a
distinction between being *in* and being *with* God. The former
seems less spirited and lively than the latter, but since Barth
offers no further clarification we are unable to determine
whether there is substantial agreement and possible convergence.
We therefore note two distinct and seemingly divergent trends of
thought in Barth regarding the interim state.

Life Post Mortem

Though every man will one day cease to be, God will still
be for him. "Hence our future non-existence cannot be our complete negation."[221] Nor, as we have just noted, can after-life
be conceived of in terms of an immortality which belongs to man
himself.[222] It is God and God alone who serves as a basis for
human hope beyond death. Properly speaking man has no beyond.
"Nor does he need one, for God is his beyond."[223] In these
comments and others like them Barth seriously restricts what
may be said concerning after-life. Some in fact, as we will
note, have questioned whether Barth allows any room for any sort
of after-life for man. This derives in part from Barth's feeling
that it is easy to say both too much and too little with regard
to after-life. On the one hand one can say too much in treating

as certain a hope which can only be based in God. Yet on the other hand it may say too little in respect to the fulfillment of this hope.[224] Barth is both timid and bold regarding after-life.

In detailing what he would envision as his eschatology we would expect Barth to focus initially upon Christ, which he does in several germane sections of the *Church Dogmatics*. Nevertheless we must caution that Barth would undoubtedly suggest, as he did in describing man in his time, that what is predicated of Christ after life need not be true with regard to other men since Jesus Christ is also God.[225]

Our discussion of after-life will focus upon the following topics: the return of Christ; the end of time; eternalising, unveiling, and completion; apocatastasis; and in conclusion the three options.

The Return of Christ

It is customary for Christians to envision a day in the future when Christ will return. Barth rather speaks of a three-fold return of Christ which, while not denying what has been customary, does nonetheless place it within a different context and with different emphasis.

The first return of Christ was that of the resurrection and the forty days. This was revealed as the dawning of the last day. Man is thereby assured that what remains since death has been deprived of its power is the running out of this last day, and then its end will appear in accordance with its beginning.[226] Barth writes that it was this first return of Christ which created and proved the basis of faith. The first return of Christ ought not be understood subjectively and/or docetic-ally.[227] The faith which developed as a result of the first return of Christ

> did not consist in a reassessment and reinterpretation *in meliorem partem* of the picture of the Crucified, but in an objective encounter with the Crucified and Risen, who Himself not only made Himself credible to them, but manifested Himself as the αρχηγὸσ τῆσ σωτηρίασ αυτῶν (Heb. 2[10]) and therefore the αρχηγὸσ καὶ τελειωτήσ πίστισ (Heb. 12[2]).[228]

The key word here is the objective encounter with Christ. The resurrected Christ was no phantom and figment of imagination. Jesus was not simply raised subjectively within his disciples. His victory over death and His exaltation should be understood objectively.[229] The grave was empty and new life beyond death became visible.[230] With his death and the empty tomb now behind him, Jesus Christ

> moves out from the latency of His being and action of yester-day and from the inoperativeness of His power, appearing to

His disciples and in them potentially to all men and the
whole cosmos, declaring Himself, making known His presence
and what has been accomplished in Him for all men and for
the whole created order, putting it into effect.[231]

Indeed Barth notes that the sole reason for the extension of the
last day "is to allow space before the kingdom comes to repent
and believe the Gospel (Mk. 1[15]) on the basis of this event and
its indication."[232] It is thus the event of Easter and the
forty days which Barth describes as the first return of Christ.

Barth notes that the New Testament also bears witness to a
second form of parousia or effective presence of Christ in the
impartation of the Holy Spirit.[233] This second return of Christ
is often if not generally overlooked, as Barth himself had done
in the *Credo*. Barth, however, will not belittle the significance
of the Holy Spirit. In fact by terming it the second parousia of
Christ he effectively places the coming of the Holy Spirit on a
level equal to the resurrection and final return of Christ.

The New Testament also bears witness to a third and future
return of Christ.

It will also take place in a different and definitive form
(of which we shall have to speak in eschatology), as the
return of Jesus Christ as the goal of the history of the
Church, the world and each individual, as His coming as the
Author of the general resurrection of the dead and the
Fulfiller of universal judgment.[234]

Several things come to light in this quotation. First we note
that Christ will return for a third and final time. Second we
note that the third return is the goal and purpose for the
world and what fills it. Christ is the goal of history, creation
is the external basis of covenant and covenant the internal basis
of creation, and this will be revealed for all in the third
coming. Third we note that the third return of Christ will
introduce Him as the source of the general resurrection, about
which we will speak shortly. All will be required to face
Christ as their judge. But for the Christian Barth affirms that
this will entail joyful tidings.[235] Fifth we note that Barth
intended to speak of this at greater length under eschatology,
a subject which would have been included in *Volume V* of the
Church Dogmatics, the volume which Barth was unable even to
start. Thus our gleaning of appropriate comments from *Volumes
III/2* and *IV/3* for what we do include here becomes justified.

We must further clarify that this three-fold return of
Christ represents one event, and in each of the forms it is the
return of the One who had previously come. Though the New
Testament usually refers to the third return of Christ when
referring to the parousia, it clearly maintains distinction
between the first, second, and third return. It also clearly
resists reduction of the parousia to a past, present, or future
form alone. The parousia of Christ formally corresponds to the

three modes of being of God in relation to His one essence in triunity.[236] Barth suggests that it may be helpful to treat the unity of these three forms of mutual relationship analogous to the perichoretic relationship within the Trinity.

> It is not merely that these three forms are interconnected in the totality of the action present in them all, or in each of them in its unity and totality, but that they are mutually related as the forms of this one action by the fact that each of them also contains the other two by way of anticipation or recapitulation, so that, without losing their individuality or destroying that of the others, they participate and are active and revealed in them.[237]

For Barth the final return of Christ represents the completion of what God in Christ had begun in the resurrection and continued in the outpouring of the Holy Spirit.[238] God will be all in all.[239]

The End of Time

We noted at the beginning of our study of death and after-life in the *Church Dogmatics* that creation is the external basis of covenant, and we noted that God created four dimensions in order to establish this covenant. Thus time had a definite point at which it began. Corresponding to the beginning of time when there was a present without a past, so at the third return of Christ there will be a present without a future and time will come to a definite end. As John writes in Revelation 10:6: "there shall be time no longer."[240] At that particular moment "the secret of Calvary will be revealed as indicated in the forty days."[241] Revelation will become completely available for all to perceive at that final moment of time. The truth will be unveiled.

Eternalising, Unveiling, and Completion

In a short book published in 1940 and entitled *La Confession de Foi de l'Eglise*, which was translated as *The Faith of the Church: A Commentary on the Apostle's Creed according to Calvin's Catechism*, Barth describes the nature of after-life in terms which sound very orthodox. He then speaks of the resurrection of the *flesh* when human existence is ushered into eternity.[242] The sanctification of man will be complete in the resurrection. Even so Barth stresses the point that resurrection is an "absolute change, which rather than an ending, is a beginning again of life."[243] Man will clearly not be resurrected as he lives now. It is impossible for man to imagine the resurrection, and Barth reiterates that fact.[244] Obviously for Barth resurrection involves a marked change from this life. Nevertheless Barth suggests a clear aspect of continuity when he writes:

> Often I have tried to imagine this for myself in this following manner: our life is hidden under a veil. This veil is the present times. At the resurrection, this veil will be

removed, and our whole life, from the crib to the grave, will be seen in the light and in its unity with the life of Christ, in the splendor of Christ's mercy, of his grace and of his power.[245]

This suggests that there will be continuity between this life and life post mortem. Barth even suggests that resurrection is a passage, a word which suggests again the idea of continuity.[246] The idea of passage also seems evident in *The Heidelberg Catechism for Today* when Barth writes: "But the important thing is that it also speaks of the whole man, soul and body, who moves through death to a resurrection in which he will be conformed to the glorious body of Christ."[247] Here, however, Barth offers no clear explanation as to whether continuity or discontinuity will be evident.

We draw attention to *The Faith of the Church* since it was written in the midst of Barth's work on the *Church Dogmatics* and, while we note that it resonates with what Barth had written previously in his career, it says more than Barth appears willing to say on these subjects in appropriate sections of the *Church Dogmatics* and other works of Barth written during the era of the *Church Dogmatics*.

In the *Church Dogmatics* the notion which comes to the fore is of a novel nature. It is the notion of eternalising. Barth writes that with the end of time "There is no question of the continuation into an indefinite future of a somewhat altered life."[248] Barth believes that the New Testament hope is much different. The third return of Christ signifies a change, a radical change. The creation will be transformed. What the New Testament anticipates is what Barth terms "the 'eternalising' of this ending life."[249] The corruptible and mortal will become incorruptible and immortal. Our earthly tabernacle will be clothed with a building prepared by God Himself, a house not made with hands. Our past life, which was limited in time, will then "fully, definitively and manifestly participate in that καινῶτησ ζωῆσ (Rom. 6⁴)."[250] This new life will be eternal life in God and in fellowship with Him. But then Barth adds that it is "the past life of every man in its limited time"[251] which is eternalised. It is the past life which undergoes transition and transformation and participates in eternal life with God. Eternalising involves the transition and transformation, the unveiling and glorifying of the life which man has already had in Christ. This resurrection of the dead represents our human hope.[252] Our hope according to Barth relates to "*this life* of ours. This life is not left behind or given up. It was and is and also will be *lived* before *him*."[253] This life will be conformed to the glorious life of Christ.[254] It is what Barth envisions in interpretation of 1 Corinthians 15:28: ο θεὸσ πάντα εν πᾶσιν (God will be all and in all). It is evident that this position is removed from pantheism where everything is God, though it is less clear how Barth could be distinuished from panentheism, the view that everything is in God. When it beomces eternalised everything will be present before God and seemingly coexist in God. Panentheism seems an appropriate nomenclature, at least as Barth describes eternalising in *Church Dogmatics III/2*.

Barth elaborates further upon the idea of eternalising in *Volume III/3* of the *Church Dogmatics*, and here we note some important qualifications. He describes eternalising in terms such that God will not be all alone again and that all else will cease to be.

> It means rather that in the final revelation of His ways He will be seen by the creature to have attained His ultimate goal in all things with the creature, the creature not ceasing to be distinct from Himself.[255]

Barth believes that the creature will be actual though within limits. This it owes to the divine preservation.[256] Barth continues by offering clarification of divine preservation in negative and positive terms. Negatively it means that "it was not in vain that God gave to it time and duration, and in time and duration reality and activity."[257] If man were to become mere appearance this would mean that the non-existent had triumphed over the creature of God, that God had revoked His own work--especially His reconciliation of man in Christ, and that God had withdrawn His Yes and elected isolation. But Barth believes that the binding of God to man is far too serious and unreserved for this to occur.[258] This negative interpretation of eternalising is a critical point for, as we will note later, it implies that man will be more than a memory for God.

Positively the eternal preservation by God of the creature signifies that the creature continues eternally before Him. Even when time will have ended with the third parousia of Christ the totality of all that has ever been will be open and present to Him and thus preserved.[259] Nothing will escape God, not even a

> wing-beat of the day-fly in far-flung epochs of geological time. Everything will be present to Him exactly as it was or is or will be, in all its reality, in the whole temporal course of its activity, in its strength or weakness, in its majesty or meanness.[260]

In this description Barth notes the same sober realism as characterizes the Old Testament. It retains even more seriously the majesty of God while pointing to a greater degree the lowliness and finitude of man. Barth concludes the section with the following noteworthy comment:

> If we wish the New Testament had more to say about this than the Old, it may well be that we are pursuing pagan dreams of a good time after death, and not letting the New Testament say the radically good thing which it has to say with the realism which it has in common with the Old Testament.[261]

This particular comment illustrates one of the difficulties
which Barth encountered in describing what transpires to the
individual after life. Barth was concerned that he not say too
much, though also his saying too little also represented a
concern for him. Barth nonetheless rather seems to lean toward
saying too little, and there are two reasons for this. First
he is concerned not to give in to a pietistic "Jenseitschristentum" (otherworldly Christianity). He does not wish to elaborate
upon the glories of a future life which might detract from our
current life. Barth does not advocate a flight into the
Beyond.[262] Closely related to this is a second factor. Barth
avoided referring to the third return of Christ as a renewal in
favor of Enthüllung (unveiling). Renewal suggests a greater
degree of transformation than unveiling while Barth wished to
stress the presence of God's gracious reality in this life.[263]
As we noted in *The Faith of the Church* above, the veil of the
present times conceals from us eternal life in this life,[264] but
this nonetheless implies a continuity between life here and after-
life. The future will bring the revelation of that which already
is.[265] The emphasis which Barth thus places upon the second
return of Christ is herewith also set into a broader context.

Barth also utilizes the idea of completion to describe
resurrection in the *Dogmatics in Outline*. He writes that in
spite of his death a Christian can look forward to the completion
of his own life. There is to be "bestowed upon him unconditional
participation in the glory of God."[266] Again Barth writes that
what was initiated in this life is completed after life. In
Volume I/2 of the *Church Dogmatics* Barth speaks along the same
line when he speaks of promise and future realization.[267] The
future completes the promise, but the content of the future is
left unclarified. Nonetheless Barth writes at the same time in
tones reminiscent of eternalising: "In resurrection our life is
involved, we men as we are and are situated. We rise again, no
one else takes our place."[268] The truth of this life will be
uncovered.[269]

Enthüllung (unveiling) and Vollendung (completion) seem
evident in the three time periods which Barth outlined in *Volume
III/1*. The first was the time of creation, yet creation is the
basis for grace and reconciliation, which is God's foremost goal.
This was obviously to be revealed in Christ in time. For Barth
the covenant or time of grace is initiated within the time of
sin[270] as the ratification and renewal of creation.[271] Thus it
appears again that unveiling and especially completion seem
evident in Barth's thinking. The eschaton, though without time,
would seem to require some sort of continuity, especially with
the third time form.

Though we will return to this subject subsequently, we note
at this juncture that in the *Church Dogmatics*, which is the most
complete and thorough statement of Barth's position at this point,
it is the notion of eternalising which is most prominent in
Barth's discussion of life post mortem while in the *Dogmatics in
Outline*, which derives from lectures at the University of Bonn

during the summer semester of 1946 which were published in 1947,
the idea of unveiling and that of completion take prominence.
However it must be noted that *Dogmatics in Outline* is sandwiched
between the publication of *Church Dogmatics III/2* in 1945 and
Church Dogmatics III/3 in 1950, the two volumes of the *Dogmatics*
in which eternalising is prominent. Thus we would suggest that
for Barth eternalising, unveiling, and completion must be complementary ideas, else Barth would have clearly distinguished them.
This, however, will be treated subsequently. Here we conclude
that for Barth it is plain that man is not negated after life.

Apocatastasis

Apocatastasis or the doctrine of universal salvation has
been evident in the writing of Barth since *The Epistle to the
Romans*. The *Church Dogmatics* and other writings of Barth from
this era demonstrate a clear inclination toward endorsement of
this idea. Yet Barth consistently refuses to cross the threshold
and unreservedly endorse apocatastasis. In our discussion we
will note the various reasons which Barth provides for the
belief that he does in fact hold a view of apocatastasis. On
the other hand we will also point out the principal reasons
why Barth is reluctant to advocate apocatastasis and why he in
fact never explicitly does so.

Volume II of the *Church Dogmatics* treats the *Doctrine of
God*. The third of the four issues treated in that volume
concerns the unfolding of God's fundamental attitude towards
man. Thus *Volume II/2* contains chapter VII which is entitled
"The Election of God." It is in this chapter, and especially
section 35 where Barth relates the election of the individual
that Barth provides us with justification for terming him a
universalist.

Barth notes the rejection of man by God on account of
human sin and guilt. Sinful man is justly denied and repudiated
by the righteous judgment and sentence of God. He is transferred
to the untenable state of Satan and his kingdom. Man is abandoned by God "to eternal perdition."[272] Indeed this is the
state which befits sinful man.

However Barth writes that this is merely a "threat." It
would be unjustifiable to suggest that this threat will never
be actualised, for in fact the threat has already been carried
out. It has been diverted to Jesus Christ "and in that way
averted from others."[273] For Barth there is only "one Rejected. .
. . and this One is Jesus Christ."[274] In Christ God has made the
life of a godless and rejected man "objectively impossible."[275]
Man may act as if he is rejected, yet Barth writes that even if
someone deserved it a thousand times over he would not have the
power to bring down upon himself the wrath of God a second time
since the sword of divine wrath has already fallen upon Christ.[276]
With such beliefs concerning the effect of the death of Christ
Barth clearly aligns himself with apocatastasis. God has removed

the reason for rejecting and repudiating man by means of the work of Christ.

In the same context Barth notes that the purported opposition between the elect and others is not absolute but can only be relative. Barth acknowledges a sharp distinction, yet both nevertheless must rely upon Christ, and therefore the difference between the elect and others must be relative.[277]

Barth also writes in *Volume II/2* concerning 1 Timothy 2:4 that the will of God is directed intentionally toward the salvation of all men and that it is sufficiently powerful for the salvation of all men.[278] In *Volume III/1* Barth contends furthermore that it is impossible to envisage an unfulfilled divine plan and purpose.[279] Barth accordingly resists following classical doctrine and closing the number of elect. He would rather the number remain open.[280] The possibility of universal salvation is thus once more indicated. Barth similarly warns that it cannot be the business of man to choose or reject others since this is distinctly for God alone to perform. Though he does not openly commend apocatastasis with this point,[281] Barth here appears to be criticizing those who restrict and limit the salvation of God to a particular segment of humanity. More affirmative of apocatastasis is Barth's comment that there exists no eternal covenant of wrath on the one hand which contrasts with the eternal covenant of grace on the other.[282] This basically reiterates what Barth had written in *The Faith of the Church* when he suggested that the creed does not mention hell and eternal death because man can believe only what is an object of faith-- and hell and eternal death are not.[283] God is not ambivalent. Rejection is rejected.[284] With such comments Barth clearly aligns himself with the belief in apocatastasis or universal salvation.

And yet, nevertheless, Barth refuses to wholeheartedly affirm apocatastasis, and he offers reason for this in *Volume II/2* as well. He writes:

> If we are to respect the freedom of divine grace, we cannot venture the statement that it must and will finally be coincident with the world as such (as in the doctrine of the so-called *apocatastasis*). No such right or necessity can legitimately be deduced. Just as the gracious God does not need to elect or call any single man, so He does not need to elect or call all mankind.[285]

Barth earnestly desires to respect the freedom of God. Nothing which might constrain God may be applied to Him. For Barth apocatastasis, the belief in universal salvation, impinges upon the divine freedom and cannot therefore be affirmed, even though Barth clearly empathizes with such a belief in *Volume II/2* of the *Church Dogmatics*.

In *Volumes III* and *IV* of the *Church Dogmatics* Barth turns from time to time to the subject of apocatastasis, though never

as completely as in his chapter relating the election of God.
In the *Doctrine of Creation* and the *Doctrine of Reconciliation*
we hear clear echoes of what Barth had previously written concerning this subject. In *Volume IV/1* Barth writes:

> "He hath concluded them all in disobedience." "Concluded"
> means that He has placed them under an authoritative verdict
> and sentence which cannot be questioned or disputed, let
> alone resisted, with all the consequences which that
> involves.[286]

Barth compares the verdict of sentence and condemnation and the
mercy of God to two sides of a coin, the one being the reverse
of the other. God cannot have mercy on anyone without first
sentencing him to condemnation.[287] Thus we again find a bipolar,
though not ambivalent, orientation in God, and this evidences a
clear universalistic trend in Barth.

This trend becomes even clearer in *Volume IV/3* of the
Church Dogmatics, the last complete volume of this monumental
work. Here Barth describes the condition of man as that of
lying. "To lie is to try to substitute for the election of man
fulfilled by God a rejection which is not God's will for him and
which according to God's Word is averted by His act."[288] It is
thus clear that God intends man not for rejection but for election. Barth continues:

> The decisive purpose of lying is that the free God should be
> replaced by One who is externally and internally bound, and
> that the man freed by and for God should be replaced by one
> who in his self-determination is "selfless" in the worst
> sense of the word, i.e., incapable of genuine self-determina-
> tion and therefore unfree.[289]

Man attempts to bind God to particular determinations which constrain what He is able to do, and God thereby loses His self-
determination, which for Barth is absurd. Man has attempted a
fatal change of place. He lives in falsehood and curses himself.
"What man actually utters when he lies even if he does not put it
into words as is unfortunately so often the case, is no other
than the dreadful cursing of himself: 'Well, I'll be damned.'"[290]
By right God could let the sword of judgment fall upon man. But
notably this threat has not yet been fulfilled. Barth writes
that

> the sword has not yet fallen. Fearful as it is, the danger
> is still only a danger. Man lies, but he is not yet damned
> and lost. From the standpoint of his lying, he can and
> should be every moment. But so far he is not.[291]

God does not yet will to make man suffer for his lying ways.
Still Barth believes that there is no basis upon which man
could reckon that the not yet will become never. If the sword
will not fall and man's condemnation is not pronounced,

it can only be a matter of the unexpected work of grace and its revelation of which we cannot count but for which we can only hope as an undeserved and inconceivable overflowing of the significance, operation and outreach of the reality of God and man in Jesus Christ.[292]

Man has no claim upon the grace of God, even if he were to argue that by nature God must be grace-full and redeem man. Barth disallows such presumption. If man were to attempt to deny his lying condition and to disarm it with the postulate of an apocatastasis or universal reconciliation as the goal and end of all things, he would be merely perpetuating the lie.

No such postulate can be made even though we appeal to the cross and resurrection of Jesus Christ. Even though theological consistency might seem to lead our thought and utterances most clearly in this direction, we must not arrogate to ourselves that which can be given and received only as a free gift.[293]

Barth clearly favors a universalistic view of salvation, but he believes that he cannot endorse such an idea without doing injustice to God.

Nevertheless Barth is unwilling to discard the notion of apocatastasis, and thus in his essay "The Humanity of God," which was originally published in 1956, Barth asks the question "Does this mean universalism?" and offers three observations in which he attempts to give no indication of his own position for or against universalism. First Barth cautions that panic is an inappropriate response to the belief in universalism before the sense or non-sense of it has been investigated. Second Barth believes that we ought to be stimulated by Colossians 1:19, which states that through His Son Jesus Christ God has determined to reconcile all things, to consider whether this could have a good meaning. Barth feels other passages beg the same consideration. Third Barth warns against the danger of "the eternally skeptical-critical theologian who is ever and again suspiciously questioning, because fundamentally always legalistic and therefore in the main morosely gloomy."[294] Barth believes that the presence of such gloomy legalism is more detrimental than even antinomianism. He writes that there is no theological justification to limit God's loving-kindness in Christ. He in fact lists as a theological duty the extension of God's love.[295]

The same sort of notion was put forward by Barth in the *Dogmatics in Outline* where Barth notes that the return of Christ, though providing comfort, does not lead to apocatastasis. There will be a decision and division, yet these will be effected by the One who has interceded on behalf of man.[296]

This same train of thought appears as well in *Church Dogmatics IV/3, part 1* where Barth suggests that there is no legitimate reason why man is forbidden to be open to the possibility that man may be delivered from God's final threat against

him. Barth continues to affirm that man has no claim for this,
but that is no reason that man may not hope and pray for it,

> to hope and pray cautiously and yet distinctly that, in
> spite of everything which may seem quite conclusively to
> proclaim the opposite, His compassion should not fail, and
> that in accordance with His mercy which is "new every
> morning" He "will not cast off for ever" (La. 3$^{22f.}$, 31).[297]

Barth demonstrates a clear and strong inclination for apocatastasis, though he never unqualifiedly supports this teaching.

This disinclination for Barth to endorse apocatastasis is
particularly apparent in at least two points. First in *Church
Dogmatics III/2* Barth notes that death implies the threat of
eternal corruption, though this is precisely what Jesus suffered.
Furthermore Barth notes that the ideas and conceptions of man
after life are not mitigated or moderated in severity when the
Old Testament is compared with the New. Though the good news of
the New Testament might seem to ameliorate the future, just the
opposite occurred. Instead of conceiving of a shadowy, weak
life after death, the New Testament presents a picture of hell
as punishment of a very positive kind. In this regard the New
Testament did not become more humane than the Old.[298] A second
point where we note this disinclination to endorse apocatastasis
occurs in *Volume IV/3, part 1* when Barth writes concerning damnation: "To be damned is to be committed to an eternity in which
we are rejected by God and therefore lost."[299] Barth knew about
hell and damnation. Yet even in these two contexts which we
have cited Barth employs the thought of hell in demonstrating
the representative character of the death of Jesus and that the
worst has not yet and perhaps may never befall man. Thus a
universalistic tendency is evident in both of these instances
as well, though it is apparent that Barth believes in the reality
of hell--at least for Jesus--and its being a possible destination
of man.

It was along this same line that Barth responded to a
request from G. W. Bromiley who had in turn been asked by the
editor of *Christianity Today* to answer some critical questions
posed by the United States theologians Clark, Klooster, and
van Til. Since the subject of universalism apparently was to
be among the questions the response of Barth is noteworthy at
this point. He declined to answer any questions because in
Barth's words:

> . . . They can adopt toward me only the role of prosecuting
> attorneys, trying to establish whether what I represent
> agrees or disagrees with their orthodoxy, in which I for my
> part have no interest! None of their questions leaves me
> with the impression that they want to seek with me the truth
> that is greater than us all. They take the stance of those
> who happily possess it already and who hope to enhance their
> happiness by succeeding in proving to themselves and the world
> that I do not share this happiness.[300]

Barth again laments and chastises those who are not open to
dialogue, and apocatastasis was one of the proposed areas of
discussion. This hardly signifies that Barth held to a position
of apocatastasis, but he clearly is critical of those who are
self-assured that the belief in universalism is prohibited.

Due to these strains of thought in his works Barth has not
infrequently been termed an advocate of apocatastasis by other
theologians. John Hick is among those who understand Barth in
this manner. Though he recognizes that Barth felt that God's
sovereign freedom should never be jeapordized by suggesting
what God *will* do, Hick nonetheless feels that the designation is
appropriate.[301] G. C. Berkouwer similarly writes: "There is no
alternative to concluding that Barth's refusal to accept the
apokatastasis cannot be harmonized with the fundamental structure of his doctrine of creation."[302] Though Berkouwer writes
that Barth wishes to safeguard the proclamation and reception of
God's Word,[303] he also remarks that the theology of Barth makes
vague the seriousness of human decision[304] since Barth is so
clearly universalistic.

In his book *Jesus Is Victor! Karl Barth's Doctrine of
Salvation* Donald Bloesch agrees with the conclusion of Berkouwer
et. al. that Barth is a universalist, but he recognizes that
Barth did not openly endorse this principle and therefore refers
to him as a tacit universalist.[305] Bloesch criticizes Barth for
his failure to maintain the objective and subjective poles of
salvation. Everything needful to salvation has been accomplished
in Christ, and this still requires subjective appropriation by
man.[306] Yet Bloesch contends that for Barth the wrath of God is
the penultimate word and love the ultimate word.[307] Bloesch
recognizes the reticence of Barth regarding universalism, though
he nonetheless recognizes the implication and terms him accordingly a tacit universalist.

Joseph Bettis notes that Emil Brunner and G. C. Berkouwer
both agree that Barth is a universalist, though each for different reasons. Bettis, however, would take exception to both
Brunner and Berkouwer. He contends: "For both of them there
are three alternatives, and because Barth fails to accept either
Brunner's Arminianism or Berkouwer's double decree, he must be a
universalist."[308] Yet Barth never allowed himself to draw such
a conclusion as a *doctrine*, though he would leave it open as a
possibility. "Barth rejects the attempt to bridge the gap
between divine possibility and a theological statement of its
actuality."[309] Since universalism constricts God's options and
freedom it is therefore shunned as a doctrine by Barth.

It is also interesting that even during his lectures Barth
was not infrequently asked by a student to clarify his position
with regard to apocatastasis. Barth would admit that universalism
was a trend in his theology, but he would never admit to being a
universalist as such. Barth tried to protect himself by saying
that universalism was an abstract principle whereas his position
was more dynamic. He believed in the victory of Jesus Christ but

was unwilling to suggest what that specifically implied and/or entailed. One of his students has accordingly termed Barth an incipient universalist.[311] Universalism was implied and was becoming evident at various points in the works of Barth, but Barth remained unwilling to give it his absolute assent and endorsement.

In conclusion we ask, "Did Barth advocate apocatastasis?" Though Barth's writing clearly moves in that direction, the question might best be answered by noting that Barth eliminated the reasons generally given in defense for rejection of this teaching. That, however, does not constitute an endorsement of apocatastasis by Barth. Barth remained reluctant to give support for apocatastasis, and that principally because he wished to protect the freedom of God. Barth would neither constrain nor constrict God's options, even if the options would normally be considered favorable for His creature man.

The Nature of Eternal Life: Three Options

In conclusion to our study of what transpires to the individual after life we will clarify what we believe Barth would advocate in this regard. This is a complicated issue, and it is especially complicated because Barth failed to complete the *Church Dogmatics*. Barth had indicated his intention to speak further in this whole regard under the topic of eschatology.[312] Specifically it was the second of the three circles Barth had intended for *Church Dogmatics Volume V: The Doctrine of Redemption* which never flowed from the pen of Barth. This particular circle was to have related the content of the promise and its future realization.[313] Notably Barth suggests that the promise will be realized in the future. For Barth it was impossible to conceive of God's plan and purpose going unfulfilled.[314] Barth indicates that as heirs man may expect eternal life in God's kingdom. We "advance towards a genuine, qualitatively and indeed infinitely better future."[315] Barth clearly affirms that something better is coming. The difficulty is to discern that future, to give it some shape. When we extrapolate from the existing volumes of the *Church Dogmatics* we find that there are at least three different interpretations for what Barth might advocate concerning the nature of eternal life and man's involvement in it. These we will describe in turn under the headings of Christian mortalism, eternalising *in* God, and eternalising *with* God.

First we note that one might conclude that Barth is a Christian mortalist, i.e. a Christian who believes that nothing of man, be it his soul or whatever, continues to exist after life. At death man as body of a soul and soul of a body dies and disintegrates while the spirit, the impersonal life force given by God to man, is withdrawn to God from Whom it derived. Man as such has no beyond; only God who is self-existent and self-generating has a beyond. For Barth the end of man parallels his beginning. In our estimation this parallel creates a serious difficulty for Barth. What is there for man before his birth? Barth argues

that before birth we are not nothing but rather non-being, and
it is the work of God in His Spirit which actualizes our being
and gives us life. But we are basically inconsequential before
birth. Therefore if we will be after life as we were before
life, we will again be inconsequential and insignificant. We
will be again non-being and non-existent. Thus the designation
of Barth as a Christian mortalist seems apropos. It is noteworthy that G. C. Berkouwer critiques Barth along the same line.
He recognizes that clear insights with regard to the solution
Barth would advocate for the ending time in relation to eternity
are not easily attained, but Berkouwer is disturbed that Barth
draws a parallel between birth and death, between "not-yet-being"
and "no-longer-being." Scripture Berkouwer writes denies this
parallel in favor of continuity, although an incorrect repre-
sentation of that continuity is rejected.[316] Though in previous
writings Barth had stressed both continuity and discontinuity,
the emphasis upon continuity is greatly diminished in the
Church Dogmatics. In any case Berkouwer rather indicates that
for Barth there is no real continuity into after-life, and our
reading of Barth as a Christian mortalist is thereby reinforced.

The second interpretation we can suggest for man in eternal
life is eternalising *in* God or *in* Christ. At the third return of
Christ God resurrects man in His memory and man is eternalised.
This way man is not destroyed. He is preserved. Everything will
be present to God exactly as it transpired during life. Everything being present to God in this manner might refer to something like a movie or a play being enacted in the same role as
always. In short this second interpretation need allow no
autonomy for man in eternity. He could be like an image on a
screen or an actor on stage for a repeat performance. Man and
all that has ever transpired would be present *to* God, but they
would be only *in* God.

The third optional interpretation of man's involvement in
eternal life is eternalising *with* God. In this understanding
everything would be present to God, and man would be accorded a
degree of autonomy. He would be an entity with whom God could
have fellowship after the manner in which man enjoys fellowship
with God during this life. He could be a creature for whom the
past, present, and future are simultaneous, i.e. he would dwell
in eternity. Concerning the constitution of man we must again
speculate, but since with the passing of the years Barth has
tended toward envisioning greater continuity between man in this
life and man in any after-life, we therefore suspect that there
would be the three spatial dimensions in eternity and that soul
would be related to these three dimensions. There is no certainty
of such, but life without space is unknown to man. Only God could
theoretically exist without the three dimensions of space, since
it was He who created them.

Notably the first option of Christian mortalism would be
inconsistent with apocatastasis since it would effectively render
it moot. The latter two interpretive options would be consistent
with apocatastasis, but eternalising in God would not entail the

sort of personal autonomy which has traditionally been associated
with apocatastasis. Eternalising in God, our second option,
would thus produce the same effective results as Christian
mortalism, our first option. Eternalising with God, the third
option, would also leave open the possibility that all things,
including animals and other three-dimensional aspects of creation,
could have autonomy.

It is also possible that the third option would become the
same as the second option *if* one takes with utmost seriousness
fellowship with the Father in solidarity with Christ. As Christians are taken up in solidarity with Christ they might lose
their personal autonomy. Hence the third option would become the
second option, but again this depends upon the degree of solidarity with Christ.

The third option, eternalising with God, deserves careful
consideration on several counts. First though Barth expressed
reticence about a hope after life, which can only be based in
God, at the same time he realized that he might be saying too
little with respect to the fulfillment of this hope.[317] Second
it seems that Barth was influenced by the portrayals of the
Christian hope which have appeared among certain conservative
Christians. Barth felt that these portrayals were extravagant,
saying too much with too little basis. Due to the manner in
which Barth expresses himself on this issue he has been criticized
and challenged for forming his statements in an antithetical
manner.[318] Barth may have overreacted to Jenseitschristentum
(otherworldly Christianity) and left himself with little or no
room for any form of afterlife. Third eternalising with God
would allow the greatest effect to be realized from the death of
Jesus, which rendered impotent the second death. Barth believes
that man was created for covenant relationship with God, that the
relationship between the Father and Son finds a parallel between
the Son and the creature.[319] This relationship would be voided
if man were not accorded autonomy after life. We also recall
that the death of Jesus enables covenant relationship with God
to be instituted after the fashion God intended it. Thus unless
man is granted the ability to act and respond when he is eternalised, death would for practical purposes destroy man and mean
that for all His labors and efforts God as Father, Son, and Holy
Spirit would have elected isolation, to be by Himself, in eternity.
That to us does not seem like a conclusion Barth would endorse
since it would signify that death as naturalized by Christ would
frustrate God's desire for covenant relationship *ad extra*, i.e.
outside Himself. Furthermore we note in the brief summary of the
proposed *Church Dogmatics* which Barth offerred at the conclusion
of *Volume I/2* that "we are inevitably summoned by God's command
not merely to live and bow before the Word, but, living and bow-
ing before His Word, to advance towards a genuine, qualitatively
and indeed infinitely better future."[320] Our first two options,
notably, would only with extreme difficulty be consistent with
"a genuine, qualitatively and indeed infinitely better future."
Thus if compelled to select from these three options we would opt
for the third, eternalising with God, though we recognize full

well that our conclusion is hypothetical since Barth could legitimately be understood to be moving toward either of the other two options.

However if we were to imagine that God in eternalising man grants to him the ability to choose and act autonomously, there yet accrues one particular difficulty--the possibility for sin must in some way be eliminated. Sin for autonomous man might remain a possibility, but it should be an impossible possibility. We would not wish to leave open the possibility that man might "fall" again. But combining such an impossible possibility with autonomy for eternalised man is beyond human experience and perhaps well beyond human comprehension. Furthermore as a corollary we note that for Barth our projection of eternalising with God might not represent a sufficiently gracefull conclusion. Autonomous man might be tempted to view himself as self-existent and therefore not in need of God, which of course would not be true. In short an inadequate emphasis upon the divine grace might lure man back into sin. Notably our third option would entail a radical transformation of man, but it certainly seems not beyond the limits of divine possibility to recreate man without sin and also without its possibility. However it should also be noted that limiting the possibility for sin shades us toward man as a puppet or actor, our second option of eternalising in God.

But as Barth would certainly say, only God can know what the nature of afterlife will be. And for his part Barth seemed content to await clarification by God.

CONCLUSION

No one can be certain to which of these positions Barth would have been more inclined or whether he would have preferred another. In contrast to our studies of the cause and significance of death and what transpires to the individual in death, our investigation of the nature of after-life remains ambivalent. The obvious reason for this is that Barth never completed his *Church Dogmatics*.

Interestingly people have speculated as to why Barth did not finish writing the *Church Dogmatics*. One reason offered for not finishing the work is simply that Barth could not. It is implied thereby that Barth realized the impossibility of bringing together the various ideas and conceptions which he had developed in the first four volumes in a fifth volume.[321] His doctrine of redemption might in short be termed irredeemable. Though such a conclusion seems unnecessarily derogatory and farfetched, there may yet be an element of truth in it. We noted in our presentation of the three options in the previous section that the implications of Barth's writings clearly direct us to disparate conclusions. George Schurr, writing on life after death in Barth, indicates that Barth had not yet

> provided the categories within which the identity of subjec-
> tive continuity beyond death could be affirmed, but he
> nevertheless insists on it, and with his present emphasis
> on durable eternity could allow for it. There is a dual
> reference, we *do* and *shall* live *with*, not simply in Christ.[322]

We take this comment very seriously for it confirms our conclusion
that, given the material Barth has provided, different conclusions
as to the nature of after-life are warranted. It further indicates that Barth would likely have moved toward our third option,
eternalising with God, the position we also feel Barth would most
likely advocate, though we are unable to advocate it forthrightly
for the reasons suggested above.

Barth has also suggested that there are not last things but
only the last One.[323] We also have noted in Barth's thought that
the future already exists and that men must step into that
future.[324] If the future already exists in Christ, then the
future can hold nothing new, and it can only be a repetition of
the past. In other words eschatology would become Christology,
and the fifth volume of the *Church Dogmatics* could only repeat
elements of the previous four, much like theology for the
Reformers flowed from the doctrine of the reconciliation in
Christ. This also illustrates what we noted above concerning
the organization of the *Church Dogmatics*. The Word of God is
the center of a circle on which appear the doctrines of God,
creation, reconciliation, and redemption. We must be cautious,
however, in expecting too little of a novel import in Barth's
Doctrine of Redemption. The integrated character of the *Church
Dogmatics* suggests that much of the proposed *Volume V* would
reiterate previous notions, but there is no reason to believe
that Barth would not have introduced something new as he studied
the Word of God via the doctrine of redemption.

Nevertheless it seems incredible that a man of Barth's
analytic and synthetic ability would have been unable to complete
his *Dogmatics*, especially in light of the manner in which Barth
had shown himself capable of innovative and creative thought in
the first four volumes of the *Church Dogmatics* as well as elsewhere. It seems a bit naive to assume that Barth would not have
been able to conclude successfully and coherently his *Doctrine
of Redemption*, and it also seems a bit bewildering that Barth
would have offered nothing new in such a volume.

There is still an additional reason why Barth may not have
completed the *Dogmatics*, one which has been suggested by one of
his students, I. John Hesselink. He suggests that with his
retirement from academic teaching Barth lacked the stimulus of
his students and classes to persist with the work. Hesselink
believes that Barth was much more dependent upon that stimulation
than many people realize.[325]

However ultimately it was the fact that, as Barth himself
realized, man lives within limits, and his *terminus ad quo*, his
own death, intervened before he had completed the task to which

he had set himself. His magnum opus, the *Church Dogmatics*, thus remains an *opus imperfectum*. Barth no doubt lamented this, but he also defended it:

> Others I have reminded of the unfinished nature of most of the mediaeval *Summae* as well as many cathedrals. To others again I have pointed out that Mozart's premature death interrupted work on the *Requiem* in the middle of the *Lacrimosa*. . . Finally, I have called the attention of others to the fact that not only in holy scripture, but also in *Church Dogmatics* II, 1, perfection is the epitome of the divine attributes, so that it is better not to seek or to imitate it in a human work.[326]

We, too, can only regret and lament that Barth in his four dimensions of space and time left an *opus imperfectum*. But we wish not to leave the *Church Dogmatics* on anything other than a positive note. The *Church Dogmatics*, even though they remain incomplete, mark Karl Barth as the foremost theologian of the twentieth century, and they provide an abundance of ideas and teachings for the Christian faith and faithful, as we trust that our study of just the one aspect of death and after-life in the *Church Dogmatics* has illustrated.

FOOTNOTES

[1]Eberhard Busch, *Karl Barth: His Life from Letters and Autobiographical Texts*, 2d ed., trans. John Bowden (London: SCM Press, Ltd., 1976), p. 486.

[2]Karl Barth, *Church Dogmatics I/2*, trans. G. T. Thomson and Harold Knight (Edinburgh: T. & T. Clark, 1956), p. 866.

[3]Ibid., p. 869.   [4]Ibid., p. 862.

[5]Ibid., pp. 862-866, 870.

[6]Ibid., p. 870.   [7]Ibid., p. 844.

[8]Ibid., p. 877.   [9]Ibid.

[10]Ibid.

[11]Karl Barth, *Church Dogmatics I/1*, trans. G. W. Bromiley (Edinburgh: T. & T. Clark, 1975), pp. 368-370.

[12]Barth, *Church Dogmatics I/2*, p. 878.

[13]Ibid., pp. 881-883.

[14]Karl Barth, *Church Dogmatics III/1*, trans. G. W. Bromiley and T. F. Torrance (Edinburgh: T. & T. Clark, 1958), p. 73.

[15]Ibid., p. 75.   [16]Ibid.

[17]Ibid., p. 76.   [18]Ibid.

[19]Ibid., p. 50.   [20]Ibid., p. 44.

[21]Ibid., p. 66.   [22]Ibid., p. 191.

[23]Ibid., p. 62.

[24]Karl Barth, *Church Dogmatics IV/1*, trans. G. W. Bromiley (Edinburgh: T. & T. Clark, 1956), p. 512.

[25]Karl Barth, *Christ and Adam: Man and Humanity in Romans 5*, trans. T. A. Smail (Edinburgh: Scottish Journal of Theology Occasional Papers No. 5, 1956), p. 6.

[26]Ibid., p. 15.   [27]Ibid., p. 18.

[28]Ibid., p. 43.

[29]Barth, *Church Dogmatics IV/1*, p. 508.

[30]Ibid., p. 509.

[31]Barth, *Church Dogmatics III/1*, pp. 81, 200.

[32]Karl Barth, *The Heidelberg Catechism for Today*, trans. Shirley C. Guthrie, Jr. (Richmond: John Knox Press, 1964), p. 76.

[33]Barth, *Church Dogmatics III/1*, p. 181.

[34]Karl Barth, *Church Dogmatics III/2*, trans. Harold Knight, G. W. Bromiley, J. K. S. Reid, and R. H. Fuller (Edinburgh: T. & T. Clark, 1960), p. 437.

[35]Barth, *Church Dogmatics III/1*, p. 203.

[36]Herbert Hartwell, *The Theology of Karl Barth: An Introduction* (Philadelphia: Westminster Press, 1964), pp. 123, 150.

[37]Barth, *Church Dogmatics III/2*, p. 437.

[38]Ibid., p. 438.   [39]Ibid., p. 469.

[40]Ibid., p. 448.   [41]Ibid., p. 459.

[42]Ibid., p. 461.   [43]Ibid.

[44]Ibid., pp. 477, 484.   [45]Ibid., p. 486.

[46]Ibid., p. 487.   [47]Ibid., p. 490.

[48]Ibid., p. 512.   [49]Ibid., p. 513.

[50]Ibid., p. 514.   [51]Ibid., p. 515.

[52]Ibid., p. 517.   [53]Ibid.

[54]Ibid., p. 518.   [55]Ibid., p. 519.

[56]Ibid.   [57]Ibid., pp. 519-520.

[58]Ibid., p. 521.   [59]Ibid.

[60]Ibid., p. 523.   [61]Ibid.

[62]Ibid., p. 527.   [63]Ibid.

[64]Ibid., p. 526.   [65]Ibid., p. 530.

[66]Ibid., p. 532.   [67]Ibid.

[68]Ibid., p. 534.   [69]Ibid., p. 535.

[70]Ibid., p. 537.   [71]Ibid., p. 538.

[72]Ibid., pp. 539-540.   [73]Ibid., p. 540.

[74]Ibid., p. 543.   [75]Ibid., p. 545.

[76]Ibid., p. 547.

[77]Ibid., p. 548.

[78]Ibid.

[79]Ibid., p. 555.

[80]Ibid.

[81]Ibid., p. 556.

[82]Ibid., p. 557.

[83]Ibid., p. 558.

[84]Ibid.

[85]Ibid., p. 559.

[86]Ibid., p. 561.

[87]Ibid., p. 562.

[88]Ibid., p. 565.

[89]Ibid.

[90]Ibid., p. 566.

[91]Ibid., p. 567.

[92]Ibid., p. 569.

[93]Ibid.

[94]Ibid., p. 573.

[95]Ibid.

[96]Ibid., p. 574.

[97]Ibid., p. 576.

[98]Ibid.

[99]Ibid., p. 578.

[100]Ibid.

[101]Ibid., p. 583.

[102]Ibid.

[103]Ibid., p. 584.

[104]Ibid., p. 586.

[105]Ibid., p. 587.

[106]Ibid., p. 589.

[107]Ibid., p. 590.

[108]Ibid., p. 589.

[109]Ibid.

[110]Ibid., p. 590.

[111]Ibid., p. 591.

[112]Ibid., pp. 591-593.

[113]Ibid., p. 589.

[114]Ibid., p. 595.

[115]Ibid., p. 596.

[116]Ibid., p. 597.

[117]Ibid.

[118]Ibid.

[119]Ibid., p. 598.

[120]Ibid., p. 600.

[121]Ibid., p. 602.

[122]Ibid., pp. 602-603.

[123]Ibid., p. 604.

[124]Ibid., p. 607.

[125]Ibid., p. 609.

[126]Ibid.

[127]Ibid., p. 610.

[128]Ibid., p. 614.

[129]Ibid., p. 621.

[130]Ibid., p. 611.

[131]Ibid., p. 628.

[132]Ibid., p. 629.   [133]Ibid., p. 631.

[134]Karl Barth, *Church Dogmatics III/3*, trans. G. W. Bromiley and R. J. Ehrlich (Edinburgh: T. & T. Clark, 1960), p. 85.

[135]Barth, *Church Dogmatics III/2*, p. 634.

[136]Ibid.   [137]Ibid., p. 635.

[138]Ibid., pp. 635-637.   [139]Ibid., p. 637.

[140]Ibid., pp. 638-639.   [141]Ibid., p. 640.

[142]Ibid., p. 326.   [143]Ibid., p. 327.

[144]Ibid., p. 328.   [145]Ibid., p. 332.

[146]Ibid., p. 338.   [147]Ibid.

[148]Ibid., p. 334.   [149]Ibid., p. 346.

[150]Ibid., p. 347.   [151]Ibid., p. 348.

[152]Ibid., p. 349.   [153]Ibid., p. 350.

[154]Ibid., p. 354.   [155]Ibid., p. 355.

[156]Ibid.   [157]Ibid.

[158]Ibid., pp. 354-355.   [359]Ibid., p. 356.

[160]Ibid., p. 357.   [161]Ibid., p. 363.

[162]Ibid.   [163]Ibid., p. 365.

[164]Ibid.   [165]Ibid., p. 359.

[166]Ibid.   [167]Ibid., p. 357.

[168]Ibid., p. 362.   [169]Ibid., p. 366.

[170]Ibid., p. 419.   [171]Ibid., p. 369.

[172]Ibid.   [173]Ibid., p. 370.

[174]Ibid.   [175]Ibid., p. 372.

[176]Ibid., p. 373.   [177]Ibid., p. 374.

[178]Ibid., p. 375.   [179]Ibid., pp. 376-377.

[180]Ibid., p. 378.   [181]Ibid., p. 377.

[182]Ibid., p. 378.   [183]Ibid.

[184]Ibid., p. 380.   [185]Ibid.

[186]Ibid., p. 382.   [187]Ibid., p. 381.

[188]Ibid., p. 384.   [189]Ibid., pp. 385-386.

[190]Ibid., p. 385.   [191]Ibid., p. 386.

[192]Ibid., p. 387.   [193]Ibid., p. 390.

[194]Ibid., p. 391.   [195]Ibid.

[196]Ibid.   [197]Ibid., p. 384.

[198]Ibid., p. 395.   [199]Ibid., p. 399.

[200]Ibid., p. 405.   [201]Ibid., p. 401.

[202]Ibid., p. 406.   [203]Ibid., p. 408.

[204]Ibid., p. 419.   [205]Ibid., p. 424.

[206]Ibid., p. 426.   [207]Ibid., p. 428.

[208]Ibid., p. 429.   [209]Ibid.

[210]Ibid., p. 432.   [211]Ibid., p. 433.

[212]Ibid.   [213]Ibid., p. 325.

[214]Ibid., p. 362.

[215]W. A. Whitehouse, *Creation, Science, and Theology: Essays in Response to Karl Barth*, ed. Ann Loades (Grand Rapids: William B. Eerdmans Publishing Co., 1981), p. 27.

[216]Barth, *Church Dogmatics III/2*, p. 362.

[217]Barth, *Heidelberg Catechism*, p. 88.

[218]Barth, *Church Dogmatics III/2*, p. 639.

[219]Ibid., p. 638.

[220]Barth, *Church Dogmatics III/3*, p. 86.

[221]Barth, *Church Dogmatics III/2*, p. 611.

[222]Ibid.   [223]Ibid., p. 632.

[224]Ibid., pp. 612-613.   [225]Ibid., p. 512.

[226]Ibid., p. 622.   [227]Ibid., p. 448.

[228]Ibid., p. 449.

[229] Barth, *Heidelberg Catechism*, p. 75.

[230] Karl Barth, *Dogmatics in Outline*, trans. G. T. Thomson (London: SCM Press Ltd., 1966), p. 123.

[231] Karl Barth, *Church Dogmatics IV/3, part 1*, trans. G. W. Bromiley (Edinburgh: T. & T. Clark, 1961), p. 291.

[232] Barth, *Church Dogmatics III/2*, p. 622.

[233] Barth, *Church Dogmatics IV/3, part 1*, p. 293.

[234] Ibid.

[235] Barth, *Dogmatics in Outline*, p. 134.

[236] Barth, *Church Dogmatics IV/3, part 1*, p. 294.

[237] Ibid.   [238] Ibid.

[239] Barth, *Dogmatics in Outline*, p. 155.

[240] Barth, *Church Dogmatics IV/3, part 1*, p. 294.

[241] Barth, *Church Dogmatics III/2*, p. 624.

[242] Karl Barth, *The Faith of the Church: A Commentary on the Apostle's Creed according to Calvin's Catechism*, ed. Jean-Louis Leuba, trans. Gabriel Vahanian (New York: Meridian Books, Inc., 1958), p. 162.

[243] Ibid., p. 166.   [244] Ibid.

[245] Ibid.   [246] Ibid.

[247] Ibid., p. 88.

[248] Barth, *Church Dogmatics III/2*, p. 624.

[249] Ibid.   [250] Ibid.

[251] Ibid.   [252] Ibid.

[253] Barth, *Heidelberg Catechism*, p. 88.

[254] Ibid., p. 89.

[255] Barth, *Church Dogmatics III/3*, p. 86.

[256] Ibid.   [257] Ibid., p. 89.

[258] Ibid.   [259] Ibid.

[260] Ibid., p. 90.

[261]Barth, *Church Dogmatics III/2*, p. 625.

[262]Barth, *Dogmatics in Outline*, p. 154.

[263]Hendrikus Berkhof, personal letter (Leiden, Netherlands: December 29, 1983).

[264]Barth, *Faith of the Church*, p. 166.

[265]Barth, *Dogmatics in Outline*, p. 135.

[266]Ibid., p. 153.

[267]Barth, *Church Dogmatics I/2*, p. 883.

[268]Barth, *Dogmatics in Outline*, p. 154.

[269]Ibid.

[270]Barth, *Church Dogmatics III/1*, p. 73.

[271]Ibid., p. 72.

[272]Karl Barth, *Church Dogmatics II/2*, trans. G. W. Bromiley et. al. (Edinburgh: T. & T. Clark, 1957), p. 346.

[273]Ibid.   [274]Ibid.

[275]Ibid.   [276]Ibid., p. 349.

[277]Ibid., p. 350.   [278]Ibid., pp. 421-422.

[279]Barth, *Church Dogmatics III/1*, p. 72.

[280]Barth, *Church Dogmatics II/2*, pp. 421-422.

[281]Ibid., p. 415.   [282]Ibid., p. 450.

[283]Barth, *Faith of the Church*, p. 173.

[284]Barth, *Church Dogmatics II/2*, p. 450.

[285]Ibid., p. 417.

[286]Barth, *Church Dogmatics IV/1*, p. 501.

[287]Ibid.

[288]Barth, *Church Dogmatics IV/3, part 1*, p. 464.

[289]Ibid.   [290]Ibid.

[291]Ibid., p. 465.   [292]Ibid., p. 477.

[293]Ibid.

[294] Karl Barth, *The Humanity of God*, trans. John Newton Thomas and Thomas Wieser (Atlanta: John Knox Press, 1960), pp. 61-62.

[295] Ibid.

[296] Barth, *Dogmatics in Outline*, p. 136.

[297] Barth, *Church Dogmatics IV/3, part 1*, pp. 477-478.

[298] Barth, *Church Dogmatics III/2*, pp. 602-603.

[299] Barth, *Church Dogmatics IV/3, part 1*, p. 473.

[300] Jürgen Fangmeier and Heinrich Stoevesandt, eds., *Karl Barth Letters 1961-1968*, trans. Geoffrey W. Bromiley (Grand Rapids: William B. Eerdmans Publishing Co., 1981), p. 8.

[301] John Hick, *Death and Eternal Life* (London: William Collines Sons & Co. Ltd., 1976), pp. 260-261.

[302] G. C. Berkouwer, *The Triumph of Grace in the Theology of Karl Barth*, trans. Harry R. Boer (Grand Rapids: William B. Eerdmans Publishing Co., 1956), p. 116.

[303] Ibid., pp. 116-117. [304] Ibid., p. 279.

[305] Donald G. Bloesch, *Jesus Is Victor! Karl Barth's Doctrine of Salvation* (Nashville: Abingdon Press, 1976), p. 138.

[306] Ibid., p. 10. [307] Ibid., p. 63.

[308] Joseph D. Bettis, "Is Karl Barth a Universalist?" *Scottish Journal of Theology* 20 (1967):426.

[309] Ibid., p. 427. [310] Ibid., p. 428.

[311] I. John Hesselink, Jr., personal letter (Holland, Michigan: August 6, 1979).

[312] Barth, *Church Dogmatics IV/3, part 1*, p. 293.

[313] Barth, *Church Dogmatics I/2*, p. 883.

[314] Barth, *Church Dogmatics III/1*, p. 72.

[315] Barth, *Church Dogmatics I/2*, p. 883.

[316] Berkouwer, *Triumph of Grace*, p. 338.

[317] Barth, *Church Dogmatics III/2*, pp. 612-613.

[318] Berkhof letter (December 29, 1983).

[319] Barth, *Church Dogmatics III/1*, p. 50.

[320]Barth, *Church Dogmatics I/2*, p. 883.

[321]I. John Hesselink letter (August 6, 1979). The same point is made in T. H. L. Parker, *Karl Barth* (Grand Rapids: William B. Eerdmans Publishing Co., 1970), p. 124.

[322]George M. Schurr, "Brunner and Barth on Life After Death," *Journal of Religious Thought* 24, no. 2 (1967-1968): 107-108.

[323]Barth, *Church Dogmatics III/2*, p. 490.

[324]Ibid., p. 547.

[325]I. John Hesselink letter (August 6, 1979).

[326]Busch, *Barth*, pp. 486-487.

ADDENDUM: THE CREDO AS INTERLUDE OR OVERTURE

Now that our study of the *Church Dogmatics* is complete we
are able to reflect momentarily upon whether the *Credo* is more
like an interlude or an overture.

The rationale for terming the *Credo* an interlude, and a
surprising one at that, should be apparent from our now
completed presentation from the *Church Dogmatics*. Barth has
argued strongly against death's being interpreted as separation
of body and soul in the *Dogmatics* as well as *Romans* and *Resurrection of the Dead*. The *Credo* contrasts with this, and we
have amply noted this, most especially by raising the question
whether this represents "a surprising interlude."

Yet overall the *Credo* appears much more like an overture
for the *Church Dogmatics*. The themes introduced there appear
in the *Church Dogmatics* in more developed form. The following
examples should illustrate.

First time and eternity are distinguished in *Credo*, though
Barth also notes a degree of continuity between the two. The
theoretical basis for this is spelled out in the *Church Dogmatics*. Time with its sequence of past, present, and future
is clarified as regards eternity, the mode of God, in which
past, present, and future are simultaneous. Time and eternity
differ, but they are also similar and related. In the *Credo*
Barth states that the life we now have will not be annihilated
in eternity, nor will we be absorbed into God and disappear.
We will have our own life with God.[1] Barth elaborates further
upon these ideas in the *Church Dogmatics*, especially under the
notion of "eternalising." And notably when we came to our
"three options" we tended toward the third interpretation,
eternalising with God. This inclination is reinforced by the
comments of Barth in *Credo*.

A second way in which the *Credo* may be understood as an
overture to the *Church Dogmatics* relates to the return of
Christ. In the *Credo* Barth refers to the second coming of
Christ in the traditional sense of the restoration and final
revelation of Jesus Christ as he was during the forty days
after Easter.[2] In the *Church Dogmatics* Barth talks of the
three-fold return of Christ. There is an obvious difference
on this point between the *Credo* and the *Church Dogmatics*. But
it may tend to reinforce the idea that the *Credo* may be understood as an overture. In this case the *Dogmatics* fills out a
theme insufficiently developed in the *Credo*.

With any analogy there are likely to be inadequacies, and
that is to be expected here as well. Yet we proffer the analogy
of the *Credo* serving like an overture to the *Church Dogmatics*
because it provides an instrument for interpreting both the
similarities and differences between the two works.

FOOTNOTES

[1]Karl Barth, *Credo*, trans. Robert McAfee Brown (New York: Charles Scribner's Sons, 1962), p. 170.

[2]Ibid., p. 121.

CHAPTER III

DEATH AND AFTER-LIFE IN THE THEOLOGY OF JOHN HICK

Introduction

One of the most significant monographs of recent years to treat the subject of death and after-life is the book *Death and Eternal Life* by John Hick. In this work Hick attempts something rare, at least in terms of the history of Christianity--a global theology of death. However novel in might be in terms of the history of Christianity, the global theology which Hick presents in *Death and Eternal Life* represents the product of a goal which Hick had established for himself several years earlier with the publication of his *Philosophy of Religion*. In the final chapter of this work Hick states his belief that

> the great religions are all, at their experiential roots, in contact with the same ultimate divine reality, but that their differing experiences of that reality, interacting over the centuries with the differing thought forms of differing cultures, have led to increasing differentiation and contrasting elaboration.[1]

It is clear that according to Hick the differences which are manifest between the great religions are apparent and consequential, not essential. Notably as well Hick understands religion as a matter of experience, experience of phenomena which are basically the same. It is the theologies or interpretations of these experiences as formulated by men which distinguish one religion from another. It was, however, at the time of the publication of *Philosophy of Religion* beyond the scope of the work to effect a reconstruction of Christian and other religious doctrines.[2] *Death and Eternal Life* is the fulfillment of the task which Hick had set himself in his *Philosophy of Religion*, though it is limited in scope to the subject of death and after-life.

We must also understand the method which Hick uses because it in turn affects the way we will present the writings of Hick on this subject. In the second edition of his book *Faith and Knowledge* Hick notes favorably that F. H. Bradley had once spoken of metaphysics as the finding of bad reasons for what we

believe upon instinct,[3] the suggestion being that our intuition
and instincts inform us better concerning metaphysical truths
than does reason and/or logic. Cardinal Newman and his work
Essay in Aid of a Grammar of Assent, which was first published
in 1870, accordingly become the focus of a chapter entitled
"Faith and the Illative Sense." Newman believed that human
convictions, especially in a matter of religion, do not result
primarily from theoretical procedures of logic.[4] Rather Hick
notes with Newman

> that the reasoning by which we arrive at many, perhaps
> most, of the certainties by which we live, does not consist
> in acquiring "clear and distinct ideas" and perfectly cogent
> claims of reasoning, but rather in appreciating the drift of
> a miscellaneous mass of evidence. . . Our capacity to see a
> large field of evidence as a whole and to divine its signif-
> icance is what Newman calls the illative sense.[5]

Hick is well aware that truth is generally viewed as being
propositional. Propositions are the basis of knowledge; they
compel assent.[6] Hick contends that faith when it is used as
fides rather than *fiducia*, which Hick prefers to translate as
trust, has generally been viewed propositionally. The illative
sense is a special sort of inference and/or inductive reasoning.
By means of the illative sense men may come to the truth, which,
though it is arrived at by a very different means, is no less
certain than if it had been accomplished deductively or propositionally. Hick contends that theology has made a fundamental
error in viewing religious truth propositionally. He believes
that certain religious truths may lend themselves to verification in the manner of other propositions, but "we *know* a great
many things which we are not able to prove, and that the religious person's knowledge of God falls within this category."[7]
This should not be misconstrued, however, to suggest that Hick
is in total agreement with Newman. In order to attain a
"global impression" or interpretation, Newman and his commenta-
tors have applied the illative sense to a logically homogeneous
range of data.[8] Theistic interpretation as Hick views it
demands much more complex data, and *Death and Eternal Life*
will illustrate this.

The Format

Our study of the three foci regarding death and eternal
life will differ in format in this chapter from our previous
studies of the works of Barth in which we tended to focus
directly upon the three foci. Hick's method, as we have
already noted, emcompasses a most broad scope of data. Upon
the basis of the wide range of data which he adduces, Hick
draws his conclusions. In our discussion we will follow the
format of Hick as presented in *Death and Eternal Life*, and we
will amplify and clarify with reference to other works by Hick.
We will indeed be confronted with a wealth of material, certainly some of which is not ordinarily subject matter to a
theological discussion, and we will then present the conclusions

as Hick senses and presents them. We will in conclusion then briefly focus upon our three foci and the responses which Hick offers. But as is the case with Barth, postponed until our fourth chapter will be most of the critical comments which we will wish to make regarding death and after-life in Hick.

The Two Goals

In the preface to *Death and Eternal Life* Hick lays out two basic and complementary goals for the work. The first is an apologetic task. Along with the religions of the world Hick believes that "this life is part of a much larger existence which transcends our life-span as animal organisms."[9] What is rather distinctive in Hick's approach is the belief not only that this belief is true but that "it is not ruled out by any established scientific findings or by any agreed philosophical arguments."[10] Hick argues that belief in life after death does not contradict and is not contradicted by the investigations of nontheological realms. Hick further contends that any religious understanding of human existence "positively requires some kind of immortality belief and would be radically incoherent without it."[11] This belief is common to all religious traditions. Hick is obviously working in an apologetic vein; he defends the belief in afterlife.

The second goal of *Death and Eternal Life* is the creation of a global theology of death. In order to effect such a global theology of death Hick distinguishes two aspects of a religion. The first of these aspects is the central affirmations concerning the nature of reality, including human destiny, which are ultimately true or false, and the second is the mythical expressions which have developed alongside the central affirmations. These latter cannot properly be termed true or false any more than civilizations, which are comprehensive forms of human life, can be evaluated as true or false. Hick noteworthily writes:

> It is because affirmations about the nature of reality are true or false or, more probably, partly true and partly false, that the theologies of the different religions can be compared with one another, that agreements and disagreements can be registered, and that the possibility of syntheses and even of a comprehensive global theology cannot be excluded in advance.[12]*

According to Hick the practice of religion invariably involves culturally-bound myths and practices. He therefore clarifies that he is not attempting a global religion, which would require a unified, global consciousness, but a global theology. He

---

*In a footnote to this quotation Hick remarks: "It will be evident that I am here, and throughout this book, using 'theology' in a deliberately wide sense to include the study of systems of religious thought (such as Buddhism) which recognize no *theos*."

desires to compare the various affirmations of theology to
ascertain whether or not there is agreement amongst them concerning their central affirmations. Such an enterprise Hick
does not believe may be excluded without investigation.

As applied specifically to the area of death and after-life
this approach requires that one consider the teachings of all
the main religious traditions and philosophies as well as the
sciences, particularly that of parapsychology.[13] Nothing which
might be pertinent to this discussion should be eliminated a
priori. The range of Hick's investigation is consequently very
broad. Furthermore Hick warns against adoption of a "ptolemaic"
view, which Hick describes in the following manner: "By a 'ptolemaic' standpoint I mean the conviction that one's own religion
is at the centre of the religious universe and provides a touch-
stone for the truth of all other faith worlds."[14] Hick acknowledges that this is inevitable and that he undertakes this
study from a Christian standpoint, but he rather believes that
it is best to view the various religions as "different responses
to variously overlapping aspects of the same Ultimate Reality."[15]
The book *Death and Eternal Life* is Hick's attempt to demonstrate
the viability and validity of this approach in regard to death
and after-life.

What Is Man?

After outlining his method Hick undertakes an anthropological study of man. Usually man is understood as being
composed of physical and non-physical parts or realms. The
physical part is apparent, but the non-physical has been given
several names, e.g. mind, soul, self, I, person, spirit, ego,
consciousness, psyche, subconscious, uncouscious, id, superego,
mentality, transcendental unity of apperception, etc. in the West
and *jiva* and *atman* in the East. The non-physical refers to the
thinking, feeling, willing, and remembering consciousness,
though Hick extends its use to include unconscious mental
activity which is directly able to influence consciousness.[16]
Hick also observes that man is a composite of his genetic code
and environment. In fact these two ingredients influence one
to such an extent that there appears no room left for character
traits independent of these two factors. "At the same time,
so long as we assume the reality of human freedom it must be
impossible decisively to rule out such a conception."[15] Thus
it is becoming increasingly difficult to postulate a human
soul in addition to heredity and environment, much less a soul
divinely created and infused. Accordingly Hick proposes that
'soul' be understood as a valuational term for self.

'Soul', then, is the valuing name for the self. The
self has been gradually formed by the interaction of a
partly random selection of genetic information with a
particular historical environment; and in the course of
this interaction an element of individual freedom, or
creativity is exercised.[18]

Soul exists only potentially in the fetus and newborn, and it
refers to the moral and spiritual personality that a child
becomes in time. Noteworthily this conception of soul places
its emphasis upon the potentiality of man, shifting the emphasis
from the origin of man to his ends.[19]

Hick also points out that there need be no contradictions
between the origin of man as portrayed by modern science and
the teaching of Christianity. Modern science teaches that
"life on this planet began with natural chemical reactions
occurring under the influence of radiations falling upon the
earth's surface."[20] Hick then notes apologetically that
Christianity teaches that man was created from the dust of the
earth, but it does not offer details as to the manner of this
genesis.[21]

Though Hick is primarily concerned with the end or goal of
man, in his book *Evil and the God of Love* Hick elaborates further
upon the origin of man, especially as it pertains to the relation
between the teachings of science and Christianity. Here he
notes:

> For the past century evidence has been available concerning
> the earlier stages of mankind, before the brief span of
> recorded history, and none of this evidence lends any sup-
> port to the theory that the human race is descended from a
> single original pair, or that mortality and liability to
> disease and disaster are other than natural to the human
> animal in his place within the larger system of nature.[22]

Hick notes that there is a marked contrast between the discoveries of science and the teachings of Christianity. Hick contends,
nonetheless, that there never has been an era without sin in
which a single couple lived in paradisal bliss along with the
other animals. Death has always characterized life on this
planet as have other evils such as earthquakes, storms, floods,
droughts, and pests. Consonant with his belief that the
potential of man ought to be the prime concern, Hick does not
believe that the emphasis of man should be placed upon a non-
existent better state that *was* but upon a radically better
that *will be*.[23]

Hick is well aware that such thoughts place him outside
the mainstream of the Christian tradition, but he would insist
that his views are not foreign to the Christian tradition. In
some of the Hellenistic fathers of the second century and
especially Irenaeus he notes greater emphasis being placed upon
developmental process with regard to man. Though he characterizes the Irenaean distinction between the *image* and *likeness* of
God as "exegetically dubious,"[24] Hick nevertheless makes fre-
quent reference to this thought pattern to justify his own
approach. Briefly stated by Hick:

> Irenaeus distinguishes between the image (εἰκών) of God and
> the likeness (ὁμοίωσισ) of God in man. The 'imago', which

resides in man's bodily form, apparently represents his
nature as an intelligent creature capable of fellowship
with his Maker, whilst the 'likeness' represents man's
final perfecting by the Holy Spirit.[25]

The reason for Hick's reference to Irenaeus is the two-stage
conception involved in the creation of man. Indeed Hick believes
that such a two-staged notion has become almost inevitable to
Christianity.[26] Thus man as he has been created by God is a
personal being in the image of God with the possibility for
cognitive freedom with regard to God. He possesses an innate
tendency to give his experience a religious interpretation,
though he is not compelled to do so. His existence is teleo-
logically and eschatologically oriented. Man is moving toward
a future which it is Hick's goal to clarify in his monograph
describing death and eternal life.

Origins of Beliefs in After-Life and Immortality

In his investigation of the origins for belief in after-
life and immortality Hick comes to conclusions substantially
at variance with the theories of major, contemporary schools of
psychology and philosophy. Study of prehistoric man as well as
studies of surviving primitive peoples in Austrailia, Polynesia,
Africa, and South America shows that there has universally been
belief in continued existence beyond death.[27] Nonetheless the
survival envisioned by these primitive peoples generally was
conceived as being ghostly. There was seldom a conception of
positive immortality. Death was envisioned as resulting from
particular and contingent causes. As Hick expresses it, "people
did not just die but were killed."[28] It was commonly accepted
among primitive man that existence continued beyond death, and
Hick reckons both a positive and a negative source for this
belief. On the positive side it was recognized that persons
who had already died continued to exist in dreams. Though one
would now classify such an existence to an "inner" realm of man,
primitive man believed that dreams represented an objective
reality. On the negative side, it was probably inconceivable
for primitive man to imagine himself as non-existent.[29] Thus
the primitive belief did not arise out of the wish for survival
or a better, improved existence, as many contemporary schools
of thought imagine.[30] In fact after-life was only a partial or
half existence. The early Greeks, whom Hick believes demonstrate
little if any development upon the Stone Age, believed that the
soul, which they described as "the body's shadow-image" or a
"feebler double of a man," descended at death "into erebus or
hades where, whilst still recognizable and still hearing its
earthly name, it persists as a depleted, joyless entity, a mere
bloodless shadow of its former embodied self."[31] The ancient
Hebrew understanding of sheol is similar.

Sheol was thought of as a vast underground cavern or pit--
probably the tribal burial place magnified into a dark sub-
terranean world--where the dead exist or persist. The
prospect was wholly uninviting.[32]

The descent into sheol was irreversible; continuation of intercourse with the living and even with God was severed. Death
for primitive man was undesirable, a thing to be shunned. Hick
also notes that death was not portrayed as the great equalizer,
i.e. the entity which would put an end to the privileges enjoyed
by the few in this life. Rather the inequalities of this life
were transferred to the following life.

With time the descriptions of after-life improved, and
after-life took on positive aspects. Notably this development
coincided with the emergence of individual self-consciousness
and faith in a higher reality as source of value, these latter
two in turn conditioning each other. Gradually the idea of a
reality superior to death developed. This reality, which is
referred to as God or the gods or the eternal Good, naturally
gave rise to questions of value in the universe. And this in
turn occasioned questioning the purely natural assumptions
about death. Notions of judgment and heaven and hell arose.
But this development may not be separated from an increasing
value being placed upon the individual. Originally the notion
of soul was corporate; it referred rather vaguely to the larger
life of a society in which an individual was a member. The
soul of the individual was that of the group, and it lived on
beyond the death of individual units. Among the Hebrews this
mentality was challenged by the prophets and shattered by the
exile. Among the Greeks the mystery cults stressed the enlightenment of the individual. Hick cites examples from other
religions traditions as well. Still the important point is
that there simultaneously developed a belief in the value of
the individual and a positive conception of after-life.[33]

The Contribution of Sociology and Philosophy

Hick surveys as well the fields of sociology and contemporary philosophy and outlines the primary conclusions within
these fields of study. He notes that whereas sex was the taboo
subject of the Victorian era, death has now assumed this
dubious distinction, though there are indications that the
taboo of discussing death is being lifted. However, as the
subjects of discussion in this section of *Death and Eternal Life*
do not impinge upon the theological significance of death and
after-life as developed by Hick but merely highlight its growing
discussion, they will not be presented here.

One observation of Hick does merit attention at this point,
however.

This considerable decline within society as a whole, accompanied by a lesser decline within the churches, of the
belief in personal immortality clearly reflects the assumption within our culture that we should only believe in what
we experience, plus what the accredited sciences certify to
us.[34]

This comment is noteworthy since it reflects the position which

Hick himself adopts with regard to death and after-life. He believes that this challenge can be met. He contends that on the basis of contemporary research within the pertinent areas of investigation one cannot preclude some aspect of man continuing to exist beyond death.

The Contribution of Psychology

Hick focuses his investigation of this field upon the relation of the concepts of mind and brain. There are various ways in which these two are seen to be related. Some suggest that the two are identical, i.e. the monistic option; others suggest that the mind is unilaterally dependent upon the body and is never independent of it, i.e. the epiphenomenalist thesis; still others believe the mind and body to be interrelated influences upon each other which both terminate at death; and finally some believe that at least a certain capacity of the mind exists beyond physical death. Of these Hick believes the monistic option to have the least initial plausibility. To identify thoughts with electrochemical activites in the physical brain is unlikely. The two may be correlated with one another, but this does not constitute proof that the two are in fact one and the same. Hick even suggests that it is inconceivable as to what might constitute such evidence for identity. To counter the epiphenomenalist thesis Hick focuses upon the deterministic scheme which it presupposes. Such a deterministic scheme is self-refuting.

> The only sort of belief in total determinism that can exist (if total determinism is in fact true) is a programmed belief which does not arise from reasoning and judgement but from physicl causes which go back in an unbroken chain coterminous with the history of the physical universe.[35]

But to hold such a belief Hick argues would mean that there is no intellectual freedom, and no one could be said to believe anything rationally since belief derives from the deterministic scheme.[36] Hick finds this conclusion absurd and therefore turns to the belief that mind and body interrelatedly influence one another.

The Contribution of Parapsychology

In order to substantiate this belief in interrelatedness Hick proffers the results of various experiments in the realm of parapsychology. The first of these is the quantitative, experimental work with Zener cards. One would expect 20% of the responses to be correct if only chance were involved with "guessing" which of the five symbols appears on the card. "But very good ESP subjects have exceeded chance expectation in their scores by margins which give 'odds against chance' of millions or even billions to one."[37] Hick also cites crisis apparitions. These refer to cases in which persons A and B, who are usually relatives or close friends, are at a distance when A undergoes some crisis, often a fatal accident, and B, who had no reason to expect this, has within the next twelve hours or so a vivid hallucination of A, sometimes in a form which indicates the nature of the crisis. Telepathic communication is also investigated. Of particular interest to Hick are the Russian experiments in telepathy conducted by L. L. Vasiliev which point strongly against an electromagnetic explanation of telepathy. Hick concludes that the phenomena related to Zener card experimentation, crisis apparitions, and telepathic communication disprove any theory of the relation between the mind and body which would preclude the mind or some aspect thereof surviving bodily death.[38]

Hick also devotes time to the investigation of trance mediumship and its significance for death and after-life. If it is indeed possible that an individual, generally referred to as a medium, can become the spokesperson of a deceased person(s) to the living, then this certainly would have profound significance for this study. Hick, however, tends to categorize most instances of genuine, honest mediumship as cases of "unconscious fraud," which can be manifest in two ways. First the medium may manifest some kind of fragment or secondary personality of the medium; the medium may induce a type of "hypnosis" in which he describes a world which he imagines to exist beyond death, i.e. after-life. Or second the medium may unconsciously acquire and communicate information about the deceased via telepathy. "Reading" the thoughts of relatives and friends of the deceased who have assembled to communicate with the deceased, the medium unknowingly portrays himself as being the spokesperson of the deceased when in reality he is the reflection of the thoughts, including even unconscious thoughts, of the living. The two instances of fraud may also be combined. But in either case the medium is inadvertently deceptive or unconsciously fraudulent. Hick finds evidence of unconscious fraud in the fact that the "deceased" does not appear to exist on his own between seances. Nor is much communicated concerning the nature of after-life, and that which is communicated appears culturally bound.[39] Furthermore Hick gives two examples of unconscious fraud. In the first example two women developed in their minds over a period of weeks the personality and atmosphere of an entirely imaginary character. A medium then proceded to describe accurately this imaginary figure, but as one from beyond the grave. In a second example the voice of one Gordon Davis was produced, but later it was discovered that Gordon Davis was yet alive.[40] Though these latter two examples would seem to dispel belief in trance mediumship, they nevertheless give evidence for telepathic communication.

Despite these latter two examples Hick will not eliminate the possibility of trance mediumship.

What it indicates is that if there is such communication it must be a matter of spirits somehow using the machinery of dramatic personation in which, together with ESP sensitivity and a capacity for self-hypnosis, mediumship apparently consists.[41]

Thus Hick posits the continuing existence of an individual as a "persisting consciousness and will."[42] The dead have a life of their own; they continue to develop as persons. And in the course of their existence the dead will occasionally indulge in a process of mediumistic communication. Yet the spirits of the dead do not bespeak another environment. Rather they seem to remain related to this world, though they do not appear to be living a "full existence" in comparison to earthly life. The dead are characterized as a psychic factor, which Hick suggests consists of "mental and emotional formations, including memories and dispositional traits, which persist as a system for a longer or shorter time after death and with a greater or less degree of coherence."[43] Hick compares this body to the *linga sharira* or "subtle body" of vedantic theory and the Mesopotamian *kur-nu-gi-a*, the Hebrew sheol, and the Greek hades. This leads Hick to make the following noteworthy observation:

> If such a shade, or psychic factor, is all that persists of the empirical self, then any true immortality must presuppose a more complex view of human nature, such as is explored in some strands both of eastern and of western thought, in which the 'true' self is other than the present conscious ego.[44]

Because of the several conclusions which might be drawn regarding trance mediumship Hick does not offer a final conclusion, but rather he leaves open various possibilities.

Humanism and Death

The place and significance of death within the humanist tradition are also investigated. Generally death is interpreted here as being a necessary part of the evolutionary process. For the continuance of life individuals must die.[45] Thus the individual in his death contributes to the advancement and perfection of humanity. Beyond its significance in contributing to the welfare of humanity, the individual in his death as well as in his life has little meaning. Hick points up several questionable aspects of the humanist hypothesis, however. First he notes the curious fact that humanist writers strongly tend to belong to "the small educated and affluent minority of mankind."[46] For such persons as well as for many enjoying the affluence and wealth of modern western society it is undoubtedly true that life is good even without any reference to after-life. But of most of the world population this could not be said. They live and die without proper nutrition and without an education. They die unable to make an appreciable contribution to the welfare of humankind. Their lives remain unfulfilled, and only some type of continuing, personal existence after life could justify their existence. Accordingly Christianity has posited three solutions to the problem of the existence of evil. The first which Hick lists is that it corresponds to the will of God, and "his omnipotent wish might be said to be

its own justification."[47] This type of despotic arbitrariness
is not very appealing humanistically, though, so Hick proceeds
to a second suggestion, this being the normal humanist response
that evil may be compensated by examining the ultimate future
destiny of humankind. In light of the end, the means appear
less foreboding and reprehensible. Hick notes that both of
these responses belittle the significance of the individual.
As long as the significance of the individual is not great,
either of these responses is acceptable.

When the significance of the individual is elevated, then
the third response to the problem of evil, which Hick personally
advocates, becomes desirable and plausible. This response is
furthermore "the only morally acceptable justification of the
agonies and heartaches of human life. . ."[48] According to this
third response "the individuals who have suffered *themselves*
participate in the justifying good and are themselves able to
see their own past sufferings as having been worthwhile."[49]
Hick carefully distinguishes the idea that this future represents a compensation for past evils endured from the idea that
the future represents the "eventual all-justifying fulfilment
of the human potential in a perfected life."[50] In such a scheme
the individual represents an end in himself, though it is still
possible that the individual will share in the fulfillment of
others. It also leaves open the possibility of human freedom,
which Hick believes is necessary to the life of man.[51] It is
also apparent that the individual continues to exist after life
and that there ensues a growth or development toward perfection.
Thus Hick has employed the teaching of humanism regarding death
to demonstrate the alternative of a humanism in which evil
remains unjustified in contrast to the teaching of the religions
of the world in which evil becomes justified in terms of the
progress and ultimate destiny of man.

New Testament Views of After-Life

In his attempt to establish a global eschatology Hick then
moves on to a consideration of New Testament views of after-life.
Hick notes first that the resurrection of Jesus was a real occur-
rence, though he doubts that dogmatic certainty regarding the
precise nature of the resurrection is attainable. The idea of
physical resurrection was prevalent throughout the New Testament
era, though not with the Sadducees. Hence in whatever form
Jesus may have manifested himself to the disciples at Easter,
it was inevitable that it would have been described as resurrection. It is thus impossible to ascertain what transpired in the
resurrection via study of the idea of resurrection. A number of
possible understandings suggest themselves, two of which are
considered most probably today. The first is the idea that
Jesus' mysteriously transformed body rose from the tomb, and
the second that some of his disciples saw a vision(s) of their
exalted Lord. Hick, however, feels that the debate as to which
of these alternatives is correct avoids the essential features
of the resurrection gospel. These Hick lists as

that God raised up Jesus, giving him power and authority
('exalted at the right hand of God'), and that Jesus was
alive ('having loosed the pangs of death, because it was
not possible for him to be held by it').[52]

Hick thus concludes that whether or not the disciples encountered a physical, resurrected body is unimportant. Furthermore
Hick adds that with this understanding even Christians are
enabled to investigate the resurrection without prejudice.

Hick does take note that the basis for arguing bodily
resurrection is the gospel accounts. Jesus appears with the
marks of crucifixion, invites Thomas to touch him, and eats.
Nevertheless the resurrected body of Christ has passed through
a profound transformation. He was able to appear and disappear
behind closed doors at will. It is also noteworthy that according to this tradition the tomb which had contained the body of
Jesus was found empty.

But in contrast to the physical nature of the resurrection,
the earliest New Testament sources for the resurrection, i.e.
the Pauline epistles, consist in waking visions of the living
Lord. Paul lists a number of resurrection appearances, but
notably he nowhere writes of an empty tomb. This is particularly
significant because, had such a tradition been known to Paul as
he wrote some of his correspondence, it is difficult to understand why Paul did not avail himself of it--unless of course it
did not exist. This in fact is precisely what some contend.
Because they view the appearance tradition as being more original and thus more authentic, the tradition emphasizing the
physical aspects of the resurrection is classified as legendary.
This tradition has even asserted that

Jesus' body was probably placed in a common grave for
executed criminals, and short of an elaborate exhumation
it would seven weeks later, at Pentecost, have been impossible to establish anything corresponding to the empty tomb
of the developed tradition.[53]

Hick himself believes that the basis of the conviction that
Jesus is the exalted Lord and that one can obtain salvation
through him most likely derives from a vision(s), perhaps only
momentary, of Jesus as a majestic figure resplendent in light.
According to Hick less than this could hardly account for the
surprising and vigorous genesis of the early Christian community
after the crucifixion of Jesus while more than this is likely
not required.[54]

The teaching of Jesus himself lends additional credence
to this position. Though his comments regarding death and
after-life come in the context of statements involving issues
about which he has something more emphatic and significant to
say and thus do not allow for constructing systematic images
of the future, Jesus did believe in a future resurrection and
judgment of the dead. Since it was the prevalent conception

of resurrection at the time, it appears likely that the resurrection would involve the bringing forth of the revivified dead
from their graves. Nonetheless it is clear that there were
more sophisticated views of resurrection circulating at the
time, especially among the Pharisees.[55] In fact Jesus' response
to the Sadducees as well as Paul's description point in this
direction. Paul describes the nature of the resurrection as a
spiritual body as opposed to a natural or animal body. This has
not solved the problem yet, however. Does the resurrected,
spiritual body represent a transformed earthly body or a new
heavenly body? Opinion varies, though Hick tends to prefer the
latter, believing that the heavenly body will be a re-embodying
of the personality.[56] This as we will note subsequently corresponds with the 'replica' theory which Hick has developed.

Hick also notes that an increasing propensity appears
among the New Testament writers to view the end state not as
"a heaven on earth but a new 'earth' in heaven."[57] The earliest
apocalyptic expectations tied the future to this world, but a
couple centuries later in the time of Christ this conception
had changed. In fact the Revelation of John is a clear example
of a two-stage universe with a new heaven and earth replacing
the old.[58] We will note later that this view is similar to
that of Hick himself though Hick prefers recreation in a new
world as opposed to a recreation and transformation in this
world.

After-Life in Christian Thought

In this section Hick focuses upon the contrast in resurrection and immortality, several key elements with regard to
death and after-life, and then the responses of several contemporary theologians.

First despite the fact that the resurrection of Jesus has
been used as a basis for life after death, Hick notes that
within the Christian tradition since the end of the second
century it has been much more the notion of the immortality
of the soul rather than the resurrection of the dead that has
provided this basis. Recent debate, especially among Protestant
theologians, has attempted to draw a sharp distinction between
these two concepts. Hick believes this contrast to be somewhat
misleading, for resurrection also entails the idea of immortality
as unending existence. The real contrast is between those who
believe that man possesses a natural, innate immortality and
those who believe that immortality will be bestowed upon man
at the future resurrection. Hick eliminates this problem with
the suggestion that whether God bestows immortality as a
natural trait or reserves it for the future is of secondary
importance since in either event God grants to man immortality.[59]
Existence is of God, both here and after-life.

The key elements with regard to death and after-life in
later Christian thought which draw the attention of Hick are the
shift in eschatological expectation, the resurrection of the

body or flesh, the concept of hell, the concept of purgatory, and the concept of heaven.

The shift in eschatological expectation is the first key element. During the New Testament era Christ was expected to return soon, almost "any day now." As time passed and Christ did not reappear, those who had already died were viewed increasingly as already being in paradise or hades after the parable of Lazarus and Dives. Thus there arose a greater emphasis upon double judgment, i.e. an individual judgment of the soul at death followed by a public, universal judgment at the parousia. Thus the critical point of life and after-life came to be the moment of death at which time the individual soul experienced individual judgment.

A shift is also noted in the resurrection as concerning the "body" or the "flesh." Hick interprets Paul as teaching the resurrection of the body, i.e. the total personality of an individual, and hence a spiritual body, and not resurrection of the flesh, i.e. revivification of a corpse. However due to the millenarian expectation and controversy against Gnosticism which stressed spiritualizing notions, the resurrection of the flesh gained ascendancy and appears in the Apostles' Creed.

The development of the conception of hell Hick finds scientifically fantastic and morally revolting. Having been given enduring expression in the *Divine Comedy* of Dante and *Paradise Lost* by Milton, Augustine's conception of hell entailed the embodiment of the damned and their burning ever-lastingly in literal flames. To Hick this conception contradicts the laws of science, i.e. a burning without consumption, as well as the law of diminishing returns, i.e. the agony of torment would not maintain a consistently high psychological level. During the seventeenth, eighteenth, and nineteenth centuries Christians became disturbed with such a conception, though they were reluctant to publish their views lest it might weaken the moral ramparts of society.

The concept of purgatory fell into disrepute during the Reformation. Tracing the idea back to Old Testament Judaism and noting its being well established in the Christian tradition by the second century, Hick advocates a readoption of the idea. Otherwise one is left with a gap between man in a state of incompletion and imperfection at death and the perfect heavenly state. Purgatory could bridge this gap by allowing for a continuing growth and development.

Christian understanding of heaven is also briefly outlined by Hick. While conceptions of heaven tend to be deliberately reticent and open-ended, the basic conception portrays it as an existence totally oriented to God. Sometimes this is portrayed as worship of God, and at other times the beatific vision is the center of the portrayal. This latter was expounded little until Thomas Aquinas, who described it as intellectual knowledge of the divine substance. It is the ultimate end of every intellectual substance,[60] and it is interminable.[61] And, as Hick notes, it shows some similarities to eastern conceptions of after-life.[62]

Finally in his survey of death and after-life in the Christian tradition Hick notes the two most prominent understandings of death itself. The first of these, stemming from the Apostle Paul and Augustine, suggests that death represents punishment for sin. "In this picture our mortality is an expression of our sinfulness, and it is only by the free mercy of the divine judge that we may hope to escape from the wrath to come."[63] Hick notes another Christian understanding of death, a minority report to be sure, but one which Hick feels is deserving of more reflection. He writes:

> Alongside the dark, punitive conception of the meaning of death there has always been the very different picture of human life as a pilgrimage, with bodily death as the end of one stage of that pilgrimage and, by the same token, as a passing on to another stage.[64]

Hick believes that these two conceptions are not really compatible, but both can claim legitimate support in the Christian tradition. Hick himself believes the pilgrim path to be better suited to contemporary understanding and pursues it as a basis for developing a global eschatology.

In concluding this section Hick cites several contemporary approaches to death and after-life among Protestant and Roman Catholic theologians. But before making his survey Hick makes an observation after reiterating that with the empirical orientation of society today there is prevalent the practice of accepting as true only that which has been self-experienced or empirically verified by authorities.

> The after-life falls outside this sphere and is accordingly dismissed as a fantasy of wishful thinking. In face of this contemporary cultural rejection, christian theology since the second world war presents a spectrum of disarray.[65]

Hick classifies the responses of theologians into three basic groups: the strongly traditional or conservative, the moderately traditional or liberal, and the radical. The conservatives reiterate past solutions, the liberals have followed suit except in substituting the notion of universal salvation for hell, and the radicals are so embarrassed with traditional Christian hope that they either have suppressed the eschatological element or denied after-life altogether.[66] Hick's survey of contemporary theology serves only to enhance this view, and since Hick does not use any of these theologians to strengthen his own view, we will defer any further discussion of this subject.

Universal Salvation

Before proceeding to his section which reviews both western and eastern pareschatologies, i.e. descriptions of what transpires between death and the ultimate state, Hick turns his attention to a study of universalism or apocatastasis within the Christian tradition. Generally the theory of universalism suggests that God in His relationship to the world as creator and sustainer is able to fulfill His intentions. And since He intends to save all men, all men will eventually be saved. However such a perspective denies human freedom. Man will be saved whether or not he so chooses.

The New Testament appears at first sight to support both arguments, but the antithesis does appear resolvable. Hick first notes that the sayings of Jesus which speak of eternal rejection by God are often classified together with those in which he speaks of rewards and punishments after life without indication as to their duration. When this separation is noted, one observes only one explicit case in which eternal punishment is threatened by Jesus, and this noteworthily occurs in the parable of the last judgment in Matthew. Apart from this only the sin against the Holy Spirit occasions "eternal sin" (cf. Mark 3:29 and parallels). This particular passage has perplexed interpreters throughout the ages as to its intent, however. Thus it is difficult to know how to treat it in this regard as well. Therefore attention focuses upon the Matthean parable of the last judgment. However since Matthew reflects more the theme of punishment than Mark, and since Mark is generally given priority as being more original, one may conclude that the Matthean passage reflects a time of persecution when the Church would have been receptive to the idea that its oppressors would be punished eternally.[67]

The Apostle Paul leans in two directions regarding universalism. On the one hand the fall of Adam is paralleled by the universal restoration in Christ. On the other hand Paul can write in a predestinatarian sense. Thus it is difficult for Hick to classify Paul on one side or the other. He does offer this noteworthy comment though: "sometimes as he wrote about the saving activity of God the inner logic of that about which he was writing inevitably unfolded itself into the thought of universal salvation."[68]

If one assumes that Jesus taught of eternal damnation, Hick believes it is still possible to reconcile his teaching with that of the universalism of Paul by a consideration of the occasions which prompted their writings. The Apostle Paul was the theologian writing for the Christian community. Paul was reflecting upon the whole of creation and attempting to relate all of human life and history to the universal purpose of God. In contrast Hick suggests that Jesus was an existentialist. He wrestled with individual men and women in an attempt to avert and overcome their self-destructive sinfulness. While Paul was theoretical, Jesus offerred practical and personal admonition and exhortation.[69] But even while noting the discrepancies occasioned by their different approaches, Hick nevertheless attempts to find common ground between Jesus and Paul.

It may well be true at a given point within the temporal process that unless you repent you will surely perish, and yet also true as a statement arrived at from other grounds, about human existence as a whole, that in the end all will turn from their wickedness and live. The two truths are formally compatible with one another because the one asserts that something will happen if a certain condition is fulfilled (namely, permanent non-repentance) while the other asserts that this same thing will not happen because that condition will not in fact be fulfilled.[70]

Thus it is apparent that Hick does not wish to eliminate the possibility of universalism's being present in the Bible. Nonetheless this involves the loss of human freedom. But such a conclusion rests on a questionable premise according to Hick. It implies that God must coerce man if He is to achieve His ultimate will for humankind. Hick, on the contrary, contends that "the christian doctrine of creation offers an alternative route to the universalist conclusion."[71] Thus Hick argues that God has so created man that he naturally responds to God and follows His will. When man seeks his own fulfillment and perfection he will innately turn to God. God does not need to coerce man for He has implanted in man the inclination to fulfill His will. This allows Hick to draw an interesting analogy--God is like a psychiatrist trying to remove inhibitions which prevent man from fulfilling himself.[72] God opens man to his potentialities, though He often will encounter myriad types of resistance to this end. Man is free *for* God--not free *from* God.[73] It is thus that Hick resolves the question of freedom anthropologically.

Disembodied Mind

The primary thrust of *Death and Eternal Life* is the development of a universal perspective of death and after-life. As another step toward that goal Hick examines western and eastern pareschatologies, i.e. images and descriptions of what happens between death and the ultimate state. The first issue which Hick addresses in this section is the survival of the disembodied mind.

Hick notes that though the dualistic idea of death as separation of mind and body has been known in the West since the time of Plato, remarkably little has been written concerning the disembodied mind. Hick therefore finds the paper "Survival and the Idea of 'Another World'" by H. H. Price to be noteworthy. Hick summarizes Price's article under three points. First perceptions of the mind after life will be of a nature similar to dreams. They will be mind-dependent and derivative of experience during life. Second there will be a form of communication and interaction with others similar to extra-sensory perception here. Third the next world will be fashioned by the power of desires,

and as Price conceives of them these desires need not be altogether pleasant.[74] Hick observes that this final characteristic
of after-life presents difficulties, unless one assumes that
there will only be private worlds after life. What would happen
when two individuals would have identical or contradictory
desires? Further how is it possible to imagine one continuing
to develop to fulfillment isolated from other individuals? If
man is a social creature who develops through interaction with
others, then it is difficult to conceive of continuing development in such a solipsistic environment. Hick offers the following suggestion, therefore, to alleviate the difficulty:

> We can however instead conceive, at least in general terms,
> a situation in which the memories and desires of a number of
> minds--and these could number thousands or millions--are
> pooled to produce a common environment.[75]

Price also suggests something similar, i.e. "a number of separate
worlds created by groups of people with sufficiently similar
memories or desires or both."[76] Hick adds the possibility of
moving from one community to another as interests change and/or
progress. While such a scheme is viable Hick doubts that a
future world created by man's desires would really aid man in
his development. It would simply represent a continuation of
earthly desires, though it might refine and purify those desires.
Hick, "a theist of the irenaean point of view, who holds that
both worlds exist through the creative activity of God to serve
the same purpose of person-making,"[77] believes that the next
world would needs be similar in nature to this world. He allows
as well that the next world might in turn lead "to a further and
radically different state, eternal rather than temporal, symbol-
ized by such ideas as heaven, nirvana, the kingdom of God, and
the *visio dei*."[78] But in any event Hick believes that the next
stage of this process would be similar in metaphysical status to
our present world.[79] In concluding this section about disembodied mind Hick makes two significant observations:

> One important conclusion that emerges from Price's paper
> is that as soon as we try to conceive of the post-mortem
> existence of the disembodied mind we find that this is not
> after all truly disembodied. If there is no physical body
> inhabiting a physical world, then the mind must supply its
> own 'dream' body inhabiting a 'dream' world, the latter
> being as real to those who experience it as the former.[80]

We will be post mortem either in a world with spatial dimensions
or else our mind will supply such a world for us via dreams and
imagination. The second conclusion which Hick draws is that the
idea of the survival after life of disembodied mind is not
radically different from embodied after-life. Disembodied mind
may in fact be understood as a special form of embodied after-
life.[81]

Resurrection of the Person

Acknowledging that the prevailing view of man among contemporary scientists and western philosophers conceives of man
as an indissoluble psycho-physical unity, Hick finds it surprising that the specifically Jewish and Christian belief in the
resurrection of the body, as compared with the Hellenistic idea
of disembodied soul, has not attracted more attention. Hick
accordingly institutes an investigation of this belief.

Hick's intention in this section, as elsewhere, is to
seek the central affirmations involved and to demonstrate their
continuing intelligibility. To conceive of resurrection Hick
employs an idea which first appeared in his book *Faith and
Knowledge*. The idea recurs in his *Philosophy of Religion*
as well as *Death and Eternal Life*. It is the 'replica' theory.
Hick proffers several hypothetical examples of a person disappearing from one locale only to appear simultaneously as a
'replica' at a second location remote from the first. Hick
contends that we would generally recognize the 'replica' as
being the person who had disappeared. He expresses it thus:

> For 'replica' is the name that I am proposing for the second
> entity in the following case. A living person ceases to
> exist at a certain location, and a being exactly similar to
> him in all respects subsequently comes into existence at
> another location. And I have argued so far that it would
> be a correct decision, causing far less linguistic and
> conceptual disruption than the contrary one, to regard
> the 'replica' as the same person as the original.[82]

The quotation marks around the word replica become necessary
lest 'replica' be confused with replica, the word used when two
entities are simultaneously identical. Hick uses 'replica' so
as to emphasize that a second, identical entity exists subsequent to an original. Hick argues that persons in this world
would recognize a 'replica' Mr. X as the now deceased Mr. X.
He then questions whether 'replica' Mr. X would recognize himself as the same individual and contends:

> It is, I think, manifestly an intelligible hypothesis that
> after my death I shall continue to exist as a consciousness
> and shall remember both having died and some at least of my
> states of consciousness both before and after death.[83]

The idea of memory plays a key role in the identification of Mr.
X and 'replica' Mr. X. Hick contends that 'replica' Mr. X would
no more doubt his identity with Mr. X than Mr. X might question
his identity during this life. Hick furthermore does not believe
that it is possible to synchronize clocks and calendars between
the worlds occupied by Mr. X and 'replica' Mr. X. He also argues
that there could not be simultaneous 'replica' Mr. X^1 and
'replica' Mr. X^2 because that would prohibit identification of
'replica' Mr. X with the deceased Mr. X.

In concluding Hick comments: "I hope that this discussion has in fact established the conceivability of resurrection as the divine re-creation of the individual after his earthly death as a total psycho-physical 'replica' in another space."[84] Hick concedes, however, that with regard to our present knowledge, the 'replica' theory is nothing more than a logical possibility. Hick further acknowledges that should this possibility ever be found to be a reality, the present theory would likely fall far short in description of the reality. Hick also points out that logically coherent extrapolations can take us only as far as reconstitution by God in another world. Beyond this only imagination could carry man.[85]

Reincarnation

The idea of reincarnation has been prominent in India for centuries and has been adopted by all religions except Christianity and Islam. The idea lacks philosophical consistency, but Hick notes the same tendency in the West. The theory of reincarnation attempts to solve one basic problem--how it is possible to account for the physical and social inequalities which invariably accompany birth into this world. In lieu of appealing to the arbitrary will of a divine creator, reincarnation teaches that one's condition at birth is the consequence of behavior in a previous life. This theory has weaknesses which Hick points up. It is difficult, for example, to recognize continuity from one life to another. Neither memory nor physical resemblance assures anyone of reincarnation. Few ever recall anything of their previous existence(s), and the theory teaches that one may alter sex, race, and even genus from one life to another. Another suggestion offerred by Hick in defense of continuity is the notion of psychological continuity according to a pattern of mental dispositions. This continuity must be of such a nature as to be able to bridge races, sexes, civilizations, climates, and historical epochs. To accommodate such a diversity of possibilities the pattern of mental dispositions would necessarily be so general as to be applicable to thousands of persons. Thus, failing to provide a means of establishing continuity from one life to another, the theory of reincarnation becomes unintelligible. Hick, nonetheless, restores some credibility to the theory with the thought that there may be an unconscious thread of memory linking the various lives which remains latent until a final moment when the soul recalls everything as it attains enlightenment. Thus Hick rescues the idea of reincarnation before it sinks. Before closing his examination, however, Hick notes that the idea of reincarnation does not actually solve the problem of the inequalities of birth. It merely shifts it. For either there is a first birth which still requires explanation or else there is an infinite regression of births which postpones the solution ad infinitum.

Hick is ultimately uncertain how one may understand the teachings of the Buddha regarding death and after-life. This stems from the different notions and understandings which appear in the Buddhist tradition. For example in contrast to the Hindu conception of the *linga sharira*, the subtle body or soul which is indefinitely reincarnated, Buddhism teaches the idea of *anatta* or "no soul." Buddhist writers have followed a nominalist approach to the soul, suggesting that though one speaks of the soul or self in everyday life it is a convenient fiction. On the other hand such a nominalist approach would signify an unproductive renunciation of nouns. Therefore even as it is possible to speak of tree, mountain, and cat despite the fact of the continuous alteration of each, so it is possible to speak of mind. Some Buddhists have spoken of *anatta* as "a wholly temporal reality, a living entity existing in its different states."[86] Hick suggests that these two seemingly contradictory notions may be brought together in an ethical consideration. Reflection upon one's transitory character enables one to transcend egoism. Hence one denies self and one can speak of *anatta* or no soul. The Buddha rejected the metaphysical notion that there was within man an enduring and unchanging entity. Rather, being an intensely practical, ethical teacher, he avoided metaphysical speculation.

Buddhism, like Hinduism, teaches a doctrine of reincarnation or rebirth. At death the psycho-physical unity constituting an individual disintegrates and ceases to exist. The individual will not be reborn. Nonetheless an aspect of the individual does continue to exist, though it does not continue interminably. That which lives on "consists of a system of character dispositions, the karmic deposit of former lives, animated and propelled onwards by the power of craving."[87] That which continues is not a conscious self but rather an unconscious system of dispositions, which as Hick notes is similar to the *linga sharira* of vedantic Hinduism.

The moment of death is very important in Buddhist teaching.

Returning now to the mechanism of rebirth, the first moment of thought in the new stream of life stands in direct causal sequence to the last moment of thought in the dying person, which thought thus determines the nature of the next birth.[88]

As a result it can hardly be surprising to note ritual associated with this moment which parallels the *ars moriendi* literature in the West.

It needs to be noted as well that rebirth does not necessarily occur into this human form. In fact only a minority of births occur into human form.

Rebecoming may occur in any of the many 'worlds'--the *kama*-worlds (sense worlds), which include our earth, purgatory, and the nearer *deva* (angel)-worlds; the *rupa*-worlds (worlds of visible form though not sense) which are the further Brahma and supra-Brahma spheres; and the *arupa*-worlds (incorporeal worlds in thought).[89]

The idea of rebirth from a womb becomes unnecessary when one
realizes that there are numerous worlds into which one may
rebecome.

The possibility that one need not be reborn again into
this world suggests an interesting possibility to Hick. Though
one may not reappear on this earth, somebody will of necessity
be required to bear the consequences of the decisions and actions
performed in this life. Thus the idea of a collective karma,
i.e. the collective, qualitative sum of volitional activity,[90]
is suggested. This idea has been posited for the Buddha himself.[91] In any event it concurs with the teaching against
egoism and encourages the unselfish love of others, both of
which were advocated by the Buddha.[92]

Reincarnation--Discriminations and Conclusions

As a conclusion to his review of western and eastern
pareschatologies Hick evaluates the teaching of reincarnation.
As a preliminary conclusion Hick discounts the theory of reincarnation for it fails to explain why babies are not born with
adult egos which had died at the end of a normal life span nor
how one can avoid becoming so general regarding reincarnated
personality traits as to become worthless. Furthermore the
memory of past life must be much greater than elementary to
establish viability for reincarnation.

Hick also examines the compatibility of the idea of reincarnation and Christianity. Reincarnation has never been an
orthodox Christian teaching, to be sure, but this ought not,
according to Hick, automatically eliminate it from consideration.
Hick notes four principal reasons why it is generally disregarded in the Christian tradition. First it is not taught in
the New Testament. And if anything it is explicitly rejected
in John 9:2-3. Furthermore it is not taught in the early Church.
Second Christianity attributes absolute importance to this life.
Such importance would be diminished if there were additional
lives. However Hick personally decries this argument on the
basis of Irenaean and even Augustinian theology. Christianity
does not believe that individuals generally have attained
perfection and fulfillment by the time of their death in this
life. As a result it has been common to posit some place after
life where further development can occur, e.g. purgatory.
Christianity may differ as to where this additional growth
takes place, but it rather suggests a parallel process. Third
it has been suggested that transmigration is at variance with
the Christian teaching of resurrection. Again, however, Hick
counters this statement. Looking beyond superficial dissimilarities, he notes that both doctrines teach that man is a
psycho-physical unity so that even after-life is envisioned as
embodied. Fourth there are those who believe that reincarnation
detracts from the uniqueness of Christ. But Hick offers a
rebuttal: "there is no logical connection between the idea that
Christ died once only for the sins of the world and the idea that
men have only one life in which to accept the benefits of that

atoning death."[93] Hick in fact suggests that salvation in Christ
might parallel the eastern experience of enlightenment or
liberation. Thus Hick has countered all purported barriers to
a Christian acceptance of reincarnation except its non-acceptance
in the early Church. This argument collapses as well, however,
when one no longer accepts the misunderstandings under which
the early Church worked and simply questions answers which have
gone unchallenged for so long.[94]

Despite the defense of the possibility of resurrection
Hick continues to throttle the idea with further considerations.
There is yet to be provided a detailed, scientific investigation
of cases before hints and clues could be provided from sources
outside the memory. Also where investigation of reported cases
of reincarnation has been done two factors are disproportion-
ately in evidence. First the persons involved are often
children. And related to this is the second factor; cases of
putative reincarnation generally occur in cultural contexts
where reincarnation is accepted. Thus Hick categorizes the
theory of reincarnation as not proven.[95] The claim of various
yogis, arhats, and other liberated souls who have been able to
reach enlightenment and recall their former lives also remains
unproven. Legend tends to embellish such reports, and the
evidence offerred is elusive.[96] Despite this, nonetheless,
Hick believes that it is possible to believe in at least partial
reincarnation. When a person dies

a mental 'husk' or 'mask' of the deceased person is left
behind and is telepathically accessible under certain
conditions to living persons. Such a 'husk' may consist of
mere fragments of memory, emotion, habit--analogous to
isolated pieces of tape-recording--or of a relatively coherent and cohesive body of such elements. . .[97]

Accordingly certain persons are able to "pick up" these husks
and integrate them into their own personality or communicate
the contents to others as does a medium.[98]

The idea that genetic codes might represent reincarnation
is also discounted by Hick. There is no positive support for
reincarnation which may be derived from this angle.[99]

In the end Hick is uncertain whether the theory of reincarnation is true or false. It is unable to provide certainty that
there is a conscious self-identity between two individuals.
Furthermore it seems to shift and avoid the problem of inequality
and inequity between persons rather than solve it. It also fails
to give mankind and life in general unity. The individual
threads his way from one life to another, and he remains
principally an individual and lacks corporate identity and
responsibility.[100] As often is the case, Hick qualifies these
negative remarks. "There are forms of reincarnation doctrine
which *may* be broadly true pictures of what actually happens."[101]
This, however, will be clarified best by means of an examination
of Hick's own possibility of human destiny.

A Possible Pareschatology

As the concluding section to his work *Death and Eternal Life* Hick draws together the results of his many investigations and formulates a possible human destiny. This for Hick involves the two basic subject matters of pareschatology and eschatology. Recalling the illative sense which was noted earlier, we will find that the possible destiny which Hick describes may be understood as derivative of the illative sense. Logical propositions are not accorded the greatest priority by Hick. Rather what Hick advocates represents the gleaning from the previous discussions and synthesizing various aspects of it.

In the section dedicated to a possible pareschatology Hick makes two basic assumptions which undergird his position and are both derivative of the previous discussions. First Hick believes that there will be a persisting self-conscious ego which will continue to exist after death. Second since the individual does not attain to its ultimate fulfillment at death, we must contemplate a pareschatological or interim state.

In order to conceive what this pareschatological state may be like Hick begins with an examination of two phenomena, the *Tibetan Book of the Dead* and western mediumistic communications. The *Book of the Dead* maps our existence between death and rebirth. During the few days during which the soul detaches itself from the body the soul is surrounded by light, the Ultimate Reality. If it so chooses the soul may enter into nirvana, but this only occurs for those who have approximated to self-purification. The vast majority are clothed in a karmic body consisting of past thoughts and deeds. Next the soul encounters good and evil powers. The good powers first attempt to attract the individual into their paradisal Buddha-worlds, but the soul declines in favor of preserving self. Then evil powers will encounter the soul, terrifying it. The soul then experiences judgment and punishment in various hells. After this the soul will be joined to another body and world corresponding to its karma. And then the cycle of life, death, and rebirth commences anew. Hick notes in closing that it is the soul itself which creates the intermediate world for itself, rather like a psychoanalytic experience.

The images in western spiritualism center around the idea of a series of seven planes of existence. The first and lowest plane is the plane of physical matter; the second is the plane of hades, which is a confused borderland between the physical stage and subsequent higher stages; the third is the plane of illusion, where souls pass a considerable time; the fourth is a plane of color; the fifth a plane of flame; the sixth a plane of light; and the seventh a plane beyond time in which the soul becomes one with God. In this scheme death represents the transition from one level to another. The transition between plane one and two occurs as the psychic double of the body, i.e. an astral or etheric body, detaches itself from the physical body of plane one and enters plane two, where it stays for

an average of three or four days. Hick concludes that though
there are differences between the *Tibetan Book of the Dead* and
spiritualism, there is also general, broad agreement between
the two.[102]

The basic thrust of Hick's thought with regard to death
and after-life is teleological, i.e. it focuses upon a goal.
With this orientation and in light of his previous discussion
and the just cited examples, Hick raises the alternative of
whether it is more likely in man's trek to fulfillment that
death occurs once and divides existence into a short, earthly
life and an interminable after-life or whether this life is
not rather the first of a series of lives which each is terminated in death. Hick advocates the latter since it appears to
fit "the various relevant considerations."[103] It is also
noteworthy that these future lives not be conceived of horizontally but vertically. One does not rebecome into this world at
a future date, but rather one rebecomes into another, higher
realm. Hick also believes that there may be an interim between
life in this world and the next, pareschatological world. This
interim he suggests is

> subjective and dream-like, and that it can take either a
> sharply defined form, reflecting an imagination effectively
> conditioned by a powerful religious culture, or be experi-
> enced as a kind of continuation of earthly life.[104]

But such an interim state is temporary. Positive intimations
of higher realms and better possibilities of existence and/or
negative moments of boredom and emptiness impel one to seek
another life. Thus one moves on from the interim psychological
state to another embodied life in another world space.[105] Hick
is inclined to believe that our life on earth is the first life,
and thus birth into the next world will not entail beginning
anew as an immature creature. The pattern of birth in this
world need not be repeated.[106] Hick is uncertain as to the
nature of sexuality and reproduction in the next world, these
uncertainties only being capable of answer in that next world.

After some time in this next world one will again die and
pass into an interim state succeeded by another rebecoming.
Hick does not claim to know whether there will be only a few or
many lives nor when fulfillment is attained if one will recall
all of one's past lives. If there are many lives, and Hick
feels that Jesus' words concerning "many mansions" or resting
places may well point to this conclusion,[107] then it is likely
that memory of past lives, particularly early ones, may be faint
and indistinct.[108]

Moksha, Nirvana, and the Unitive State

As he had done in his pareschatological section Hick begins
his section detailing a possible eschatology with a survey of
alternatives as presented by the various pertinent traditions.
Hick notes that it is generally assumed that the eschatological

understandings of Christianity, Hinduism, and Buddhism conflict
with one another. Hick, by contrast, believes that the eschatologies of the east and west are essentially open-ended and
convergent,[109] pointing to a similar conception of human fulfillment. Christianity has basically viewed human fulfillment
individualistically, whether or not such fulfillment takes a
social or mystical form. The Kingdom of God is a society of
individuals who dwell together in harmony in the presence of
God. Each person here retains individuality but in a perfected
form. The other notion of Christian fulfillment, the beatific
vision, stresses individual communion with God.[110] Hick sees
the various types of Christian mysticism as aiming at unity with
that which *is* beyond every appearance, which is unity with God.
When one dies to self, then a new creature is born who is self-
less.[111] When one gives up self, then one becomes free to be
"entirely transparent to and controlled by the presence of
God."[112]

Hinduism in its advaita or non-dualistic Vedanta form
teaches that human destiny is impersonal; it involves the
dissolution of the individual. As one does away completely with
the self, one is able to identify absolutely with the Absolute
or Brahman.[113] Souls merge into the Infinite and possess no
individual consciousness, memories, or boundaries.[114] Though
this is the best-known form of Indian faith in the West, Hick
claims that it has comparatively few followers. More Hindus
are of the *vishishtadvaita* or modified non-dualistic form. In
this form the Absolute or Brahman is not impersonal but rather
the personal Lord, Supreme Person, or Supreme Self. And moreover
in the state of liberation or ultimate destiny the self continues
to exist individually. A plurality of individuals continues to
exist in the ultimate state.[115]

A similar misconception exists with regard to the understanding of nirvana in Buddhism. The idea that nirvana entails
annihilation of the individual is inaccurate for the attainment
of nirvana is possible in this life. Instead nirvana entails
the annihilation of evil in the individual.

> Nirvana is thus a psychological state in which the self-
> positing ego has been abolished and in which there is
> accordingly freedom from the cravings which make human
> life a self-perpetuating cycle of anxious self-concern.[116]

An individual in the state of nirvana can be a living human
being, even conscious of his own past as an individual, but
without the self-serving desires which arise from viewing the
world in an egocentric fashion. A living individual in nirvana
does not live in a state of effective numbness either but in a
state of joy, peace, and happiness.[117]

Within Buddhism there is a difference in the conception of
what transpires at death to the one who has attained nirvana.
There are some Buddhists who hold that at death the one who has
attained to nirvana simply passes out of existence, similar to

western materialistic conceptions of man. By contrast, more
orthodox Buddhism distinguishes between nirvana, i.e. the state
of one still alive, and parinirvana, i.e. nirvana without qualification, lying beyond and outside the cycle of rebecoming. In
parinirvana some believe that the individual terminates completely
in the infinite and eternal Reality. As a drop merges into the
ocean so the individual ceases to exist as a separate individual
though the real aspect of the individual continues to exist
eternally in the Infinite Reality. There are still others who
maintain that the Buddha taught that there is no significant
difference for an Enlightened One before and after death. Once
one is beyond the process of rebecoming one eternally *is* in a
manner beyond the imagination of the unenlightened.[118] Nirvana
is experienceable but not really describable.[119] The state of
parinirvana has been characterized as "a diluted, undifferenti-
ated, 'resting' existence, more or less impersonal but still
unrecognizable."[120]

Hick also notes that Mahayana Buddhism teaches a type of
incarnation parallel to Christian teaching as found especially
in the Gospel of John.

Thus in the Mahayana 'the Buddha' no longer signifies an
individual arhat who lived long ago. Gautama was merely
one of the physical bodies of the eternal Buddha who is
Dharma or Truth; he was the Dharma made flesh. . . the
Buddha came to draw men into his Dharma Body. . .[121]

The Buddha becomes incarnate whenever the state of nirvana is
achieved.

A Possible Eschatology

As a conclusion to *Death and Eternal Life* Hick offers the
reader his own conception of a possible eschatology. Hick again
attempts to synthesize the teachings of various theological
systems where they demonstrate basic agreement or a similar
intention.

The first aspect which draws the consideration of Hick
is anthropological. Having demonstrated that a materialistic
approach to man is untenable, Hick also believes a dualistic
approach, e.g. mind-body, is inadequate. The mind is related
to the body, but it is likewise related to spirit or atman, a
supra-individual, presently unconscious unity of humankind and
perhaps of all created life. Thus Hick espouses man as a
trichotomy of body, mind, and atman.

Hick also employs two other groups of words to characterize
man. The first refers to the embodied mind as a self-contained
individual set apart from and opposed to others; this is the ego,
egoity, or egoism. In contrast to this person, personality, and
personal refer to the embodied mind in its interrelationship and
interaction with other embodied minds.

Common to all the religious traditions is the belief that man has fallen or is separated from Ultimate Reality. Similarly the reason given for this unsatisfactory condition is commonly the egoism of man. And amongst the religious traditions one discovers two basic paths to overcome this situation.

> One is an inner or mystical way whereby the contemplative opens his spirit progressively to the presence of God and is drawn by grace into the divine life, or whereby the mediator comes to realize his oneness with Brahman or passes through egolessness to nirvana. The other is the outer way of love for one's fellow creatures, expressed in selfless service to one's suffering brethren.[122]

By either path the ultimate goal is the same--being at one with Ultimate Reality, whether this is envisioned as personal or nonpersonal. Hick appears to be content with either of these two paths as long as one is striving for Ultimate Reality, but his preference would seem to lie with the outer way of love. Though the two basic paths need not be mutually exclusive, the former path would tend to be more private and individualistic while the latter is public and therefore can be experienced and observed. The latter consequently lends itself to being graded or evaluated as Hick advocates in an article entitled "On Grading Religions." Hick suggests that one may evaluate the various religious traditions according to the level which they are "able so to possess our minds and hearts as to exhibit a transforming power in our lives."[123] Though this is not the sole criterion which Hick offers, it is clear that for Hick religions may be judged by the fruit which they produce in their adherents. Ultimately either the inner or outer way will come to the same end according to Hick, but the one does lend itself to empirical judgment, and that Hick views favorably.

Furthermore Hick believes that only infrequently do persons attain to the goal during this life. Most make some progress toward that end, but generally whatever growth there may be is broken off by death. Hick believes that growth will continue, nonetheless. He believes that there are other realms or worlds to which one passes to develop further. Though there may be many such pareschatological realms, one does not rebecome indefinitely. There will come a time, most likely outside time itself, when the individual will reach the goal of true fulfill-ment. But before venturing to describe this realm Hick notes that life on this earth appears to be the first life. This appears consistent with the fact that life appears to be initi-ated in the womb as well as the fact that persons seldom remember any previous existence. It would also fit well with Hick's 'replica' theory.

It is when he comes to describe the ultimate end of man that Hick is somewhat reticent, as are the various religious traditions. There appear to be two poles which form the limits for those who conceive of life as being continued after death. On the one hand are those who assume that the individual empties

himself into the sea of the universe. The individual continues
to live in the universe, although one might say that the individual is nearly annihilated. On the other extreme are those who
contend that an immortal ego continues to exist as an independent
reality after life. Hick personally is more inclined to the
latter view, though he finds the notion of an independent,
immortal ego untenable. Hick attempts to present a view of the
state of human fulfillment which is pluralistic but in which
the ego has been transcended. To clarify this idea, modern
insights concerning the nature of personality are employed.
Generally in the course of history the individual has been
viewed as an atomic unit. Recently, however, the interpersonal
character of personality has been noted, particularly by Martin
Buber. An individual exists and develops as a person in relation
to and over against others. One cannot be a person in isolation.
Hick believes that the Christian doctrine of the trinity may
help to give additional clarification. The biblical narratives
speak of God as possessing more than one center of consciousness
and will. Yet God is one.

> . . . we can say that the three divine selves or conscious-
> nesses are not self-enclosed egos, existing over against
> each other, but mutually constitutive personal centres
> whose relationship with one another form a rich and complex
> unity.[124]

Fellowship in the ultimate state will correspond to intertrini-
tarian fellowship in which there is distinction yet marked unity.
This serves as a model for Hick of just how the individual might
exist in fulfillment.

> There will be a plurality of centres of consciousness, and
> yet these will not be private but will each include the
> others in a full mutual sharing constituting the atman,
> the complex collective consciousness of humanity.[125]

There are clear echoes here of the section in which Hick dealt
with disembodied mind, especially as it relates to telepathic
communication. People will share consciousness yet remain
distinct. This also provides a basis for the fulfillment of
the social dimension of human community. Our individual
histories will take on an increasingly interpersonal character.[126] Using a Christian phrase, Hick believes that "in the
mystical Body of Christ humanity is to become one in many and
many in one."[127]

Furthermore in the ultimate state there will most likely
no longer be time or embodiment. When one has reached fulfillment, i.e. when development is complete, then embodiment will no
longer be necessary. Similarly since there will be no more
change, the significance of time will be eliminated.[128]

In conclusion Hick notes that the collective human self
or atman is not God in this conception. Individuals will live
in ideal relationship to God or Ultimate Reality, but their

openness to this Reality will not result in their identification
with it, even as their relationship to others does not involve
disintegration.[129] Hick remains theistic in the conception of
the ultimate state. One becomes united with God though not
absorbed into God.

Hick notes that it is logically conceivable that one could
arrive in the ultimate state and not realize it. The plurality
of after-lives or postmortem worlds which Hick envisions might
contribute to uncertainty as to whether one had actually arrived
at the ultimate state. Hick had focused attention upon this
problem as early as 1960 in an article entitled "Theology and
Verification." In it Hick argues that there are criteria which
would assure one beyond rational doubt that God exists. This
would happen in a situation in which simultaneously one enjoyed
an experience of God's purpose for our life being fulfilled and
an experience of communion with God as revealed in Christ.[130]
Such an experience, however, is possible only after life in the
eschaton. One would know beyond rational doubt that he had
arrived when these criteria are met, and one would recognize
the fact much like a person recognizes that he is finally a
grown-up.

This type of eschatological verification must needs be
revamped with less specifically Christian criteria if they are
to be utilized for a global eschatology, and this Hick has
attempted in an article entitled "Eschatological Verification
Reconsidered," which was published in 1977. Here again Hick
is concerned for verification, i.e. the elimination of rational
doubt, and the final state holds open this possibility. Coming
to that state one will gain

> an awareness of existing in the presence of God and of
> being freely led within the divine providence towards the
> fulfilment of their human potentialities in the community
> of mankind perfected.[131]

This state will be religiously unambiguous[132] and will leave
no room for rational doubt about a religious, theistic understanding of the universe.[133] Though Hick acknowledges that
additional investigation of the relation and relevance of eschatological verification to nonChristian beliefs would be appropriate,[134] he has at least formulated the criteria of eschatological verification in a more global sense, with criteria more
befitting the results of his investigation in *Death and Eternal
Life*.

Conclusion

In many of his writings Hick attempts to demonstrate that
the reasons given for unbelief and/or atheism are either inappropriate or invalid as regards religious faith and practice.
This is clearly evident in *Death and Eternal Life*, a work in
which Hick argues in order to promote the verification of religious truth via the likely probability of a certain truth and/or

the elimination of rational doubt.

Accordingly with regard to the three foci of our study we note first a naturalistic and positive interpretation of the meaning and significance of death. Death accords clearly with the will of God. It enables man to move from one world to the next. It facilitates the growth and development of man.

What happens to the individual in death is that the soul becomes divorced from the body. Simply stated, while the body disintegrates the soul will become reembodied.

This leads directly to the third issue of what happens after life. Hick suggests that one will pass through numerous after-lives, likely with 'replica' bodies. At the conclusion of each after-life one will die again with the 'body' disintegrating and the soul rebecoming in another world with another 'body.' This will continue until one attains to the ultimate state in which one will be totally conscious of the Real or God as well as of others. This ultimate state will be both disembodied and timeless.

FOOTNOTES

[1] John H. Hick, *Philosophy of Religion*, 2d ed. (Englewood Cliffs, New Jersey: Prentice-Hall, Inc., 1973, 1963), pp. 126-127.

[2] Ibid., p. 129.

[3] John Hick, *Faith and Knowledge*, 2d ed. (Glasgow: Collins, Fontana Books, 1966, 1974), p. 69.

[4] Ibid.   [5] Ibid., p. 81.

[6] Ibid., p. 14.   [7] Ibid., p. 91.

[8] Ibid.

[9] John Hick, *Death and Eternal Life* (London: William Collins Sons & Co. Ltd., 1976), p. 5.

[10] Ibid.   [11] Ibid.

[12] Ibid., p. 29.   [13] Ibid., p. 26.

[14] Ibid., p. 30.   [15] Ibid., p. 31.

[16] Ibid., p. 35.   [17] Ibid., p. 43.

[18] Ibid., p. 45.   [19] Ibid., p. 46.

[20] Ibid.   [21] Ibid., p. 47.

[22] John Hick, *Evil and the God of Love* (Glasgow: Collins, Fontana Library, 1968, 1977), p. 181.

[23] Ibid., pp. 181-182.

[24] Hick, *Faith and Knowledge*, p. 256.

[25] Hick, *Evil*, p. 217.   [26] Ibid., p. 291.

[27] Hick, *Death*, pp. 55-56.

[28] Ibid., p. 57.   [29] Ibid., p. 63.

[30] Ibid., p. 60.   [31] Ibid., p. 58.

[32] Ibid., p. 59.   [33] Ibid., p. 73.

[34] Ibid., p. 92.   [35] Ibid., p. 119.

[36] Ibid., p. 117. [37] Ibid., p. 121.

[38]Ibid., p. 123.   [39]Ibid., p. 135.

[40]Hick, *Philosophy of Religion*, pp. 105-106.

[41]Hick, *Death*, p. 138.   [42]Ibid., p. 140.

[43]Ibid.   [44]Ibid., p. 141.

[45]Ibid., p. 147.   [46]Ibid., p. 152.

[47]Ibid., p. 158.   [48]Ibid., p. 159.

[49]Ibid.   [50]Ibid., p. 160.

[51]Ibid., p. 166.   [52]Ibid., p. 173.

[53]Ibid., p. 175.   [54]Ibid., p. 177.

[55]Ibid., pp. 182-183.   [56]Ibid., p. 186.

[57]Ibid., p. 188.   [58]Ibid.

[59]Ibid., p. 181.   [60]Ibid., p. 205.

[61]Ibid., p. 206.   [62]Ibid.

[63]Ibid., p. 207.   [64]Ibid., p. 208.

[65]Ibid., p. 92.   [66]Ibid., pp. 92-93.

[67]Ibid., p. 246.   [68]Ibid., p. 248.

[69]Ibid.   [70]Ibid., p. 249.

[71]Ibid., p. 251.   [72]Ibid., p. 253.

[73]Ibid., p. 257.   [74]Ibid., pp. 265-266.

[75]Ibid., p. 271.   [76]Ibid.

[77]Ibid., p. 275.   [78]Ibid., pp. 275-276.

[79]Ibid., p. 276.   [80]Ibid.

[81]Ibid.   [82]Ibid., p. 283.

[83]Ibid., p. 285.   [84]Ibid., p. 293.

[85]Ibid., p. 295.   [86]Ibid., p. 337.

[87]Ibid., pp. 343-344.   [88]Ibid., p. 345.

[89]Ibid., p. 346.   [90]Ibid., p. 301.

[91]Ibid., p. 381.   [92]Ibid., pp. 358-359.

[93]Ibid., p. 372.   [94]Ibid., pp. 366-373.

[95]Ibid., p. 375.   [96]Ibid., p. 381.

[97]Ibid., p. 376.   [98]Ibid., p. 378.

[99]Ibid., p. 388.   [100]Ibid., p. 389.

[101]Ibid., p. 391.   [102]Ibid., pp. 404-407.

[103]Ibid., p. 408.   [104]Ibid., p. 416.

[105]Ibid., p. 417.   [106]Ibid.

[107]Ibid., p. 421.   [108]Ibid., p. 419.

[109]Ibid., p. 427.   [110]Ibid., p. 426.

[111]Ibid., p. 443.   [112]Ibid., p. 444.

[113]Ibid., p. 428.   [114]Ibid., p. 429.

[115]Ibid., pp. 430-431.   [116]Ibid., p. 433.

[117]Ibid.   [118]Ibid., p. 439.

[119]Ibid., p. 433.   [120]Ibid., p. 439.

[121]Ibid., p. 440.   [122]Ibid., p. 454.

[123]John Hick, "On Grading Religions," *Religious Studies* 17 (1981):460.

[124]Hick, *Death*, p. 461.   [125]Ibid., pp. 461-462.

[126]Ibid.   [127]Ibid., p. 462.

[128]Ibid., p. 463.   [129]Ibid., p. 464.

[130]John Hick, "Theology and Verification," *Theology Today* 17 (April, 1960-January, 1961):26-27.

[131]John Hick, "Eschatological Verification Reconsidered," *Religious Studies* 13 (1977):197.

[132]Ibid., p. 196.   [133]Ibid., p. 197.

[134]Ibid., p. 202.

CHAPTER IV

A COMPARISON AND CONTRAST OF BARTH AND HICK
WITH CRITICAL COMMENTS

Introduction

In order to appreciate better the ideas of an individual it is generally beneficial to study them in the light of the ideas of someone else. We have thus far given an exposition of the ideas of Barth and Hick relative to death and after-life. We propose now to compare and contrast directly these two men on the three major topics which have been the foci of our study thus far.

One other topic merits our attention first, nonetheless. It is undoubtedly apparent that Barth and Hick differ on many of the issues we have raised. As we will note, even some of their points of similarity will yield under closer scrutiny to significant differences. This raises the question of method, the means which Barth and Hick use to arrive at their conclusions. For us it will entail an examination of four subjects--God as object of investigation; the nature and place of faith with a special examination of Hick's notion of eschatological verification; the place of Christ and Christianity and their relationship to other religions; and the place of grace in Hick and Barth. Beyond this but related to our methodological considerations we will examine the role and/or function in which Barth and Hick perceive themselves, for this will help to clarify why the two hold such disparate views on numerous issues.

Then before turning to our direct comparison and contrast of Barth and Hick on the three issues we have been studying we will make a few critical observations involving questions of consistency in the work of these two men and offer clarification of our own perspective.

A Study of Methods

GOD AS OBJECT OF INVESTIGATION

For Barth as well as for Hick God is the object of theological investigation. Robert Crawford argues therefore that for Barth theology is not unscientific.

Like the other humanistic sciences it seeks to apprehend
a specific Object and its environment, *directed* by the
phenomenon itself. It is a human effort after a definite
object of knowledge; it follows a definite self-consistent
path of knowledge; it is accountable for this path to itself
and to everyone.[1]

Hick would undoubtedly concur. Indeed Hick would deplore any
attempt to keep any realm of theological investigation sacro-
sanct from investigation. Theology must be like other scientific
investigation or else it will lose credibility to modern man.
Barth and Hick would thus appear to agree that theology is a
science with God as its object. However as Crawford points out,
for Barth God as object is not passive but active. Focusing
upon a difference in the German language as compared with
English, God is *Gegenstand* rather than *Objekt*. "This is very
different from scientific objectivity where the Object is not
modified by the Subject and the Subject is comparatively indifferent to the Object."[2] Barth makes this point clearly in
The Resurrection of the Dead: "God always remains the subject
in the relationship created by this testimony. He is not transformed into the object, into man's having the right to the last
word."[3] The initiative always resides with God, though God is
not impassive to our human response nor is He unaffected by it.
There is a dialogical relationship between God and man which
influences the manner in which man perceives God. The contrast
between envisioning God as *Gegenstand* and *Objekt* is much less
pronounced in Hick, and certainly Hick would not desire it and
tries to avoid it. Though Hick does believe that God as Subject
did initiate the created order and that now He sustains it, God
remains much more of an *Objekt* for Hick rather than a *Gegenstand*.
In describing the nature of faith Hick contends that an object
depends for its significance upon the context in which it is
viewed. Hence God, too, is interpreted differently depending
upon the context.[4] Hick writes "that while the object of religious knowledge is unique, its basic epistemological pattern is
that of all our knowing."[5] This is amplified further by a reference Hick makes to the parable of the blind men and the elephant[6]
and his reference to Wilfred Cantwell Smith's *The Meaning and
End of Religion* which suggests that religions ought to be thought
of as being on a continuum along which the faith-life of individuals is "conditioned by one or other of the different streams
of cumulative tradition."[7] Hick also notes the analogy of
experiments with electro-magnetic radiations in which, depending
upon the way the experiment is conducted, light can exhibit wave-
like properties or particle-like properties.[8] By analogy Hick
would suggest that God is an object like light or an elephant
which may be experienced differently, i.e. it may yield to
differing conceptions. We must also note that Hick allows for
nontheistic forms of religion, though he prefers to understand
this as the experience of the Eternal One being "known and
responded to in nonpersonal terms, as the depth or ground of
being, as the Infinite, or the Absolute (Brahman), as Nirvana,
as Sunyata ("Voidness"), and in yet other ways."[9] Hick envisions all religions as theistic, but it is the experience of the

Eternal One in personal and nonpersonal terms which marks a
great distinction between two streams of religious consciousness.
Nonetheless it remains the case that in all of these instances
God is nonetheless *Objekt*, and man alone determines what he
will believe. Hence though Barth and Hick both envision God as
the object of theological investigation, there is a significant
difference between them in the stance adopted with regard to the
object and the effect which the object has upon the investigator.

THE PLACE AND NATURE OF FAITH

The manner in which Barth and Hick employ faith also lends
itself to similarity and dissimilarity. In *The Epistle to the
Romans*, within Barth's critique of theology as it had developed
in the nineteenth century, a key element was his attack upon the
place and use of reason and natural theology in theological
investigation. As his theology evolved that critique remained
in place. In *The Epistle to the Romans* Barth clearly distinguished faith from reason and natural theology.

> it (faith) grips reason by the throat and strangles the
> beast. It effects what the whole world and all that is in
> it is impotent to do.[10]
> Reason cannot attain to it, only faith can achieve it.[11]

Barth deplores the use of reason and/or natural theology in
theology. He in fact argues that natural theology points to
something found rather than to something being sought; we might
say that natural theology points to *Objekt* while the living God
is *Gegenstand*. Barth bases his faith in God's Word, in the
revelation of God. It is the center and foundation of Christian
dogmatics. He recognizes that theology might thus appear stupid
and impossible, but he believes that revelation is self-authenticating. Revelation is something apart and not even something
which might be understood as a continuation of human experience.
This belief is reiterated in *The Resurrection of the Dead* when
Barth writes that faith does not represent insights of a higher
and the highest kind.[12] Rather Barth contends that Paul is
arguing with the Corinthians for a basis of faith in God's
revelation, in the "appeared" of chapter 15.[13] In the *Credo*
Barth reminds his readers that everything is governed by the
word *credo*.[14]

Barth maintains this method in the *Church Dogmatics*. In
Volume II/1 he talks about our knowledge of God and how it is
gained. In contrast with other writers of the day, Barth contends
that the only possibility of knowledge of God is the reality of
our knowledge of God. The possibility of the knowledge of God
does not contribute to man's knowledge of God. Jesus Christ, the
revelation of God, is the "knowability" of God on the human
side.[15] Thus Barth's focus is consistently upon Christ.

It would be unjustified, however, to suggest that Barth
envisions the relationship between faith and reason as entirely
antithetical. In 1931 Barth published a work which he entitled

Anselm: fides quaerens intellectum, a work in which he argues that though faith precedes understanding, fiath nevertheless seeks for understanding. Barth does not ignore the facts as established by nontheological sciences, but he does regret their one-sided interpretation in isolation and apart from man's relationship to God.[16] Barth holds that one cannot even contemplate man hypothetically without God. For Barth the relationship of God and man is primary. The nontheological sciences should not be accorded prominence or dominance over theology.

John Hick demonstrates a parallel to Barth at this point. In his book *Faith and Knowledge* he clarifies his dissatisfaction with the propositional nature in which faith has traditionally been understood within Christianity. Faith was viewed as assent to certain propositions, but Hick views this as inadequate. Hick also critiques the voluntarist view of faith[17] as well as basing faith upon moral judgment.[18] Hick finds much to his liking in the conception of Cardinal Newman which is termed the illative sense, though Newman according to Hick failed to realize the complexity of theistic interpretation and continues to view faith as propositional.[19] Hick rather views faith as the interpretation of our experience which is directed toward God.[20] Faith is "an apprehension of the divine presence within the believer's human experience."[21] Faith is neither a reasoned conclusion nor an unreasoned hunch nor an inference to a general truth.[22] Rather faith is an encounter between man and the divine, "a mediated meeting with the living God."[23] Faith involves experiencing the world in the light of a principle of interpretation. As such it is not propositional, nor is it a matter of fact, though in time the accuracy of the faith principle can be checked against experience. Hick notes that different types of situational experiences are appropriate to various sorts of interpretive experiences, and he definitely indicates that we are not dealing here with logically necessary truths. Hick is dealing with those statements of faith which might be verified through the removal of ignorance or uncertainty. Verification is enhanced and eventually certainty or truth assured when the grounds for rational doubt are eliminated. Precisely when verification might happen may vary between individuals and situations, but verification is possible. Even the idea of eschatological verification, which we will discuss below, serves to verify faith since it purportedly removes grounds for rational doubt concerning statements such as "God exists."

Hick also likes to utilize parables in the clarification of his ideas. Two will illustrate for us the nature of faith for Hick. One of these is the parable of the garden, which appears in at least two of the works by Hick.[24] In the parable both observers of the garden have faith, though they interpret the facts before them in contrasting manners. The one believed that a gardener, albeit of a special and unique variety, existed while the other disbelieved it. Hick suggests that scientific investigation, etc. did nothing to dissuade the faith of the observers. By implication, therefore ultimately the beliefs of any man can be independent of scientific research. The second parable

concerns the two travellers going along a road with the one
believing that it leads to a celestial city and the other
believing that it leads nowhere.[25] Here again faith will lead
the two travellers to view the elements of the journey differently. Both demonstrate faith, but the content of that faith
differs markedly. In his writings, and especially in *Death and
Eternal Life*, Hick cites an abundance of research from the
natural sciences, from psychology and parapsychology, from
philosophy, etc. which might seem to suggest that faith might
be dependent upon or enhanced by them. In fact faith does not
grow, though faith can be verified through the elimination of
rational doubt. The research which he cites Hick believes will
eliminate grounds for rational doubt and thereby verify faith,
though faith can exist apart from such research and verification.

There is a clear parallel between Barth and Hick in that
both of them do not rely upon reason or scientific investigation
for the content of faith. Both recognize that faith exists
apart from reason. However as quickly as this agreement is
noted, the two diverge and follow different paths. While Barth
affirms revelation and gives assent to numerous statements of
faith, Hick views Barth as propositional in regard to faith.
Even though Barth highlights the truths which stem from revelation and the work of the Holy Spirit, faith entails the affirmation of certain truths. Hick would criticize Barth for remaining
dependent upon propositions instead of the faith-interpretive
experience. Nonetheless like Barth Hick perceives the inadequacy
of pure reason, natural theology, etc. He suggests that certain
truths are recognized as true by the illative sense or a sense
of that nature. Hick argues that the human mind has a readiness
or tendency to interpret its experience in religious terms.[26]
Certain truths do not lend themselves to logical or empirical
verification yet remain true. The knowledge of God which a
religious person claims falls within this category.[27] But this
prompts us to ask whether the idea of revelation as Barth employs
it or the illative sense as Hick employs it could be viewed as
the same since both become necessary to overcome the inadequacy
of reason and both provide a basis for religious belief. It is
here that a clear difference between Barth and Hick becomes
apparent. For Barth revelation derives from God; God is the
source of our knowledge of Him and His relationship with the
world. God reveals Himself to man. God is the Subject of
revelation rather than its Object. For Hick man is the source
of his religious belief. God is the object of belief, and He
has established the created order so that for some belief in
Him is possible. Hick might contend that God is the indirect
source of our knowledge of Him, but for Barth God is the direct
source of our knowledge of Him. Barth would perceive Hick as
advocating a type of natural theology in his understanding of
faith and therefore reject his method. Furthermore Barth would
criticize Hick for his failure to apprehend the power and significance of sin. To Barth Hick would appear naive. The natural,
human tendencies can be fooled. Hick is aware of this and
attempts to corroborate his beliefs from other religions, etc.
Barth employs the Word as his authority, and while Hick would

criticize this "ptolemaic" stance of Barth, Hick is also aware
that faith interpretations may differ radically over the same
experience. Hick accordingly has argued for eschatological
verification as an unambiguous confirmation of faith. This,
however, occurs at the eschaton whereas Barth perceives the
eschaton already in Christ.

Thus for Barth faith is self-authenticating and leaves no
room for doubt, and consequently Barth feels no need for extra-
theological investigations. He does not oppose nontheological
investigation per se, though he would undoubtedly disagree with
some of the conclusions Hick and others draw from these inquiries
and be disinclined toward their sources. For Hick faith and
doubt coexist, at least until faith has been verified. Hick
relies upon nontheological disciplines to aid in the verification
of faith. Faith per se is not dependent upon these investigations, but they are necessary to the verification of faith.

THE PLACE AND NATURE OF ESCHATOLOGICAL VERIFICATION

Hick is conscious that the logical positivists mounted a
considerable challenge to Christian faith by calling into question whether theological statements could be meaningful, whether
they contained factual or cognitive meanings, and whether they
were in principle verifiable or at least "probabilifiable."[28]
By these criteria many if not all theological statements appear
meaningless. Hick notes that theology alone does not suffer
from the application of such criteria, and then by way of
response to the logical positivists he goes on to argue that at
least the statement "God exists" is capable of verification.
Hick notes that the beatific vision has been used traditionally
to verify theism. But though it might seem to offer direct
evidence of the existence of God, for Hick it is difficult not
so much to believe in a beatific vision as to decide what it
means.[29] Therefore he moves on to indirect evidence and argues
that it is possible to conceive of a situation which points
unambiguously to the existence of God. Though Hick realizes
that the mere survival of the individual after life would not
constitute proof of theism,[30] Hick believes that the conjunction
of two developments would assure man beyond rational doubt of
the reality of God as conceived within Christianity.

These are, *first*, an experience of the fulfillment of God's
purpose for ourselves, as this has been disclosed in the
Christian revelation; in conjunction, *second*, with an
experience of communion with God as he has revealed himself
in the person of Christ.[31]

Though it might be argued that some in such a situation might
remain uncertain even if they were to experience such a situation, Hick contends that such a situation of eschatological
verification is like "being grown-up."[32] A child may

not know, concretely, what it is to be grown-up. But when
he reaches adulthood he is nevertheless able to know that he

has reached it; he is able to recognize the experience of
living a grown-up life even though he did not know in
advance just what to expect.[33]

Hick refers to this as eschatological verification,[34] because
such a situation can transpire only after life at the end or
goal of life.[35] Furthermore Hick contends that in such a situation we would become indirectly certain of God's infinite attributes since Jesus taught this and eschatological verification
would simultaneously validate the teaching of Christ. Hick is
careful to point out that eschatological verification does not
serve to confirm faith,[36] but rather it is offered in response
to the logical positivists to demonstrate that the statement
"God exists" is meaningful and verifiable. The theistic assertion upon which the system of Christian belief rests is, regard-
less of its truth or falsity, a genuinely factual assertion.[37]

Obviously eschatological verification was bound to attract
scholarly attention, and indeed it has. It entails implications
for our study both here in terms of the method of Hick and later
as to what transpires to the individual after life. Criticism
of eschatological verification has come from various sources.
We will cite that of Gregory Kavka first, who though critical
of Hick also endorses the concept, and subsequently Kai Nielsen
and Michael Tooley, who offer more negative evaluations.

In promoting the idea of eschatological verification Hick
has argued that the proposition that "there are three successive
sevens in the decimal determination of π"[38] can be verified
though not falsified.[39] To date this proposition has not been
verified, though the possibility for doing so will always be
conceivable. On the other hand the proposition is not in
principle falsifiable. Kavka sketches a postmortem world in
which the power lies at the disposal of Satan and his evil
cohorts. Here Christianity is even portrayed as "a cruel hoax
devised by Satan and that the historical Christ was an agent
sent by Satan to raise in good people false hopes of eternal
salvation."[40] Kavka proffers the possibility that Christians
might view this as a test of their faith. But to do that Kavka
suggests would entail a double standard since the principles
which allow for verification ought to apply as well for falsification.[41] Kavka also notes that Hick seemingly had allowed for
just this sort of eschatological falsification in the first
edition of *Faith and Knowledge*, which was published in 1957,
when he suggested that the obverse of the beatific vision would
refute belief in a loving God. This passage, however, does not
appear in the second edition of *Faith and Knowledge*, which was
published in 1966.[42] Kavka concludes noteworthily, nonetheless,
that the possibility of eschatological falsification actually
enhances eschatological verification since it is both verifiable
and falsifiable and thus becomes a meaningful proposition.[43]

In an article entitled "Eschatological Verification"
Nielsen suggests that Hick assumes the very thing he is seeking
to understand. Hick assumes that man is created by God with a

purpose. Without this assumption we would not know how or when
the purpose of God had been fulfilled. Hick thus depends upon
the premise for the realization of the conclusion.[44] Hick has
responded to Nielsen by noting that he is both right and wrong.
In order to explicate the truth-conditions which would be
required for the existence of God an exhaustive definition of
the divine nature would be required. Eschatological verification does not enable us to do this. But in disagreement with
Nielsen Hick states that eschatological verification was not
intended to accomplish this. Eschatological verification is
intended to demonstrate that the existence of God is factually
true or false. The Christian concept of deity involves eschatological expectations which will either be fulfilled or not.[45]
Furthermore Hick notes that Nielsen himself has emphasized that
it is possible to use a word correctly and yet be unable to
exhaustively present its meaning.[46] But for Hick it is when
our awareness of our environment corresponds to what we have
been led to expect upon the basis of Christian revelation that
one can speak of eschatological verification. It is possible to
sense what a certain situation will feel like though never to
date having had the experience. The fact that Hick acknowledges
that an awareness of God after life may be possible only for
those who have an awareness of aith in this life[47] would appear
to confirm our conjecture.

Michael Tooley has also commented upon the concept of
eschatological verification at some length, and he makes several
points which we wish to note. First since Hick acknowledges
that there are experiences which one can have in this life
which verify theological statements, why must eschatological
verification be proposed in the first place? Tooley writes
that eschatological verification only serves to complicate the
discussion with the introduction of additional philosophical
problems concerning the survival of an individual after life.
Tooley surmises that the real reason why Hick espoused the idea
of eschatological verification is to encourage people to consider the possibility that Christian theism is not only factually
meaningful but true. As Tooley writes: "it is reasonable to
accept Christianity on faith, since the crucial evidence is not
yet in."[48] This does seem to correspond to the expressed intent
of Hick. But whether it unnecessarily complicates things
depends upon one's adherence to the principles of logical
positivism. If these principles be rejected, then Tooley's
point stands, but if they are not rejected Hick provides an
apologetic response worthy of consideration.

Tooley also notes the difficulty in attributing infinite
attributes to God. While Hick points to Jesus Christ as serving
as indirect verification of the infinite attributes of God,[49]
Tooley cites nontheological contexts such as infinite inertial
mass to clarify that infinite attributes may be meaningful.[50]
Thus though he comes to the point by a different path (method,
after all, literally derives from the Greek ὁδοσ for path or
way), Tooley concurs with Hick that infinite attributes can be
meaningful, though he is challenging the method Hick advocates.

Tooley is also critical of Hick's indirect verification for infinite attributes because the argument is implicitly circular. The confirmation Hick seeks presupposes that the factual significance of theological statements has been independently established. Since this is lacking, the indirect verification of infinite attributes is impossible.[51]

Hick according to Tooley also makes the mistake of treating God as a theoretical entity when persons, including therefore God, cannot be treated as theoretical entities. God, like every person, has some properties that "are neither observable by others, even in principle, nor theoretically relative to such observable properties."[52] God therefore cannot be viewed as a theoretical entity since not all of his properties can be theoretical.[53] But Hick would likely respond by asking whether enough properties are observable to exclude rational doubt.

According to Tooley the only way to solve the dilemma posed by the logical positivists is to reject the verifiability principle as a criterion of factual meaning. Tooley suggests that the place to begin is in noticing that the verifiability principle would pose the same problem for persons as it does for God since both are experientially transcendent.

Note must also be taken of the fact that the two criteria which Hick proposed in 1960 for eschatological verification have a definitely Christian orientation, and this would prove contrary to the development by Hick of a global eschatology. Hick even quoted favorably Barth's contention that "Jesus Christ is the knowability of God"[54] to account for the belief that man will come to a religiously unambiguous state in which he experiences communion with God.

> The redeemed (whom I assume to include everyone--though this is of course a theological rather than a philosophical opinion) will have experienced in this world, or will have come to experience at some stage between this world and the final heavenly state, what they take to be an awareness of existing in the presence of God and of being freely led within the divine providence towards the fulfilment of their human potentialities in the community of mankind perfected. . . And this belief is, surely, progressively confirmed and then verified in the experience of moving towards and then participating in the eschatological situation of a perfected human community in which the consciousness of God's presence is universally shared.[55]

Hick believes that the theistic character of the universe will be verified eschatologically if not before. It is clear that the first criterion supplied by Hick in 1960 has been generalized to theism and continues to be valid. The second criterion of "communion with God" also remains valid though the qualification "as revealed in the person of Christ" would not be used with exclusive reference to Christ.

For his part Barth would be unsympathetic to Hick with regard to eschatological verification. For him it would be superfluous as it was originally stipulated in 1960, and the more general, nonChristian orientation of more recent years would be rejected because it fails to give appreciation to the centrality and uniqueness of Christ.

THE PLACE OF CHRIST AND CHRISTIANITY AND OTHER RELIGIONS

We thus come to another aspect of the theologies of Barth and Hick which requires comment, for it will illuminate another basic difference between the two, indeed perhaps the primary difference.

Through his writings Barth attempts to clarify the revealed Word of God. In this regard there is no change in Barth. Nonetheless the *Credo* and *Church Dogmatics* demonstrate a heightened concentration upon Christ as the focus and standard of his thought. Christ was prominent in the early Barth, while he became the key and essential focus of the later Barth. Barth advocates basing his anthropology, from which most of our discussion derives, on Christology, although it cannot be directly deduced from it. The sinful aspect of man prevents direct deduction, yet it in fact impels a Christological concentration for Barth in order to ascertain man's God-given nature.

John Hick moves in nearly the opposite direction as Barth. According to an autobiographical sketch it was while a law student at University College in Hull that he underwent a spiritual conversion and became a Christian of a strongly evangelical and even fundamentalistic character. He was actively associated with Inter-Varsity Fellowship.[56] A decade later one of the first articles Hick published was "a criticism of the Christology of D. M. Baillie for failing to express the full orthodox faith."[57] In his article on eschatological verification, which appeared in 1960, Hick again offers two specifically Christian criteria for eschatological verification. Hick, as was noted, even quotes Barth with favor at this time: "As Karl Barth expresses it, 'Jesus Christ is the knowability of God.'"[58] As Hick continued his study work on one problem has brought up another. Thus, though anticipating that *Faith and Knowledge* would be his sole major work, Hick found his horizons broadening. The question of theodicy in particular drew his concern, this resulting in his second major work *Evil and the God of Love*, a work in which he advocates belief in God's universal saving activity. Interestingly Hick has noted that his own response to the theodicy question enjoys "a long and respectable ancestry, going back through Schleiermacher ultimately to the earliest fathers of the church, particularly Irenaeus."[59] We cannot help but note that Barth would not consider Schleiermacher so respectable. Though Barth wrestled at length with Schleiermacher and accorded him respect, Barth nonetheless could never follow the path of Schleiermacher. After this point in his life Hick became more puzzled with the problem of reconciling the truth claims of the various world religions. His relocation to Birmingham precipitated contact with large Muslim, Sikh, Hindu, and Jewish communities, and he discovered that

> essentially the same kind of thing is taking place in them as in a Christian church--namely, human beings opening their minds to a higher divine Reality, known as personal and good and as demanding righteousness and love between man and man.[60]

Hick was drawn to the conclusion, in concert with Wilfred Cantwell Smith's *The Meaning and End of Religion* of 1962, that the religious life of mankind ought to be considered as "a continuum within which the faith-life of individuals is conditioned by one or other of the different streams of cumulative tradition."[61] For Hick this involved a Copernican revolution in religious thinking away from a Christianity- or Jesus-centered model to a God-centered model of the universe of faiths. As was noted in our review of *Death and Eternal Life* it also entailed distinguishing the central affirmations from their mythical associations. It was from this period that *Death and Eternal Life* evolved. Since then Hick has focused upon the Christological question and attempted to demonstrate that the idea of divine incarnation is better understood as poetic truth rather than metaphysical truth. The book *The Myth of God Incarnate*, which Hick edited, has resulted from this study. It is thus readily apparent that Hick is moving in a direction nearly opposite to that of Barth.

   Furthermore we note that Hick has schematized the attitude of Christians to the other world religions according to three phases, phases which are not unlike his own personal pilgrimage. The first phase, total rejection, is expressed in the dogma that nonChristians will be consigned to hell. The second phase, which Hick compares to the epicycles which were added to the old Ptolemaic conception of the universe, arose out of a growing awareness among Roman Catholics of the religious faith first of Protestants but then also the devout of the great nonChristian religions. It was pointed out that nonRoman Catholics may nevertheless metaphysically be Roman Catholics without knowledge of it. The analogy to transubstantiation is noted by Hick. The third phase, in evidence particularly since Vatican II, is characterized by even greater epicycles. In this phase non-Christians will be saved, but they will not be known as Christians. Accordingly Karl Rahner refers to anonymous Christianity while Hans Küng distinguishes between the ordinary way of salvation within the world religions and the extraordinary way of salvation within the Catholic Church.[62] Hick clearly would now advocate a fourth phase whereby all the great world faiths are able to bring men to the fulfillment for which they were created. The religions of the world all result from human response to the Eternal One,[63] but the varying cultural contexts in which they have developed have occasioned the diversity among the various religions. *Death and Eternal Life* exemplifies Hick's attempt to produce a global, universal response to the ultimate question of eschatology.

The perspective of Hick places him clearly at odds with Barth. Barth writes in *Church Dogmatics I/2* that "the Christian religion is true, because it has pleased God, who alone can be the judge in this matter, to affirm it to be the true religion."[64] This means that Christianity

> alone has the commission and the authority to be a missionary religion, i.e. to confront the world of religions as the one true religion, with absolute self-confidence to invite and challenge it to abandon its ways and to start on the Christian way.[65]

Hick refers to this as "sublime bigotry."[66] He would likely categorize Barth in his second or third phase, this because of the incipient universalism in Barth, but Barth's rejection of nonChristian religions would also give him affinities with Hick's phase one. While Hick acknowledges that it may be possible to grade certain religions as being better than others on the basis of their ability to improve moral behavior,[67] it is apparent that he would reject the attitude which characterizes Barth.

Also of note is the fact that though Barth would reject the position of Hick, Hick would understand Barth as ptolemaic, "simply" in need of a new perspective. Hick is not antithetical to Barth. Someone of another religious tradition who made absolute and exclusive claims for his tradition would be antithetical to Barth. Hick would rather seek the central affirmations which are not culturally relative but instead are inherent within the theology of Barth. Barth for his part, however, would likely react to Hick in inimical fashion.

What this particular section illustrates is the primary difference between Barth and Hick. Barth was Christocentric and, though at one point Hick was also inclined to that perspective, that clearly is no longer the case. While for Hick Christ continues to be revealing, for Barth Christ is *the* revelation of God.

THE PLACE OF GRACE

We also note between Barth and Hick a difference in their estimates of grace. From our study of Barth we have noted dialectic in his theology. Especially prominent in the early Barth is the relationship between yes and no, etc. where the negative is but the reverse and prelude of something positive. Though it is less prominent in the later Barth, our investigation leads us to believe that the later Barth still holds similar beliefs. Barth still perceives the No of God as strongly in the *Church Dogmatics*, but equally and even more powerful is the divine Yes which justifies. It is worthwhile to recall that the earlier Barth was writing in the context of exegetical commentaries in which similar themes recur frequently. The *Dogmatics* is more structured and systematic, evidencing few successive repetitions of theme, though that theme remains prevalent. Barth remains concerned to demonstrate the priority of grace, or, as G. C. Berkouwer expresses it, the triumph of grace.[68] Though Barth would have preferred "freedom" to "triumph" and "Christ" to "grace,"[69] nonetheless it is true that God's grace is so overwhelming that there remains little, if anything, for man to do save affirm it. Christ is free to effect what He wills. This priority or triumph of grace or Christ is an element, and likely the most significant element, of Barth's style.

In Hick there is much less emphasis upon grace, and in time Hick has moved from any particular focus upon Christ and/or Christianity to God, the "Eternal One" as Hick prefers to refer to him, and religion in general, again opposite in direction from Barth. Hick emphasizes that humans should grow and develop, maturing through various lives. One might note in Hick a new sort of law which suggests that man must earn and/or merit his salvation. Barth clearly would oppose any such reinstitution of the law. We also note that other than creating the environment for this structure for growth, and perhaps in that sense exemplifying grace, God is removed from humanity. In fact we cannot help but wonder how far removed Hick's God is from the deist conception of God, the belief in a God or First Cause who created the world and instituted immutable and universal laws that preclude any alteration as well as divine immanence. The same principles guide the universe now as when it was created. Hick affirms that he is a theist of the Irenaean persuasion, though we believe it would be accurate to describe Hick as a deist since God appears as Creator but is little involved in the current course of events within the world. Hick, for example, makes no reference to the Spirit or a parallel religious phenomenon aiding and guiding man, this due largely to the accent he places upon the initiative of man itself. Nor does Hick speak of prayer. While we recognize that deism is a particular form of theism, it is quite a special form which clearly separates Hick from Barth and the western tradition of Christendom, a fact which Hick himself recognizes. But Irenaeus, whom Hick claims to follow, was hardly a deist, a fact which removes Hick even further from Barth and the western tradition of Christianity. Since this deistic element in Hick impels him in certain directions and toward corresponding conclusions and repels him from others,[70] it must be considered as an aspect of his method.

Thus we note that while Barth places a special emphasis upon divine grace Hick is much more reserved and in a sense antithetical in this regard, this being a result of the emphasis Hick places upon the natural predispositions of man.

THE ROLES OF HICK AND BARTH

The differences regarding the methods of Barth and Hick are apparent. The two men are quite distinct. Though we have noted some similarity between them, that similarity dates more from the beginning of Hick's writings. Yet already at that time there was a grand distinction between them, a distinction based in the role or function each was playing.

Barth was first and foremost a Church theologian; his teachings were directed to the edification of the Christian faith and the Church. In his later work Barth focuses more upon Christ, and though this may tend to make his earlier work appear more oriented toward philosophy in general, especially since *The Epistle to the Romans* has an existential focus, that is a relative judgment. Barth remained a Christian theologian working within the Church his entire life.

Relative to Barth Hick is much less of a Christian theologian, and certainly not a Church theologian. Other than his evangelical, fundamentalistic stage, Hick has been concerned primarily with philosophical matters. Hick seeks the truth. Even disregarding his evangelistic stage, there appear to be two stages in the work of Hick. In the first stage Hick appears to be a Christian apologete. Indeed his investigation of nontheological realms has an apologetic function. Hick expresses it this way:

> It is not that the believer needs further confirmation of his faith, but that the philosopher--whether believer or not--wants to know what aspects of Christian belief bring that system of belief within the accepted criteria of factual meaningfulness.[71]

Hick is clearly trying to demonstrate that Christian belief can be related positively to the criteria established by philosophy for meaning. Christian belief is not a form of subjectivism but can meet the challenges directed at it by philosophy. Furthermore Hick is clear that faith requires no further verification, though he also points out that the possibility of future confirmation is not to be excluded.[72] Hick accordingly adduces arguments and examples from a plethora of realms in order to demonstrate that his understanding of the Christian faith would be consistent or at least not inconsistent with the findings of those realms.

In his later stage, which begins with his years at the University of Birmingham with its diverse, cultural exposures, Hick continues to function as an apologete, but he seeks to defend a global theology rather than Christianity per se. There is yet the plethora of realms cited by Hick, but the object of his defense has changed significantly.

This difference in roles has a profound influence upon the style and content of the works written by Hick and Barth. Hick cannot escape nontheological disciplines in his investigations. They are indeed mandated by his apologetic task. Barth on the other hand finds such investigations superfluous, and this indeed was the radical break Barth made round the issue of natural theology.

It is clear that Barth and Hick have entertained differing visions of their task throughout their respective careers, and this has undoubtedly influenced the divergence which we have

noted between them. The marked divergence which now marks
them is evident from the start. While Barth kept his gaze
fixed upon Christ, believing Him to be sufficient in and of
Himself, Hick in his former stage was concerned to relate Christ
to the world and vice versa. In his focus upon the world Hick
has attempted to make his faith appear rational and meaningful.
The Apostle Paul long ago wrote in 1 Corinthians 1:18: ο λόγοσ
γὰρ ο τοῦ σταυροῦ τοῖσ μὲν απολλυμένοισ μωρία εστίν, τοῖσ δὲ
σωζομένοισ ημῖν δύναμισ θεοῦ εστιν (For the word of the cross
is folly to those who are perishing, but to us who are being
saved it is the power of God). For Paul and Barth the contemporary stance of Hick might be understood as the result of
seeking wisdom according to the standards of the world. Furthermore it is noteworthy that the Christian theologian and apologete
Friedrich Schleiermacher receives the respect of Hick.[73] Barth
struggled long and hard with Schleiermacher and concluded that
Schleiermacher was responsible in good measure for the faulty
course followed by nineteenth-century theology, including its
Religionsgeschichtliche Schule (history of religions school),
with which Hick has affinities. This was rejected by Barth in
his writings from the start.

It thus seems clear that the roles adopted by both Barth
and Hick, though they did change somewhat over the years, are
responsible for the divergence which characterizes their work
today. Though Barth was from the era of *Romans* leery of reason,
he outrightly rejected reason and natural theology in the *Church
Dogmatics*, and accordingly made no attempt to establish corre-
lation between the Word and the world. Hick, though he affirms
the priority of faith in interpretation of reality, nonetheless
related faith to reality in order to verify faith. There is a
clear distinction between Barth and Hick, though one must not
overlook the priority of faith for both, though even faith bears
different content for both.

Critical Comments

Consistency of thought is commendable, even apart from the
conclusions which may be reached. The conclusions one reaches
should accord with the basic data which are presented. Optimum
consistency should be a goal in one's thought. As we now
introduce some critical comments upon the work of Hick and Barth
the issue of consistency will recur and play a significant role
in our evaluation. We will focus upon three areas of consistency in Hick--with regard to twentieth-century Christianity,
with regard to nonChristian religions, and with regard to himself before we reflect upon consistency in the work of Barth.

HICK'S CONSISTENCY WITHIN TWENTIETH-CENTURY CHRISTIANITY

Hick acknowledges that one's faith will influence the
interpretation which is given to the information he encounters.
It is to be regretted, however, that in his survey of the work
of several twentieth-century theologians this seems evident in
Hick himself. His own views color the interpretation and

evaluation he accords others. As was noted previously Hick
feels that with the empirical orientation of society today there
is the inclination to accept as true only that which is self-
experienced or empirically verified by authorities. Since the
after-life falls outside this sphere it is dismissed as a
fantasy. Christian theology, confronted by this cultural
rejection, has according to Hick evidenced a spectrum of disarray
since World War II with regard to after-life. Hick illustrates
this with brief studies of six contemporary theologians, three
of which--Tillich, Moltmann, and Pannenberg--we must examine for
ourselves.

Hick notes divergent trends of thought in the theology of
Tillich, and he derives varying implications from these trends.
Yet instead of attempting to synthesize these divergent trends
in some systematic manner or indicating which of these trends
would seem most logically consistent given an overall view of
Tillich's thought, Hick simply drops Tillich from further consideration.

Hick's treatment of Moltmann merits two comments. First
Hick judges Moltmann's use of uncriticized Biblical imagery
paradoxical, "renunciation of the theologian's responsibility."[74]
Hick believes that it is the theologian's task and responsibility
to penetrate toward the central affirmations concerning reality,
and hence he desires to be rid of the mythical expressions
which garb those affirmations. Whereas Hick implies that basic
agreement exists as to these central affirmations, such a statement is itself as paradoxical as Hick imagines Moltmann's
method to be. Anyone familiar with theology in recent decades
knows that there is considerable debate as to what these central
affirmations are and the extent to which they are clothed in
mythic expressions. Hick is less than responsible in implying
that agreement regarding the central affirmations exists, especially since it is disagreement in this regard which serves as
the basis of the difference between Hick and Moltmann, and
Barth could also be mentioned. A second comment concerning
Hick's treatment of Moltmann is the perplexing and disappointing
lack of any reference to Moltmann's *The Crucified God*, which was
published in 1973. In this work Moltmann places emphasis upon
the uniqueness of Christ and the trinitarian event.[75] Such an
emphasis upon the uniqueness of Christ runs counter to Hick's
personal belief that the great religions do not differ in regard
to their central affirmations. Thus when Moltmann stresses the
uniqueness of Christ Hick is disinclined to agree since he views
such claims as ptolemaic. It appears that Hick's own faith has
affected his evaluation of Moltmann and occasioned an oversight
and/or misrepresentation.

The appraisal which Hick offers of Wolfhart Pannenberg is
also characterized by misrepresentation in three areas. First
Hick suggests that Pannenberg exemplifies the recapitulation
theory of after-life. He bases this upon the concept of eternity
which Pannenberg offers when he writes that eternity is the unity
of all time where past, present, and future are simultaneous.

The fact is that for Pannenberg eternity is beyond time, and thus it is beyond human experience of temporality. It entails more than a mere recapitulation of time, which Hick fails to appreciate.[76] Second Hick lacks empathy for Pannenberg's rejection of the belief in the immortality of the soul. Pannenberg does not believe that there is an immortal aspect of man which survives death in some form of continuing existence, and he feels that belief in the immortality of the soul is scientifically impossible. As a result of this Pannenberg believes that the idea of resurrection after an intermediate state is scientifically more reasonable and credible.[77] Hick notes in another section that the belief in resurrection readily accommodates itself to the view of psychosomatic unity, but Hick oddly omits that Pannenberg exemplifies this.[78] Because Hick has failed again to empathize and get inside the system of another theologian, he cannot appreciate the scientific rationale of this position and therefore fails to give an accurate portrayal of Pannenberg. He thereby misses opportunity to illuminate and support his own position by means of contrast with another. Furthermore Pannenberg does not advocate the resuscitation of corpses as Hick suggests he does. Rather Pannenberg speaks of the resurrection of spiritual bodies, an idea which Hick might have employed in support of his own position.[79] The *Weltoffenheit* or openness to the world in contrast to *Ichbezogenheit* or self-centeredness of man which Pannenberg advocates might also be used sympathetically by Hick to enhance his view of what is wrong with man and what will be righted in the future.[80]

We must conclude that Hick has failed to justify his claim that theology since World War II evidences disarray with regard to after-life. Hick's interpretation may demonstrate that conclusion, and we would agree that there exists an array of interpretations though *dis*array is a pejorative exaggeration. Hick in his conclusion is not consistent to the examples he cites. We cannot follow his interpretation until he at least offers a more empathic evaluation of the theologians cited.

HICK'S CONSISTENCY REGARDING NONCHRISTIAN RELIGIONS

The failure of Hick to interpret accurately the Christian theologians we have just cited poses an even more disturbing problem for our study. Since Hick has been shown to be deficient in his interpretation of Christian theology in recent years, we cannot help but be suspect of the interpretation(s) he offers of other religions. If Hick has not accurately analyzed theologians of the religious tradition in which he himself was raised and from which he undertook his inquiry in *Death and Eternal Life*, then this certainly does not bode well for his analysis of traditions different than that in which he was reared. His exposition of other religions must be questioned lest in such interpretation he has been influenced by his own personal views. Julius Lipner and Duncan Forrester have in fact both commented along this line.

In an article entitled "Truth-Claims and Inter-Religious Dialogue" Lipner characterizes Hick as one of the chief exponents of reduction-dialogue, which Lipner describes in the following terms:

> Broadly speaking, and allowing for different variations on the same theme, the reduction dialogist tends to reduce conflicting religious-claims by a process of what he calls 'demythologizing', i.e. emptying the otherwise irreducible facticity of such beliefs, of literal content, and supplanting them with unitive insights which have only 'mythologically' or 'poetically' been expressed by these overtly factual statements.[81]

While Lipner feels that such reductionism can be done in very many cases, he doubts that it can be "regarded as a general rule for interpreting ostensibly fact-assertive (and ancillary) claims in religion."[82] In *Faith and Knowledge* Hick clearly expresses his disenchantment with faith as propositional belief, eventually coming to advocate something similar to Cardinal Newman's illative sense. Lipner, Hick would contend, is still viewing faith propositionally, while Lipner would contend that Hick intends to remove too much which is propositional and vital. Indeed Hick's principal complaint with the illative sense as Newman proposed it was that Newman continued to view faith propositionally. Lipner is contending that Hick has gone too far, because religious faith will invariably entail propositions which are ostensibly fact-assertive. It is impossible to remove all statements of fact from religious faith without succumbing to an amorphous relativism which could little be distinguished from solipsism. Hick obviously wishes to avoid such a conclusion, but he has not supplied the means to preclude it. Furthermore the possible pareschatology and eschatology which Hick advocates in *Death and Eternal Life* certainly entail propositions which will be demonstrated as true or false in time. It is apparent that Hick has not sufficiently clarified how faith is related to statements concerning after-life, especially since he himself describes this future using propositions which will be eschatologically verifiable.

In addition Forrester "wonders whether perhaps he (Hick) has not capitulated to a relativism which is unlikely to be acceptable to committed believers except for Vedantic Hindus."[83] When Hick argues that the varying religious traditions have "mistakenly developed dogmatic definitions of the divine on the assumption that their own partial experience of it is complete and adequate,"[84] which Hick views as parallel to the parable of the elephant and the blind men,[85] we must question whether other religious traditions could agree with Hick. We very much doubt it. In fact Forrester questions whether Hick has not introduced us to the Unknown God of the Apostle Paul who will ultimately remain unrevealed or else whether Hick has not produced a God without attributes.[86]

Serious questions bearing upon both the accuracy and
consistency of Hick's treatment of nonChristian religions are
thus apparent.

HICK'S CONSISTENCY WITH HIMSELF

Besides the problem of detailing in a consistent manner
the relationship between faith and propositions concerning
after-life, which we have just noted, there are additional
questions which we wish to raise concerning the internal consistency of Hick in his various writings.

First we note that Forrester challenges the manner in
which Hick defines religion:

> An understanding of the universe, together with an appropri-
> ate way of living within it, which involves reference beyond
> the natural order to God or gods or to the Absolute or to a
> transcendent order or process. Such a definition includes
> such theistic faiths as Judaism, Christianity, Islam,
> Sikhism; the theistic Hinduism of the Bhagavad Gita; the
> non-theistic faith of Mahayana Buddhism and non-theistic
> Hinduism. It does not, however, include purely naturalistic
> systems of belief, such as communism and humanism, immensely
> important though these are today as alternatives to reli-
> gious faith.[87]

Communism certainly entails religious beliefs, for communism
encourages individuals to give themselves over to and dedicate
themselves to the communist order. Communism, which publicly
proclaims atheism, in fact entails the worship and service of
man-made gods and is therefore not atheistic, i.e. without
god(s). Hick noted the slanted interpretation given by L. L.
Vasiliev to his investigation of a physical cause for telepathy,[88] yet he fails to note that Vasiliev's naturalistic
philosophy is really the religion of communism. Not only that,
this points up the problem that the religion of communism,
which controls the lives of hundreds of millions worldwide, is
basically absent from Hick's study. Furthermore we cannot help
but be disappointed at the paucity of reference to Islam in the
writings of Hick. It appears that Hick groups Islam with
western and semitic beliefs, but that is not explicitly
stated.[89] At a time when hundreds of millions are adherents of
this faith and at a time of its ascendency, the negligible
reference to Islam is to be lamented. A reduction dialogist
such as Hick should heed the faiths of communism and Islam if
he wants to maintain credibility in the formulation of a global,
non-ptolemaic theology. Forrester accordingly concludes that
Hick has produced "a map which, unlike that of Copernicus,
totally disregards known heavenly bodies."[90]

Forrester continues with a comment similar to that of
Lipner concerning the method followed by Hick:

This 'Copernican revolution' cannot but produce a truncated
version of Christian faith with at its centre a reinter-
preted Christ incapable of sustaining the faith, hope and
love of the believer. And there is surely reason to believe
that the recasting which Professor Hick's position would
involve for other faiths as well would be in no way more
acceptable to them.[91]

It appears that neither Christian nor nonChristian faiths may
be pleased with the results of the method followed by Hick.
Indeed it would be interesting to learn how a Hindu or Buddhist
would evaluate the positions espoused by Hick in Hick's global
eschatology of *Death and Eternal Life*. A particularly crucial
example of this would be the theistic belief which Hick advocates.
This would imply that ultimately non-theistic faiths will need
to adopt a theistic perspective if they wish to follow Hick's
global eschatology. Hick does not inform us, however, as to how
non-theists will be expected to become theists, or, as Hick
might express it, how individuals who experience the Eternal
One impersonally might come to experience him in personal terms.
Nontheists could just as easily expect theists to adopt their
understanding. This issue is certainly of no little significance, and Hick has not dealt sufficiently with this matter.

Forrester accordingly offers a positive alternative to
Hick, an alternative with which Barth as well as we ourselves
would find favor:

My suspicion is that Professor Hick's 'Copernican revolution' is just this sort of muddle, and that in the present
time of cultural and religious confusion we can receive
surer guidance from theologies which are at pains to check
and develop the Christian projection as accurately as
possible and lay it charitably and boldly alongside other
projections which also claim to guide man in his pilgrimage.[92]

Barth would want the Christian truth proclaimed in undiluted
fashion, and we would concur.

In *Death and Eternal Life* Hick cited with appreciation
the work of H. H. Price concerning the survival of disembodied
mind. Hick concluded that if there were no physical body
inhabiting a physical world after life, then the mind would
supply one. This gives rise to Hick's 'replica' theory, for
Hick believes it is necessary to be embodied in the resurrection
world(s). Yet in description of the ultimate state Hick writes
that when one reaches fulfillment embodiment will no longer be
necessary. One might also ask why mind would be necessary
since further growth is impossible. To follow the logic of
Hick at this point would certainly incline Hick toward the near
annihilation of the individual, though western eschatologies,
as Hick recognizes, are more inclined toward the idea of an
independent, immortal ego. While it may be true that embodiment
is no longer necessary, it is unclear as to how Hick can suggest
that disembodied existence in the ultimate state is conceivable.

Notably however our criticism of Hick does not mean that
the conclusions which Hick advocates regarding pareschatology
and eschatology are incorrect and/or invalid. Hick can suggest
whatever he wants as a *possible* pareschatology or a *possible*
eschatology, as indeed the fifth and final section of *Death and
Eternal Life* is entitled "A Possible Human Destiny" with "A
Possible Pareschatology" and "A Possible Eschatology" among its
divisions. We can only be disappointed that after all of his
investigations Hick can come to nothing more definite than a
possibility. Hick himself acknowledges that for the believer
"faith is not a probability but a certainty."[93] One would
expect that if Hick really hopes to have others adopt his beliefs
that he would be able to offer more than a mere possibility, or
even a probability. Relativism and subjectivism have triumphed
in the theology of Hick.

This prompts one final observation regarding the internal
consistency of Hick, and a contrast with Barth at this juncture
will be illuminating. Hick ultimately produces only a possible
pareschatology and a possible eschatoloyg. He does not contend
that he has given any *proof* of his positions. Hick speculates
quite freely upon his religious and scientific investigations.
For someone to follow Hick will therefore require not an insignificant leap of faith or, as Hick would state it, leave one
with considerable grounds for rational doubt. Since one of the
expressed goals of Hick is to produce a credible global eschatology, the more the speculation and leap become apparent in Hick,
the more incredible his thought will appear to modern man. In
contrast Barth acknowledges the necessity of faith in his
thought. Yet since the thought of Barth exhibits a focus, i.e.
Jesus Christ, which controls his thought, there is less speculation in the thought of Barth than one might anticipate, while
there is much more in Hick than he initially wants to exhibit.

THE CONSISTENCY OF BARTH

Previous to 1931 Barth published a number of works which
can be contrasted with his works of 1931 and thereafter. Hence
has been spawned the reference to an early and a late Barth.
Numerous individuals in their estimates of Barth make this
distinction. We must ask, therefore, whether Barth remains
consistent. Though we, too, note an *early* and a *late* Barth,
it is nevertheless an early and a late *Barth*. Though there are
differences in Barth for which the year 1931 serves as an
approximate division, we wish not to diminish the continuity
resident within Barth. Such a conclusion is consonant with the
findings of our research regarding death and after-life in Barth.
It is also a view championed by G. C. Berkouwer in his book
*The Triumph of Grace in the Theology of Karl Barth: An Intro-
duction and Critical Appraisal*. Berkouwer considers various
analyses of the theology of Barth before arriving at the following conclusion:

Barth's theology must *from its inception* be characterized as triumphant theology which aims to testify to the

overcoming power of grace. We do not find in it a transition from crisis to grace, or from disjunction between God
and man to fellowship between them, but rather a relationship between these polarities which Barth was concerned to
set forth in varying emphases and accents.[94]

This is hardly to deny that there are changes of position in
Barth, especially since Barth himself confirms this. As we have
noted above *The Epistle to the Romans* has an existential flavor.
This Barth removed from his writings after 1931.[95] Barth even
acknowledges that natural theology had been resident in his work
previous to 1931.[96] This, too, was removed. In terms of our
study, however, the most significant switch from the era previous to 1931 to that after 1931 concerns the manner in which
Barth understands time and eschatology. In *Romans* Barth had
interpreted time and eschatology tangentially. There were
moments of revelation, but these represented the transcendent
God breaking into time from above. God was essentially foreign
to time. In *The Epistle to the Romans* Barth "So emphasised the
timeless and transcendent character of revelation that it had
no place for a conception of creaturely being and time as con-
stitutive of the incarnation."[97] We noted a shift in *The Resurrection of the Dead* toward a future eschatology. This shift is
completed by Barth in the *Church Dogmatics*. There Barth himself
criticizes his stance in *Romans* as being one-sided, though nonetheless necessary for the time. In the *Dogmatics* he notes that
the aspect of teleology was lacking from *Romans*. It was because
of this that Paul Tillich and Rudolph Bultmann believed at that
time that they could welcome Barth as one of themselves.[98]
Barth also affirms that it was the Word of God which exposed
the error of his emphasis, and this in a typical, dual fashion
for Barth. The written Word of God called for a teleological
understanding in addition to a transcendent one. Second Jesus
Christ, the incarnate Word, demonstrated God's involvement with
time in time, and not just divine involvement at tangential
moments. Here we note how Barth's heightened emphasis upon
Christ or, as Barth expresses it, his bringing Jesus Christ
"from the periphery of my thought into the centre"[99] effected
a shift in perspective. Nonetheless it was his exegesis of
scripture, the written Word, which promoted this change, and
it is the exegetical study of the Word which is characteristic
of Barth in both his early and late writings. This demonstrates
the continuity and consistency of Barth. We therefore believe
that Berkouwer is correct in exposing differences of emphasis in
the early and late Barth while holding that the basic theme
remains unchanged throughout.

There is nonetheless at least one area in which Barth
might be inconsistent--"the surprising interlude" in which Barth
speaks of death as separation of body and soul, a view inconsistent with both his previous and subsequent writings. The
inconsistency is particularly striking when it is recalled how
meticulous Barth is about clarifying his thoughts and, as we
have just noted, even clarifying changes of emphasis within his
thought. Nonetheless as we noted there are ways in which death

172 as separation of body and soul might be understood to be consistent with Barth's earlier and later works. We thus note it here as a possible inconsistency.

There is an additional area of possible inconsistency in Barth which we must also note. This revolves around conclusion(s) which Barth would espouse concerning the nature of after-life. We noted three different possibilities while also suggesting that Barth may have preferred another. We also noted that it would have been difficult for Barth to finish the fifth volume of the *Church Dogmatics*, which would have treated the doctrine of redemption. We do not know whether Barth could consistently have brought his ideas to a conclusion. Some have speculated that it would have been impossible for Barth to do so, though we have questioned that. Nonetheless we must thus speak of another possible inconsistency, though certainly it is not an actualized one.

A word of caution is appropriate at this juncture as well. The fact that we note but one inconsistency in Barth should not be misinterpreted to mean that Barth is above criticism. There are many who criticize and challenge Barth for his method and/or the conclusions he reaches. The topic of natural theology and the charge of Christomonism are but two prominent examples where much controversy and debate has surrounded the positions of Barth. We have noted that Hick would term Barth ptolemaic. This, however, does not detract from the consistency of Barth. His persistent rejection of natural theology and faithful stress upon the centrality of Jesus Christ in the *Church Dogmatics* evidence his consistency, though certainly not all would stand in agreement with Barth in these teachings.

A Personal Perspective

Though the comparison and contrast of Hick and Barth and the adjoining critical comments oriented around the issue of consistency indicate a great deal concerning our personal perspective and though it cannot be surprising at this juncture that we favor Barth in terms of method, we must nonetheless clarify and highlight some differences. We certainly do not believe that consistency is the sole issue by which to evaluate Hick and Barth, though that certainly is significant. In this section we will outline our own response to the methodological issues we have raised in regard to Hick and Barth and indicate our reason(s) for an alternative(s) when we feel that is mandated.

The primary issue we must clarify is the nature of faith. Both Hick and Barth noteworthily begin with faith as being primary. Although with Hick this is less apparent than with Barth, we have demonstrated that this is clearly the starting point for both men. Hick entertains the notion that faith is an interpretive principle which can be verified by removal of grounds for rational doubt. Barth, by contrast, though he too affirms that faith is primary, understands faith in more positive terms. Faith is what must be affirmed on the basis of the revelation of God. It needs no verification. This has been a consistent theme in the work of Barth since *The Epistle to the Romans* in which he already then disparages reason in favor of faith. Hick in his sympathetic estimation of the illative sense demonstrates a parallel to Barth, but we believe the affirmation of revelation from God is more trustworthy than apprehension of the divine by man.

In explication of our own perspective we must affirm that we hold the position of Barth to be the better alternative. Faith is much better expressed in affirmative terms rather than in terms of what cannot be doubted. The Cartesian method of doubt, with which Hick is related, may eventually doubt and deny everything on rational grounds. Indeed Descartes set out to do precisely that until he would reach something beyond doubt. Furthermore it is curious that in defense of the notion of eschatological verification Hick employed the concept of "being grown-up," a surprisingly ambiguous and relative phrase for one who demonstrates considerable precision and clarity in his writings. Being grown-up is for Hick self-authenticating; one must affirm it once it has happened, though we suspect that it would be possible to become more grown-up in time. Barth would contend that faith is similar to this notion of being grown-up, which ironically Hick himself no longer utilizes in more recent writings. In our own method we advocate affirming the positive, that which God has revealed to man through His Word. Though this leads us to interpret our experience of the world and the world itself after a particular manner, we believe faith entails more than an interpretive principle. There is a content to faith, which even Hick admits is eschatologically verifiable. Furthermore we have a deep appreciation for what Hick attempts to do, but we agree with Forrester that the preferred path is to develop the Christian understanding of death and after-life and then to set this in comparison with other projections of the subject. It may well be that the differences between the Christian projection and other projections are incapable of resolution, and we can live with this difference whereas Hick tries to camouflage or eliminate it. Furthermore we have a high regard for the apologetic function of relating faith to other disciplines. Because it must play a subordinate and ancillary role, we are not controlled by this apologetic task, though neither are we afraid to investigate it.

This leads naturally to a second point which concerns the relationship of faith and reality. Both Hick and Barth are sensitive to the accusation that theology is out of touch with reality. Hick expends a great deal of effort in countering this precise charge by ascertaining the nature of reality as it is clarified by nontheological disciplines. He argues that faith and reality are not contradictory but rather complementary, the one enhancing the other. This indeed is his apologetic task.

We also recognize that it was his role as an apologetic theologian which gave rise to Hick's idea of eschatological

verification. When it is borne in mind that eschatological
verification is intended as a response to the logical positivists in order to demonstrate that the statement "God exists"
is meaningful, then it appears that Hick has met a notable
challenge. If one were to suggest that "life exists on the
planet Mars" there would be criteria to ascertain the truth of
that statement. Someday it may be verified, though falsification will be difficult. Time will tell. Hick has given the
criteria which would verify theistic belief. We believe that
even as men came to perceive in Jesus the revelation of God, so
they could in an eschatological situation verify theistic
belief. The criteria set down by Hick should be sufficient to
serve for verification.

        Nonetheless we agree with Tooley and even with Hick him-
self that eschatological verification is unnecessary to the
faith-full, and it is doubtful whether it will exercise a
positive, faith-instilling impact upon logical positivists and
others who might lack religious faith.

        What Hick actually may have indirectly demonstrated is
the inappropriateness of applying logical positivist criteria
universally. It is impossible to suggest the criteria which
would verify a statement as simply as "John loves Mary."
Certainly not everyone would concur on those criteria, nor
could all proposed criteria be universalized or applied generally. If logical positivists and philosophers are not pleased
with the response Hick offers for verifying theistic belief,
then it likely points to the inappropriateness of logical
positivism in all realms. It should not be universalized.

        Barth is also sensitive to the issue of the relationship
between faith and reality, but his response is to bring man into
touch with *Reality*, with the God and Father of Jesus Christ.
Barth would contend that since reality is out of concert with
Reality that it is his function as a theologian to clarify
Reality in Its relationship to reality. Barth focuses primarily
upon God as the Real and only secondarily upon reality, which
ultimately has its basis in Reality. This accounts for why
covenant, for example, is viewed as the internal basis of creation and creation the external basis of covenant.

        The relationship of faith and reality which we advocate
is again similar to that of Barth. By his own admission Barth
in his early writings allowed for natural theology, though its
use was already severely curtailed. Later Barth realized that
theology must be based solely in and upon the revealed Word of
God and that that Word was self-authenticating. Because of the
historic abuses and misuses of natural theology and especially
because it could add nothing to God's revelation and might in
fact detract from it, Barth shunned the use of natural theology.
He made no allowances for *praeambula fidei* (portals of faith).
Faith based upon the revealed Word of God was His sole focus.
The alternative which Hick offers finds revelation everywhere.
Most notably in contrast to Barth, for Hick revelation can be

uncovered in other religious traditions. We ourselves find
Christ, the incarnate Word, to be unique. He has a unique task
and function within God's covenant relationship with man, as we
will note subsequently, and we must therefore disparage Hick in
his denial of this uniqueness.

We would nonetheless not wish to be construed as either
advocating any sort of gnosticism or docetism. God revealed
Himself to man in space and in time through Jesus Christ. The
Word was revealed in four dimensions. God uses space and time
as the dimensions of covenant relationship with man. Jesus
Christ is not an ethereal knowledge, i.e. a form of gnosticism,
nor was Jesus a phantom, i.e. a form of docetism. For Barth
this prohibits examination of the world or reality a-theistically, i.e. literally without God.

This seemingly however would leave open the possibility
that man may discover God outside His revelation in the world
and its reality. We believe that that is a possibility, but
it is a possibility which must be corroborated against the
revelation of God in Jesus Christ. Jesus Christ remains the
normative though not exclusive source of revelation. Supposed
revelation in other realms of space and time must be checked
against the reality of God's revelation in the Word. In other
words the Word remains the ultimate standard of revelation.

If we have a criticism of Barth at this point it comes
more as a regret than as a criticism. Barth held the revelation
of God so high, he focused on it so exclusively, that he
neglected to clarify at length from other disciplines such as
psychology, biology, physics, etc. how those disciplines have
misinterpreted the facts which they have brought to light concerning man. To suggest that facts were being accorded
a-theistic interpretations is one thing; to offer the same
facts a theistic interpretation quite another--and one which
we would like to have been granted. This would aid in clarifying
the relationship of faith and reality. It would also tend to
negate the accusation that theology is out of touch with reality,
a charge which has not infrequently been leveled at Barth,
especially for his disparagement of natural theology. It is
apparent, therefore, that we have sympathy for the apologetic
task which Hick sets for himself, and it is this which gives a
certain appeal to his work in our modern age. But we would first
determine what God in Christ has revealed before making any
attempt to relate it to other realms. Relating faith to other
realms of reality remains nonetheless a nonessential enterprise,
since faith can exist by itself. Nevertheless such an enterprise could be a beneficial one in a world which views and
interprets itself a-theistically and notes no relationship
between faith and reality. We shall make some cautious ventures
of this sort in a subsequent personal perspective, though we
reiterate that this is a nonessential endeavor as far as our
faith is concerned. We view it is *postlegomena* rather than
prolegomena.

Footnotes

[1]Robert Crawford, "The Theological Method of Karl Barth," *Scottish Journal of Theology* 25 (1972):323.

[2]Ibid., p. 325.

[3]Karl Barth, *The Resurrection of the Dead*, trans. H. J. Stenning (New York: Fleming H. Revell Company, 1933; Arno Books reprint 1976), p. 16.

[4]John Hick, *Faith and Knowledge*, 2d ed. (Glasgow: Collins, Fontana Books, 1966, 1974), p. 104.

[5]Ibid.

[6]John Hick, "The Theology of Religious Pluralism," *Theology* Vol. 86, No. 713 (September, 1983):335. The actual parable of the blind men and the elephant relates that each of the blind men touches a different part of the animal with the one who feels a leg mistakenly identifying the elephant as a tree, the one who feels the trunk identifying it as a snake, and so forth.

[7]John Hick, *God Has Many Names* (Philadelphia: Westminster Press, 1980, 1982), p. 18.

[8]Hick, "The Theology of Religious Pluralism," p. 337.

[9]Hick, *God Has Many Names*, p. 84.

[10]Karl Barth, *The Epistle to the Romans*, 6th ed., trans. Edwyn C. Hoskyns (New York: Oxford University Press, 1933; 1976 reprint), p. 144.

[11]Ibid., p. 143.

[12]Barth, *Resurrection*, pp. 139-140.

[13]Ibid., pp. 138-139.

[14]Karl Barth, *Credo*, trans. Robert McAfee Brown (New York: Charles Scribner's Sons, 1962), p. 171.

[15]Karl Barth, *Church Dogmatics II/1*, trans. T. H. Parker, W. B. Johnston, Harold Knight, J. L. M. Haire (Edinburgh: T. & T. Clark, 1957), p. 150.

[16]Karl Barth, *Church Dogmatics III/2*, trans. Harold Knight, G. W. Bromiley, J. K. S. Reid, and R. H. Fuller (Edinburgh: T. & T. Clark, 1960), p. 432.

[17]Hick, *Faith*, p. 52.   [18]Ibid., p. 62.

[19]Ibid., p. 91.   [20]Ibid., p. 97.

[21]Ibid., p. 115.   [22]Ibid.

[23]Ibid.

[24]Hick, *Faith*, pp. 164-165 and John H. Hick, *Philosophy of Religion*, 2d ed. (Englewood Cliffs: Prentice-Hall, Inc., 1973), p. 86. John Wisdom seems to be original author of this parable. The article in which it appears, entitled "Gods", was first published in 1944 in *Proceedings of the Aristotelian Society*. Since there is another variation of this parable by Anthony Flew which points to God's death of a thousand qualifications and since some may already be familiar with it according to this later version of Flew, we will quote it as Hick uses it:

Two people return to their long-neglected garden and find among the weeds a few of the old plants surprisingly vigorous. One says to the other "It must be that a gardener has been coming and doing something about these plants." Upon inquiry they find that no neighbor has ever seen anyone at work in their garden. The first man says to the other, "He must have worked while people slept." The other says, "No, someone would have heard him and besides, anybody who cared about the plants would have kept down these weeds." The first man says, "Look at the way these are arranged. There is purpose and a feeling of beauty here. I believe that someone comes, someone invisible to mortal eyes. I believe that the more carefully we look the more we shall find confirmation of this." They examine the garden ever so carefully and sometimes they come on new things suggesting that a gardener comes and sometimes they come on new things suggesting the contrary and even that a malicious person has been at work. Besides examining the garden carefully they also study what happens to gardens left without attention. Consequently, when after all this, one says "I still believe a gardener comes" while the other says "I don't" their different words now reflect no difference as to what they have found in the garden, no difference as to what they would find in the garden if they looked further and no difference about how fast untended gardens fall into disorder. At this stage, in this context, the gardener hypothesis has ceased to be experimental, the difference between one who accepts and one who rejects it is now a matter of the one expecting something the other does not expect. What is the difference between them? The one says, "A gardener comes unseen and unheard. He is manifested only in his works with which we are all familiar," the other says "There is no gardener" and with this difference in what they say about the gardener goes a difference in how they feel toward the garden, in spite of the fact that neither expects anything of it which the other does not expect.

[25]The parable appears in the article "Theology and Verification" by John Hick in *Theology Today* 17 (April, 1960-January, 1961):18-19 and *Faith and Knowledge*, pp. 177-178. It reads:

Two men are traveling together along a road. One of them believes that it leads to a Celestial City, the other that it leads nowhere; but since this is the only road there is both must travel it. Neither has been this way before, and therefore neither is able to say what they will find around each next corner. During their journey they meet both with moments of refreshment and delight, and with moments of hardship and danger. All the time one of them thinks of his journey as a pilgrimage to the Celestial City and inter- prets the pleasant parts as encouragements and the obstacles as trials of his purpose and lessons in endurance, prepared by the king of that city and designed to make of him a worthy citizen of the place when at last he arrives there. The other, however, believes none of this and sees their journey as an unavoidable and aimless ramble. Since he has no choice in the matter, he enjoys the good and endures the bad. But for him there is no Celestial City to be reached, no all-encompassing purpose ordaining their journey--only the road itself and the luck of the road in good weather and in bad.

During the course of the journey the issue between them is not an experimental one. They do not entertain different expectations about the coming details of the road, but only about its ultimate destination. And yet when they do turn the last corner it will be apparent that one of them has been right all the time and the other wrong. Thus, although the issue between them has not been experimental, it has nevertheless from the start been a real issue. They have not merely felt differently about the road; for one was feeling appropriately and the other inappropriately in relation to the actual state of affairs. Their opposed interpretations of the road constituted genuinely rival assertions, though assertions whose status has the peculiar characteristic of being guaranteed retrospectively by a future crux.

[26]Hick, *Faith*, p. 215.   [27]Ibid., p. 91.

[28]Hick, *Philosophy of Religion*, p. 85.

[29]Hick, *Faith*, p. 187 and "Theology and Verification," p. 25.

[30]Hick, "Theology and Verification," pp. 25-26.

[31]Ibid., pp. 26-27 and Hick, *Faith*, p. 187.

[32]Hick, "Theology and Verification," p. 27.

[33]Ibid.

[34]Hick, *Philosophy of Religion*, p. 91.

[35]Ibid., p. 90.   [36]Hick, *Faith*, p. 194.

[37]Ibid., p. 195.

178

[38]Hick, *Philosophy of Religion*, p. 90.

[39]Ibid. and Robert Audi, "Eschatological Verification and Personal Identity," *International Journal for the Philosophy of Religion* 7(1976):392.

[40]Gregory S. Kavka, "Eschatological Falsification," *Religious Studies* 12(1976):202.

[41]Ibid., p. 203. [42]Ibid.

[43]Ibid., p. 204.

[44]Kai Nielsen, "Eschatological Verification," *Canadian Journal of Theology* 9(1963):276.

[45]Hick, *Faith*, p. 197. [46]Ibid., p. 198.

[47]Hick, "Theology and Verification," p. 30.

[48]Michael Tooley, "John Hick and the Concept of Eschatological Verification," *Religious Studies* 12(1976):183.

[49]Hick, "Theology and Verification," p. 29.

[50]Tooley, "Eschatological Verification," pp. 185-186.

[51]Ibid., p. 198. [52]Ibid., p. 197.

[53]Ibid.

[54]Hick, "Theology and Verification," p. 29.

[55]John Hick, "Eschatological Verification Reconsidered," *Religious Studies* 13(1977):197.

[56]Hick, *God Has Many Names*, p. 14.

[57]Ibid., p. 15.

[58]Hick, "Theology and Verification," p. 29.

[59]Hick, *God Has Many Names*, p. 17.

[60]Ibid., p. 18. [61]Ibid.

[62]Ibid., pp. 29-34 and John Hick, "Learning from Other Faiths," *The Expository Times* 84(1972-1973):36-38.

[63]Hick, *God Has Many Names*, p. 22.

[64]Karl Barth, *Church Dogmatics I/2*, trans. G. T. Thomson and Harold Knight (Edinburgh: T. & T. Clark, 1956), p. 350.

[65]Ibid., p. 357.

[66]Hick, *God Has Many Names*, p. 90.

[67]John Hick, "On Grading Religions," *Religious Studies* 17(1981):461-463.

[68]G. C. Berkouwer, *The Triumph of Grace in the Theology of Karl Barth: An Introduction and Critical Appraisal*, trans. Harry R. Boer (Grand Rapids: Eerdmans Publishing Co., 1956), pp. 9-19.

[69]Eberhard Busch, *Karl Barth: His Life from Letters and Autobiographical Texts*, 2d ed., trans. John Bowden (London: SCM Press, Ltd., 1976), p. 381.

[70]Hick's article "Jesus and the World Religions" in John Hick, ed., *The Myth of God Incarnate* (London: SCM Press, 1977) might seem to suggest that Hick envisions God's involvement with the Hebrew prophets, Buddha, Jesus, Mohammed, and in the individuals responsible for the *Upanishads* and the *Bhagavad Gita* (cf. p. 181), but these again seem to be instances of an individual's or group's coming in touch with God and/or his Logos, which has remained the same since creation.

[71]Hick, *Faith*, p. 194.   [72]Ibid., p. 196.

[73]Hick, *God Has Many Names*, p. 17.

[74]John Hick, *Death and Eternal Life* (London: William Collins Sons & Co. Ltd., 1976), p. 215.

[75]Jürgen Moltmann, *The Crucified God: The Cross of Christ as the Foundation and Criticism of Christian Theology*, trans. R. A. Wilson and John Bowden (London: SCM Press, Ltd., 1974), pp. 65, 178-187, 235-249.

[76]Wolfhart Pannenberg, *What Is Man? Contemporary Anthropology in Theological Perspective*, trans. Duane A. Priebe (Philadelphia: Fortress Press, 1970), p. 74.

[77]Ibid., pp. 45-53, Wolfhart Pannenberg, *The Apostles' Creed in the Light of Today's Questions*, trans. Margaret Kohl (Philadelphia: Westminster Press, 1972), p. 106, and Wolfhart Pannenberg, *Faith and Reality*, trans. John Maxwell (Philadelphia: Westminster Press, 1977), p. 76.

[78]Hick, *Death*, pp. 278, 221-227.

[79]Wolfhart Pannenberg, *Jesus--God and Man*, trans. Lewis L. Wilkins and Duane A. Priebe (Philadelphia: Westminster Press, 1968), pp. 75-77.

[80]Pannenberg, *What Is Man?*, pp. 3-13 and Pannenberg, *Jesus*, p. 193.

[81]Julius Lipner, "Truth-Claims and Inter-Religious Dialogue," *Religious Studies* 12(1976):227.

[82]Ibid.

[83]Duncan B. Forrester, "Professor Hick and the Universe of Faiths," *Scottish Journal of Theology* 29(1976):69.

[84]Hick, "Theology of Religious Pluralism," p. 335.

[85]Ibid.

[86]Forrester, "Professor Hick and the Universe of Faiths," p. 69.

[87]Ibid., p. 70.

[88]Hick, *Death*, p. 128.   [89]Ibid., p. 28.

[90]Forrester, "Professor Hick and the Universe of Faiths," p. 70.

[91]Ibid., p. 72.   [92]Ibid., p. 71.

[93]Hick, *Faith*, p. 52.

[94]Berkouwer, *Triumph of Grace*, p. 37.

[95]Busch, *Barth*, pp. 196 and 211.

[96]Ibid., p. 211.

[97]Dan L. Deegan, "The Christological Determinant in Barth's Doctrine of Creation," *Scottish Journal of Theology* 14 (1961):119.

[98]Barth, *Church Dogmatics II/1*, p. 635.

[99]Busch, *Barth*, p. 173.

The Cause and Significance of Death

INTRODUCTION

Traditionally theology has taught that God created man without sin and placed him in the Garden of Eden where Adam sinned and incurred the divine wrath, including punishment for his sin. Orthodox theology within the Roman Catholic, Lutheran, and Reformed branches of Christendom has posited a direct, causal relationship between sin and death. Neither Hick nor Barth adheres to this line of interpretation which understands death as an accursed and negative phenomenon, something unnatural to the created order.

THE CAUSE AND SIGNIFICANCE OF DEATH IN HICK

In his book *Evil and the God of Love* Hick insists that "Only a drastic compartmentalization of the mind could enable one to believe today in a literal historical fall from a paradisal state. . ."[1] There never was a pre- or un-fallen state, no matter how remote, according to Hick. None of the evidence would suggest that there has ever been a time when mortality has been unnatural to man.[2] Since there has never been a time when death was not part and parcel of human experience, then we must conclude that for Hick death is natural and always has been.

Whether for Hick death is a negative phenomenon is another though related issue, for though death is natural it might still be perceived as a curse. Yet it is certain that even if death were a tragedy for man, for Hick it would not be a curse in the traditional understanding of orthodox Christianity. It would be very difficult for Hick to refer to death as entailing a divine curse since Buddhism, a religion which Hick utilizes in developing his global eschatology, admits of no personal divinity, i.e. no god or *theos*, as conceived in the West. Even granting this qualification, however, and recognizing that Hick is a theist of the Irenaean persuasion, death for Hick is certainly not negative. In fact death for Hick is both positive and negative. Death represents the conclusion of life on one level and initiates a transition to life on another level, which for Hick should be a higher, more advanced level since this is the first level. Hick finds it difficult to conceive of a lower level(s) though higher levels are discussed. In fact for Hick the negative side of death is death's curtailment, for however briefly, of one's progress toward fulfillment.

THE CAUSE AND SIGNIFICANCE OF DEATH IN BARTH

With Barth the cause and significance of death are more complicated than with Hick. Death is both radically positive and radically negative.

In *The Epistle to the Romans* Barth, like Hick, argues that there never was a pristine era of human history in a Garden of

Eden. Though Barth speaks of man's dwelling in the Garden of
Eden in *The Epistle to the Romans* he indicates that this "time"
was not historical. "Primordial and non-historical" are the
words which Barth uses in description. Time as man knows it
is time in separation from God, and similarly this time will
end when man becomes reunited with God. Death for Barth is
the reverse side of sin; there is a direct relationship between
the two. Thus death bears a negative significance. However
death is not wholly negative either. Death serves a positive
function in that it inhibits the apotheosis of man; it clarifies
who is God. Death serves a second positive function in its
serving as a necessary counterpart to the divine "Yes." God
rejects in order that He might exercise mercy. This is the
road of double predestination to which Barth refers in *Romans*.[3]
A third positive evaluation of death for Barth in *Romans* is
its compelling man naturally to encounter the final barrier,
its leading man to wonder what might be beyond life. Barth of
course believes that only revelation and faith can answer that
question, but of his nature man can place the issue before
himself. Barth speaks of death as a veritable and profound
barrier. It is like an impenetrable wall over which one cannot
climb.

Like *Romans*, *The Resurrection of the Dead* speaks of death
in both negative and positive terms. In concert with Paul
Barth views death as unnatural, the last enemy, "the peak of
all that is contrary to God."[4] Whereas the Corinthians were
adept at finding the eternal in the finite, the incorruptible
in the corruptible, etc., Paul emphasizes the discontinuity
inherent in death. The Kingdom of God is neither the continuation nor the fulfillment of this life, and therefore death was
a frontier for Paul. Furthermore as a result of their inadequate appreciation of sin, the Corinthians failed to recognize
the sting of sin in death. In general the overall estimation
which Barth offers of death in *The Resurrection of the Dead* is
more negative than in *Romans*. Nevertheless Barth does reiterate
that the recollection and contemplation of death has a positive
value in pointing to the resurrection which lies behind death.
Emphasizing as it does 1 Corinthians 15 *The Resurrection of the
Dead* seeks to point out the errors and misunderstandings in
Corinth. Those misunderstandings generally reflected too
positive and passive of an evaluation of death. In this context
Paul's generally negative evaluation of death as well as Barth's
more negative attitude may be better understood.

Barth continues to write in this same vein in the *Credo*
and makes two interrelated points. First he notes that those
who are in Christ yet "fall asleep," but this is not at all
natural but rather astonishing. Second Barth notes that most
of the New Testament miracles are signs directed against the
power of death.[5] In the *Credo* there is no positive evaluation
accorded to death.

It is in the *Church Dogmatics* that Barth offers his fullest consideration of the cause and significance of death. We

meet again with some of Barth's former thoughts concerning death, both in negative and positive evaluations, but there are new and more penetrating insights as well.

First we will note the negative appraisals Barth offers for death. In section 47 of the *Church Dogmatics* in which Barth discusses man in his time Barth as usual begins with a Christological focus in a section entitled "Jesus, Lord of Time." Barth had in *Volume III/1* indicated that the lost time of man is surrounded by grace, first in the time of creation and then in the time of Christ, though the time of Christ dominates all of time. Here Barth defends further his Christological focus and concludes that time is of the essence of man. In the subsequent section entitled "Man in His Time" Barth makes the astute and significant observation that though our anthropology must be based upon Christology, it cannot be deduced from it. This results from the fact that man experiences time differently than Jesus since time as man experiences it is characterized by sin. Man lives in contradiction to God and the nature with which God created him. Hence death as it actually encounters man is negative and evil. It is the sign of God's judgment. As he actually encounters death now man "can hope for nothing better than to be hewn down and cast into the fire."[6] Death is the reward man receives which is appropriate to life as it is actually lived. Furthermore Barth contends that man desires, even craves time. Human life seeks duration. Death threatens this human demand for duration and permanence. Man therefore protests against the limitation which death represents. Barth even suggests that a resigned acceptance of death is incompatible with the fact that life is created by God since it involves an acceptance of sin and its consequent punishment as though they were the original and authentic destiny of man. Barth notes that it is in the realm of the living that fellowship with God is possible. Since the dead exist in a state of weakness and utter helplessness they are unable to maintain fellowship with God. Hence the Old Testament uses terms such as the wilderness, Egypt and Babylon, the ocean and chaos in description of death. Death as man actually encounters it is the sign of divine judgment. It is a negative and evil phenomenon.

Nevertheless this is hardly all that Barth has to say on the matter, and it is when Barth describes the positive and natural aspects of death that he is most perceptive and novel. We note first as does Barth the life and death of Jesus Christ and their significance for our topic. Jesus lived in time and fulfilled it. Hence Barth refers to him as "Lord of time." Barth realizes therefore that time is not evil. In fact man must have time in order to establish covenant relationship with God. Time is a condition sine qua non for covenant. However for several reasons Barth is not convinced that unlimited time would benefit man. Primary in this is the realization that Jesus fulfilled time though his time had a beginning and an end. Man is right to seek a duration of time, but limitless duration is no guarantee of the determination and perfection for which

man aspires, a point with which Hick would not agree. Limitless
time according to Barth would only present limitless opportunities but could offer no guarantee of any fulfillment. In fact
unrestricted time might be used to portray hell since man as he
exists will never attain the goal for which he was intended.
Barth then suggests that God demonstrates His care for man by
allotting him only a span of time. Otherwise man would be
centrifugal and incapable of identity. Furthermore Barth notes
that fulfillment is to be found only in God, not in an infinite
extension of time. Death, by reminding man of this, serves a
positive function. And in a similar vein death prevents the
apotheosis of man and throws man back upon the grace of God.

It is readily apparent that Barth accords death both
negative and positive evaluations in the *Church Dogmatics*.
This might seem contradictory, but for Barth it is not. Barth
actually views death as a neutral, unaccursed phenomenon.
This is in fact the primary fashion in which Barth interprets
death. As God gave man a starting point in birth which is
positive, so He gives man an end in death, and unless one is
willing to curse all of life including birth Barth argues that
God must have intended good in death. Barth also notes that
God drove Adam and Eve from the Garden of Eden in order to
prevent their eating other forbidden fruit and thereby becoming
immortal, this an action which demonstrates God's continuing
care and concern for man. As man actually experiences death,
however, the primary significance is overshadowed by what Barth
terms the second death, the negative and accursed elements
which have come to be associated with death. The essential
cause of this is the sin of man. God never intended that man
should sin, though He did intend that man would die. It is in
the threat which God utters in Genesis 2:17, which is confirmed
in Genesis 3:19 and 6:3, that the interconnection of sin, guilt,
and death is directly stated. This is confirmed in the New
Testament when Paul writes that sin is the sting of death, but
it is most especially confirmed in the death of Jesus who was
made a curse and sin on behalf of man in order that man need no
longer experience this second death. Hence death can be
spoken of as natural, even as a "falling asleep."[7] "The end
of Jesus Christ has made our end simply the *sign* of God's
judgment."[8] We need no longer evaluate death as utterly negative and evil. It remains a sign of that reality, but it need
not be experienced as that reality any longer.

COMPARISON OF HICK AND BARTH

The interpretations of the cause and significance of death
which Hick and Barth offer are indeed quite distinct. Hick
views death as a natural phenomenon. The only negative significance which Hick attributes to death is its disruption of man's
progress. Otherwise death serves as a transition to another
realm, which accords with the way the world has evolved and/or
been created. Barth envisions death quite differently.
Because he is not attempting a universal eschatology, Barth
can say that death is a natural phenomenon, in accord with the

way God created it. Yet even as it was naturally intended, at
least as Barth conceives death, death points to the grace of
God. This will become clearer in our discussion of what transpires to the individual in death, to which we will turn shortly.

But first we want to focus attention upon the radical
distinction between Barth and Hick relative to sin. Hick is an
optimist as far as man and sin are concerned. He believes,
almost naively, that man will simply progress towards the
ultimate state. But this optimism hampers and disables Hick
from a profound appreciation or depreciation of sin. Regarding
Aushwitz, Belsen, and other concentration camps where six
million Jewish men, women, and children were exterminated
between 1942 and 1945, Hick comments: "It would have been
better--much much better--if they had never happened."[9] Barth's
evaluation, perhaps better expressed as his devaluation, of sin,
especially as it relates to the second death, is much more penetrating, prudent, and thoughtful. Barth recognizes the powers
and forces of evil which occasioned this death of Christ,
powers and forces which are awesome. Yet in Jesus Christ these
powers and forces have been and are overcome. That is the
message of Easter which enables Christians to refer to the
passion of Jesus as *Good* Friday. So though Barth is able to
speak in positive terms of death, it is done only because the
negative forces of death were overwhelmed by God in the death
of Jesus. Death has been naturalized through Christ so that
men may now "rest in peace."

A Personal Perspective

THE PROBLEM

Confronted as we are with scientific evidence that the
heavens, the earth, and all that fills them were not created
in six days and that death antedated the appearance of Adam upon
earth we are left with three alternatives. First we may bury
our heads in the sand like an ostrich and hope that things will
appear better the next time we look around. However to do this,
which we might term ostrich theology, is ill-advised since it
would signify that God is not involved with His creation, and it
would deny relationship between faith and reality, which we have
already affirmed above on theological grounds. Second we might
hold that scientific investigation and evidence are simply
wrong. Genesis 1 suggests that the creation took place in six
days, and science must therefore be deceived either by God
and/or the devil if it holds another position. This, too, is
a troubling alternative in its implications for faith and reality. Notable as well is the fact that neither Hick nor Barth
elects either of these alternatives. The third option would be
to reexamine the teachings of the early chapters of Genesis to
ascertain whether they are indeed at variance with modern
scientific research and investigation. Indeed it is not just
scientific investigation but modern literary criticism which
has prompted a fresh look at these chapters.

186

We may not overlook either the fact that, as Barth
expresses it, *fides quaerens intellectum*, faith seeks for understanding. Indeed this is our primary impetus for taking up this
question. Man has always felt compelled to investigate what he
believes, and, though there are other forces which might impel
him to engage in such an investigation, it is the compelling
desire to understand what he believes which provides the primary
incentive for man to seek to understand his faith and provides
the reason why we must make an examination of the cause and
significance of death ourselves.

OUR COURSE OF SOLUTION

From two directions we feel compelled to examine the Old
Testament background for death.

First we note that the resurrection of Jesus makes such a
study necessary. The Easter event is without question the
source from which the New Testament community sprang. Without
Easter Jesus and his followers would simply have disappeared
and been forgotten. But Easter made such a possibility impossible. We will want to examine what significance Easter has for
us, though this will be postponed until the final section of
this chapter. For the early Church the astounding thing was
that the resurrected one was at the same time the crucified one.
The one who appeared from the tomb in glory on Easter Sunday
morning was he who had been placed in the tomb from the igno-
minious death on the cross. The early Church was thus confronted with the problem of clarifying the meaning and significance of the death of Jesus, and the Old Testament definitely
influenced the way they came to understand the death of Jesus.
Their teaching on this issue we shall note as well as the manner
in which this relates to the cause and significance of our own
death.

The second reason for investigating the Old Testament for
background on the issue of death and after-life derives from
orthodox theology. Christian orthodoxy has posited a direct
relationship between sin and death, and it has based this upon
its understanding of the first chapters of Genesis, especially
as these have been interpreted in light of various New Testament
writings, e.g. Romans 6:23. We must therefore examine the early
chapters of Genesis to ascertain the significance attributed to
death. Literary criticism will certainly influence our conclusions as will the writings of Gerhard von Rad, Barth, and others.
Then subsequently we will note the relationship which the New
Testament plays in regard to our understanding of the cause and
significance of death.

THE CONTRIBUTION OF LITERARY CRITICISM

Literary criticism of the Old Testament suggests that the
early chapters of Genesis came into their present form relatively
late. Much of the later chapters of Genesis and Exodus seems to
have antedated the first chapters of Genesis. These first

chapters represent a crystallizing of tradition(s) in the sagas
of these chapters. Much of what appears in these chapters was
appropriated from other domains. Commentaries will readily draw
attention to the various sections of these chapters, but we wish
to relate the parts to the whole in which they stand rather than
focusing solely upon a part(s) itself. The parts influence the
whole, and vice versa. Specifically we will want to examine
carefully the meaning and importance which may be attributed to
the idea of curse in Genesis 2 and 3.

THE NATURALNESS OF DEATH IN THE OLD TESTAMENT

Despite the unnatural and accursed character of death
which has been characteristic of orthodox theology, Old Testament scholars have noted that the understanding of death was
quite different. The conclusion of Gerhard von Rad is typical:

> Whereas the view of Yahweh's relation to life is rich
> and theologically varied in the OT, the estimation of death
> in Yahweh religion remains unitary and constant even through
> many centuries of vigorous religious development. The
> termination of life by a normal death in old age is accepted
> as something regrettable but natural against which no
> protest is made.[10]

This prompts the question whether the early chapters of Genesis,
which have influenced extensively the orthodox understanding of
death as an accursed phenomenon, are at variance with the
remainder of the Old Testament. We will argue that the early
chapters of Genesis concur with the Old Testament overall in
this regard.

COVENANT AND CURSE

In *Church Dogmatics III/1* Barth astutely notes that Genesis 1-2:4a teaches that creation is the external basis of
covenant. The remainder of chapter 2 and chapter 3 in Genesis
demonstrate that covenant is the internal basis of creation.
The notion of covenant is thus evident in these first chapters
of Genesis, and indeed it plays a major role.

Furthermore it is the Old Testament scholar von Rad who
seems to have first noted that the structure of the book of
Deuteronomy reflects the procedure of a covenant ceremony which
opened with a recital of history; was followed by the proclamation of the Law, which was accompanied by sworn obligations;
and then was concluded with blessings and curses. The Sinai
covenant of Exodus 19-24 follows this same structural pattern.[11]
Notably for our study blessings and curses were a regular aspect
of covenant formulae. Remarkable also is the fact that the
structure of covenants parallels various other treaties in the
ancient Near East.[12] This is significant for our study for
several reasons. First as we have just noted above the idea of
covenant is prevalent in the early chapters of Genesis. We may
therefore expect to find there the procedures and elements of

covenant formulae. Second we note with Barth that the story
of the Fall of Adam and Eve universalizes the action of the
children of Israel at Mt. Sinai. Adam is representative, a
type, of all humanity. Third the curse which appears in
Genesis 2 and 3 should thus be understood in light of the curse
and God's action upon man's disobedience at Sinai. At Sinai
God, though intending to carry out the threats and curses
commensurate with disobedience, does not do so. He could
justifiably have utterly destroyed Israel. Rather however God
chooses to be merciful and forgiving. We note that that same
pattern prevails in the first chapters of Genesis. For our
study this raises the issue of how to understand the threats
and curses which have traditionally been viewed as the occasion
for God's instituting the punishment of death.

In one sense the threats and curses are diminished. Such
threats and curses were regular aspects of covenants, and even
if the covenant were broken the threats and curses were not
always actualized. We note that not even God lived up to His
threats! Be it noted, however, that we believe it would be
better to suggest that God is acting here in His grace and mercy
rather than attributing any inconsistency or unfaithfulness to
God.

We must also note that God is not explicitly charged with
instituting physical death for Adam and Eve at this point.
After establishing a perfect environment in Eden for covenant
relationship, complete with mutual obligations, God leaves a
specific charge not to eat of the tree of the knowledge of good
and evil lest in the day they eat of it מות תמות (you shall
surely die, cf. Genesis 2:17). The effect of the participle
upon an imperfect verb is to intensify the action; it does not
create the action per se. Thus death becomes intensified; it
becomes more threatening. But it is not thereby created.
Claus Westermann reaches a similar conclusion in his commentary
on Genesis 1-11. He writes that

> the oft used formula for the death penalty, מות תמות, has a
> fixed meaning. The meanings "you will become mortal" or
> "you will die sometime later," are quite impossible. The
> majority of exegetes have rejected this explanation.[13]

von Rad for one writes: "One cannot say that man lost a 'germ
of immortality' any more than one can say that a material modification occurred in him, as a consequence of which he must now
fall prey to death."[14] This interpretation is confirmed in the
context of the whole when in Genesis 3:22-23 God drives man out
of Eden in order that he not eat of the tree of life and hence
live forever. Immortality appears here to be more of a curse
than death. We therefore conclude that physical death is not
attributed negative significance; it is not a curse.

Nevertheless we must note that the curse which God threatened was taken with the utmost seriousness by God Himself. God
threatened to destroy the children of Israel at Mt. Sinai.

But Moses intervened as a mediator and caused God to relent. Barth points out in *Church Dogmatics III/3* that God takes man's rebellion and sin seriously, and that is exemplified most especially in the crucifixion of Jesus. The New Testament writers use different images to express their belief that the death of Jesus establishes a new and different relationship between God and man. Paul in particular stresses that Jesus took upon himself the curse of the law υπέρ ημῶν (on our behalf). In 2 Corinthians 5:21 he writes that God αμαρτίαν εποίησεν (made him sin). In Galatians 3:10 Paul writes that on the cross Christ **became** επικατάρατοσ (cursed). In the institution of the Lord's Supper the cup is referred to by the synoptic writers and Paul as τὸ αῖμά τῆσ διαθήκησ (the blood of the covenant). The idea of covenant recalls the elements of covenant and invariably the curse when the covenant is broken. Clearly the idea is that sacrifice could establish and/or renew a right covenant relationship with God by placing upon the animal the curse due to sin. The Johannine references to Christ as ο αμνὸσ τοῦ θεοῦ ο αίρων τὴν αμαρτίαν τοῦ κόσμου (the lamb of God who takes away the sin of the world, cf. John 1:29) suggests as well that the curse of sin was borne away by Christ in the crucifixion. These images from the New Testament all point up that death was not entirely natural or as God intended it to be. God caused the curse to become associated with death on account of the sin of man. It was the curse of sin which aroused within man dread of death because in death he realized that he would face the holy God. When death is regretted in the Old Testament it is not because one will depart his beloved but rather because the focus is upon the curse of death. But death need no longer be accursed. It has been renaturalized through the vicarious death of Christ. Paul is jubilant that "death has lost its sting" (cf. 1 Corinthians 15:55). Christ has absorbed the curse of sin on behalf of man.

CONCLUSION

The cause of death thus becomes God, but God has introduced death into the world not as a punishment but in accordance with His divine plan. Barth again has illuminated several positive functions of death for man in this regard. The significance of death is both positive and negative. It is positive when it accords with the divine will, but it is negative when through sin man brings to death the curse.

Our conclusions, then, are very similar to Barth and distinct from Hick. Hick has missed the unique significance of the death of Christ, and we cannot follow his lead. We find ourselves indebted to the writings of Barth in coming to our own position. Nonetheless the course we chart is different from Barth. We are enabled to interpret death in both positive and negative terms because of the manner in which the curse becomes attached to death through breach of the covenant. This allows us to avoid placing emphasis upon the notion of second death, which though being a notion with which we can sympathize, would hardly be a universally acceptable interpretation of second death.

Furthermore our interpretation can be found and applied throughout the New Testament and is not limited to just the book of
Revelation as is second death.

Footnotes

[1]John Hick, *Evil and the God of Love* (London: Macmillan and Co. Ltd., 1966; 1977 reprint by Fontana Books), pp. 181-182.

[2]Ibid., p. 181.

[3]Karl Barth, *The Epistle to the Romans*, 6th ed., trans. Edwyn C. Hoskyns (New York: Oxford University Press, 1933; 1976 reprint), p. 250.

[4]Karl Barth, *The Resurrection of the Dead*, trans. H. J. Stenning (New York: Fleming H. Revell Company, 1933; 1977 reprint by Arno Press), p. 169.

[5]Karl Barth, *Credo*, trans. Robert McAfee Brown (New York: Charles Scriber's Sons, 1962), p. 167.

[6]Karl Barth, *Church Dogmatics III/2*, trans. Harold Knight, G. W. Bromiley, J. K. S. Reid; and R. H. Fuller (Edinburgh: T. & T. Clark, 1960), p. 597.

[7]Ibid., pp. 638-639.   [8]Ibid., p. 629.

[9]Hick, *Evil*, p. 397.

[10]*Theological Dictionary of the New Testament*, s.v. "ζάω, ζωή {βιόω βίοσ} B. Life and Death in the OT," by Gerhard von Rad, 2:846.

[11]*Theological Dictionary of the Old Testament*, s.v. "ברית," by M. Weinfeld, 2:265-266.

[12]Ibid., p. 266.

[13]Claus Westermann, *Genesis 1-11: A Commentary*, trans. John J. Scullion (Minneapolis: Augsburg Publishing House, 1984), p. 225.

[14]Gerhard von Rad, *Genesis: A Commentary*, rev. ed., trans. John H. Marks (Philadelphia: Westminster Press, 1972), p. 95.

What Happens to the Individual in Death?

INTRODUCTION

The question of what transpires to the individual in death is closely linked to that of anthropology, i.e. the question of "what is man?" Traditionally even within orthodox Christian circles man has been understood to be a combination of body and soul. This in turn has lent support to the idea that death is the separation of body and soul. Though Hick has an affinity with this traditional understanding, there is note-worthy difference as well. Barth, too, takes exception to the orthodox teaching with regard to anthropology and what happens in death. We will review briefly the positions of Hick and Barth in response to this question before offering our own perspective.

THE QUESTION IN HICK

Hick believes that man is composed of a physical and a non-physical realm. Though the physical realm is apparent, the non-physical has been accorded different names in various cultures. For Hick the non-physical refers to the thinking, feeling, will-ing, and remembering consciousness, though he also includes unconscious mental activity which is able to influence conscious-ness. Soul as Hick uses it is a valuational term for the self. "'Soul' connotes the moral and spiritual personality which the child becomes in interaction with its human environment."[1] For Hick genetic code and environment influence soul. At death the soul and body are separated. We may assume that the body decom-poses while the soul migrates to another realm.

THE QUESTION IN BARTH

Karl Barth is certainly neoorthodox in his understanding of what transpires to the individual in death. Though Martin Luther is a noteworthy exception, the orthodox understandings of death in the Roman Catholic, Lutheran, and Reformed tradi-tions interpret it as the separation of body and soul. The anthropology of Barth does not lend itself to this sort of understanding. In *Romans* we noted that Barth speaks of the body and soul as composing a totality. He also mentions that "THIS mortal must put on immortality," thereby suggesting that there is no innate immortal aspect to man. In *The Resurrection of the Dead* Barth clearly renounces the idea of the immortality of the soul. The human soul and the human body will be restored at the resurrection by the Spirit of God. Hence if they both must be restored, then neither is immortal. In the *Church Dogmatics*, especially *Volume III/2*, Barth is very clear that soul and body are related and interconnected. Man is the soul of a body and the body of a soul. It is inconceivable for the one to exist apart from the other. Though soul and body are differentiated the one from the other, there remains nonetheless an inner unity between soul and body with the soul being the dominating party over the body. Soul and body are so intimately connected that the Bible will at times number bodies and souls when whole human beings are actually being numbered. Furthermore Barth is explicit that both soul and body are simultaneously mortal. Though Barth distinguishes it from nothing, non-being precedes and succeeds life. Human beings derive from and return to non-being. Barth envisions birth and death as limits to human life. Death, though shifting from a wall to a frontier in the *Dogmatics*, is nevertheless final.

As we noted in our study of his anthropology, Barth views man primarily as a whole with various centers which make reference in terms of the whole. Soul and body are the two principal centers or foci, though arm, heart, mind, etc. are also mentioned. There is also a third aspect *to*, though not *of*, man which Barth stresses. This is the spirit. Spirit is the principle of animation which constitutes man soul of a body. It derives from God and is therefore immortal. The presence or absence of spirit determines whether or not there is life. Thus death represents a withdrawal of the spirit from man.

POINTS OF AGREEMENT AND DISAGREEMENT

It thus appears that Hick and Barth are very different, almost at opposite poles, when it comes to their understandings of what transpires to the individual in death. Yet there are some remarkable similarities which come out at this point. In *Death and Eternal Life* Hick argues against the identity of mind and brain. Specifically he rejects the monistic option and the epiphenomenalist thesis. Another option which Hick does not follow is that of interrelated influences of mind and body upon each other, influences which both terminate at death. Hick believes that there is an interrelation of mind and body, but it must be one which allows some aspect of mind to continue beyond death. Hick terms it a psychic factor.

Barth agrees with Hick in several ways at this juncture. Though Barth disparages the dualistic, Greek view, he is equally disparaging of two forms of abstract monism often contrasted with the Greek view. The first of these is monistic materialism, the belief that only the corporeal and physical and that which can be brought under this denominator is real. According to this view mind or human consciousness is only a function of the brain, a view which Hick likewise disputes. Barth dismisses spiritual monism as "too good to be true."[2] According to this view only spirit is real and corporeality is a mere garment or appearance. Barth would have done well to articulate better his beliefs in this regard, for it could appear that grace also is "too good to be true." Furthermore it could be argued that Barth himself is a spiritual monist. R. Prenter has accused Barth of "creation docetism."[3] For Barth undoubtedly the covenant of grace precedes and exercises priority over creation, Barth's time of grace being a parallel to this. But though for Barth creation is certainly more than appearance, because of its secondary significance one might contend that creation is nonetheless little more than appearance, and the spiritual monism which Barth believes to be "too good to be true" thus might for Barth himself prove true. Hick also disparages spiritual monism. Nevertheless the fact that they share an opposition to certain views hardly constitutes their agreement with regard to others.

Such a possibility for agreement may not be precluded nonetheless. While we must admit that Hick holds a dualistic view of man, the fact that he suggests that the non-physical realm of man has been given many names allows for a wide range of understandings. Hick's review of H. H. Price as well as his 'replica' theory both point to a proximity between the physical and non-physical even after life. For Barth soul and body have an intimacy which is lacking in Hick, though it may be that Hick has great sympathy for this position. Furthermore the indefinite character of what Hick intends by terming soul "a valuing name for the self"[4] leaves open the possibility that the physical may entail much of what has traditionally been attributed to a non-physical realm of man. Here it is apparent that Barth is consistent while Hick is more indefinite as he attempts to include breadth of viewpoints in his terminology.

For Hick it is apparent that the soul of man separates from the body in death. Barth believes that this is impossible. Soul and body are intimately interrelated and it is the return of the spirit to God from whence it came that determines death. But notably it is Barth's spirit which is impersonal while the soul of Hick is intimately personal. Nevertheless it is not without significance that for both Hick and Barth death involves a separation. Life is a union which is divided at death.

A Personal Perspective

THE INDIVIDUAL IN DEATH

Not a little research and investigation has gone into the question now before us. Philosophers throughout the ages have attempted to develop an anthropology which answers the question of "what is man?" Modern scientific investigation continues to research issues which impinge upon an answer to this question, as Hick has demonstrated.

We take our start in faith, a Biblical faith centered in Christ, and we find the analysis of Barth particularly acute in this realm. Man thus is a unit with two rather elliptical foci--his soul and his body. We are unable to conceive rationally the precise relationship between the body and soul since body and soul do not lend themselves to neat, mathematical analyses as does an ellipse. Even advocates of a separate soul and body are unable to give an adequate description of their purported interrelationship. Furthermore we would concur with Barth that man has life, he becomes soul of a body and body of a soul, as he is granted spirit by God. The withdrawal of spirit by God thus represents death for the individual.

THE INDIVIDUAL, DEATH, AND SCIENTIFIC RESEARCH

John Hick exemplifies those who believe that faith becomes verified as reasons for rational doubt are eliminated. Thus we noted the considerable investigation which he makes in the realms of psychological and parapsychological phenomena. We indicated above our preference for Barth's understanding of faith as that which must be affirmed upon the basis of what is revealed by God. Barth emphasizes that the initiative lies with God. What we know of God and His relationship with man stems from divine revelation.

Barth, nonetheless, was neither a gnostic nor a docetic. Yet he never offered a theological interpretation of facts from nontheological disciplines, facts which would seem in certain instances to counter the revelation of God. That it might indicate a dependence upon natural theology likely contributed to Barth's reluctance to do this. We must be wary of such an implication ourselves. But we are also wary of gnosticism and docetism. Thus we feel it is appropriate to examine critically several comments of Hick and a few other individuals where these comments would seem to contradict our conclusions.

First we note that the psychological and parapsychological phenomena which Hick cites in *Death and Eternal Life* would seem to suggest that man may be some sort of combination of body and soul. The evidence for ESP, i.e. extrasensory perception, seems to point in that direction, even if we discount for instances of unconscious fraud as does Hick. Nevertheless ESP and parapsychological phenomena may indicate merely that certain individuals enjoy a form of communication which is peculiar to them, much like we might say that on the basis of intelligence one individual is capable of a type of reasoning beyond the capability of another. Other conclusions may be equally justifiable. To suggest conclusions for a body-soul theory or moreover for the continued existence of soul beyond death is unwarranted by the facts. Special functions of the soul may very well die with the body. Indeed this is what we believe.

The same sort of unwarranted conclusions are popularly advocated by Raymond Moody, Jr. and Elisabeth Kübler-Ross and have even attracted investigation by pollster George Gallup, Jr.[5] Here the evidence is the accounts of those who have undergone near-death experiences. Two comments seem appropriate in response. First it seems that insufficient reflection has been accorded to those who have not experienced the phenomena cited by Moody, though they also have been nearly dead and then brought back to life. Moody suggests that persons who do not recall such phenomena may be suppressing them.[6] Nevertheless suppression is generally of negative, threatening phenomena and not of things positive and delightful like Moody suggests occur. If suppression is involved here one might just as likely conclude that these individuals saw hell and/or were frightened beyond description. Indeed there are contrary examples to those cited by Moody which do point in this direction. In his work *Eternal*

Life? Hans Küng adduces just such examples. In one instance an individual was taunted for hours by waves of vicious, yellow wolves, which the near-dead individual was imagining. Other individuals tend to "see plainly as heralds of death--like the figures in some of Van Gogh's paintings--gigantic black birds, rats and animals from the underground."[7] When these individuals regain their consciousness they usually will talk of their experiences with horror and disgust.[8] Moody and Kübler-Ross and even Gallup have not presented all the types of images which appear in near-death phenomena, and the omitted examples portend a significantly different if not contrary conclusion(s). Indeed one might reason that those who imagine the positive phenomena which Moody, Kübler-Ross, and Gallup recount are suppressing or repressing their negative experiences by imagining positive ones. Other conclusions also are conceivable. Certainly the conclusions which Moody and Kübler-Ross suggest seem unwarranted.

Furthermore as a second comment we would like to have the findings of Moody, Kübler-Ross, and Gallup compared more extensively with the images and phenomena prevalent in isolation research and the images and phenomena associated with various drugs. Though not life-threatening situations the images and phenomena of these areas offer parallels to the findings of Moody, Kübler-Ross, and Gallup. Needless to say, the more parallels to be noted, the less warranted the suggested conclusions of Moody and Kübler-Ross would appear to be. Again Küng cites evidence which illuminates our thoughts. He notes that Ronald Siegel posits that the human brain has a protective mechanism which shields dying individuals from the reality of their situation through escape into a dreamland, much like the effect of certain drugs.[9] Though this is unproven it certainly demonstrates that there are conclusions which may be drawn which are quite at variance with those of Moody and Kübler-Ross.

We find no legitimate challenge to our conclusions, then, stemming from the research of the behavioral sciences.

CONCLUSION

Barth wrote that he would not dissociate himself from the facts being brought to light by modern science, though he dissociated himself from the one-sided and mediating interpretations being given the facts.[10] Our brief reflection upon the interpretations being offered by Hick, Moody, Kübler-Ross, etc. in explanation of various psychological and parapsychological phenomena demonstrates that Barth is justified in his assessment. Indeed we wonder how, even based upon a presumed a-theistic and/or scientific basis, the types of conclusions being offered by Hick, Moody, and Kübler-Ross, particularly the latter two, have been accorded much credence. Life here and now and any purported life after life can only come from God. People would be well-advised to seek life from God rather than to imagine that there is an aspect of man which continues to exist after life in some other realm.

Footnotes

[1]John Hick, *Death and Eternal Life* (London: William Collins Sons & Co. Ltd., 1976), pp. 45-46.

[2]Karl Barth, *Church Dogmatics III/2*, trans. Harold Knight, G. W. Bromiley, J. K. S. Reid, and R. H. Fuller (Edinburgh: T. & T. Clark, 1960), p. 391.

[3]R. Prenter, "Die Einheit von Schöpfung and Erlösung. Zur Schöpfungslehre Karl Barths," *Theologische Zeitschrift*, 1946, pp. 161ff. Cited by G. C. Berkouwer, *The Triumph of Grace in the Theology of Karl Barth: An Introduction and Critical Appraisal*, trans. Harry R. Boer (Grand Rapids: Eerdmans Publishing Co., 1956), pp. 9-19.

[4]Hick, *Death*, pp. 45-46.

[5]The books *Life After Life: The Investigation of a Phenomenon--Survival of Bodily Death* (New York: Bantam Books, 1975) by Raymond A. Moody, Jr. with a foreword by Elisabeth Kübler-Ross, and *Reflections on Life After Life* (New York: Bantam Books, Inc., 1977) by Raymond A. Moody, Jr. are the prime sources of this notion. The topic has attracted so much attention that pollster George Gallup, Jr. along with William Proctor has investigated the subject in a book entitled *Adventures in Immortality: A Look Beyond the Threshold of Death* (New York: McGraw-Hill Book Co., 1982).

[6]Raymond A. Moody, Jr., *Reflections on Life After Life* (New York: Bantam Books, Inc., 1977), p. 87.

[7]Hans Küng, *Eternal Life? Life After Death as a Medical, Philosophical, and Theological Problem*, trans. Edward Quinn (Garden City: Doubleday & Company, Inc., 1984), p. 16.

[8]Ibid.   [9]Ibid., p. 17.

[10]Barth, *Church Dogmatics III/2*, p. 432.

What Happens After Life?

INTRODUCTION

What happens to people after life has been the third focus of our study of Hick and Barth. This is the ultimate question which concerns man, even in death. Man can tolerate a great deal, including death, if he believes that it will be a means toward some good end. Both Hick and Barth offer descriptions of what happens after life, and though we will note differences we must seek to determine whether those differences are genuine or merely apparent. Hick of course is concerned for the central affirmations of the religious traditions he examines, and it is incumbent upon us to do the same with regard to Hick and Barth in order to determine their relative similarities and dissimilarities.

AFTER-LIFE IN HICK

In his examination of after-life in Christian thought Hick indicates that the recent debate which attempts to draw a sharp distinction between the immortality of the soul and the resurrection of the dead is misleading. Hick believes it is of secondary importance whether God bestows immortality as a natural trait upon man in birth or whether He reserves it for the future since in either case God grants immortality. Existence is of God both now and hereafter, though, to be sure, Hick believes that man is immortal already in this life. This prompts a double response from us. First while we believe that Hick is correct to suggest that immortal existence is of God whether it is initiated with this life or after-life, whether one believes that he has another chance(s) to put things in order with God or whether he believes that this life is all there is will profoundly influence the way he acts and reacts not only in this life but in relation to death. If death be final man is dependent upon the grace of God for any hope for after-life, but if human beings innately possess the quality of immortality, then they ultimately control their own destiny. It does make a considerable difference whether human beings are already immortal or become so by the grace of God post-mortem. Second we question whether the mere extension of time will result in fulfilled time. Hick displays a very optimistic view of man's inevitable progress, an optimism we and also Barth do not share. The mere extension of existence in time could be viewed like life on a treadmill which goes nowhere and would therefore be accursed. Our view stresses eternal life (ζωὴ αἰώνιοσ) in communion with God as the end, goal, and fulfillment of humanity.

After life according to Hick the soul must do something or go somewhere. Hick is quite confident that the soul exists in a pareschatological or interim state, though the appropriate word is likely states or stages. After life one proceeds to another level of existence where life begins anew, though not as the immature creature with which this life on earth began.

Hick rather compares after-life to a ladder with numerous rungs
which must be climbed in order to reach the top. Whether it is
possible to skip a rung(s) Hick leaves open, though such a skip
seems possible if not probable. What determines where one
exists after life is one's karma, the composite of one's past
thoughts and deeds. After a life at this new level one will
die again and rebecome. Hick quite obviously is unable to
determine how many times one might rebecome, even if one were
to complete every rung, but he is inclined to believe that
there are many rungs and hence many times of rebecoming. What
Hick is advocating appears ultimately to be the idea of purgatory in a less offensive garb. Furthermore though Hick avoids
Origen's heresy of the pre-existence of souls by suggesting
that life begins in this world, Hick seems to be drinking of
the same cup as Origen. Such fellowship places Hick in most
unorthodox company, indeed anathematized company. Whether Hick
would thus appear orthodox to any branch of Christendom is
questionable and in fact doubtful.

Ultimately, nonetheless, the individual for Hick will
reach the goal of true fulfillment. Hick is reticent to describe
this state, but this is common to the various religious traditions. Hick's prime concern is to clarify individuality in this
final state. He recognizes that certain traditions nearly
annihilate any individuality while others speak of an immortal
ego. Hick attempts to present a view which is pluralistic
though ego-transcending, similar to the three persons of the
Christian trinity. Hick suggests that there will be a plurality
of centers of consciousness, all contributing to the collective
human self or atman, but noteworthily embodiment will no longer
be necessary. While Hick's notion of 'replica' entails a
bodily afterlife, ultimately the body is discarded. This
would seemingly incline Hick toward the annihilation of the
individual, as noted previously. Neither will there be any
time, for its significance will also be eliminated. Though
Hick may want to maintain at least theoretically the individual
personality in the ultimate state, a bodiless and timeless
eschatological existence leaves little room for individuality.
One's karma, of course, might lend one personality, but Hick
does not inform us whether one or only One will exist, i.e.
are there units of consciousness or only a single composite
unit?

AFTER-LIFE IN BARTH

Karl Barth contrasts significantly with Hick regarding
the interim after life and before the resurrection. As we
noted in our study of Barth, some have questioned whether Barth
in fact leaves any room for after-life. Though we believe that
Barth does, he is very circumspect in the description he offers
of after-life. We shall focus upon two aspects of the period of
after-life, i.e. the interim between death and the resurrection
and the resurrection and beyond.

In the interim it is apparent that for Barth there is no life. The soul and body in their unity both slip into non-being while the spirit, which is the principle of animation for the soul and body, returns to God from whence it came. Notably the spirit is for Barth an impersonal force.

In the commentary *Romans* and the Corinthian study *The Resurrection of the Dead* Barth is explicit that the resurrection will entail the repredication of the body. There is similarity here between repredication and Hick's notion of 'replica,' though this similarity disappears for Hick in the ultimate state, which is disembodied. Man will maintain individuality despite the belief that resurrection will result in a type of Christian monism in which God is all in all. We note that the idea of discontinuity is prevalent in these earlier works. In the *Credo* a greater degree of continuity is asserted. Barth talks of the resurrection as a realization of what man already is in Christ.[1] Eternity already is available for man in this world; the future will only mark its completion.[2] Barth speaks of continuity in the *Church Dogmatics* as well. What remains to be accomplished is the running out of the last day, and then its end will appear in accordance with its beginning.[3] To be sure the beginning to which Barth refers is Easter, the resurrection of Jesus and the forty days, and thus one must acknowledge discontinuity, but it will not be as radical of a discontinuity as the earlier Barth envisioned. Death has been transformed from a barrier wall into a frontier. Nevertheless it is apparent that the earlier Barth expects an embodied resurrection. This is not so clear in the *Dogmatics*, and some have questioned whether Barth conceives of any life after life. We noted three options to Barth at this juncture, and two of them did not necessitate embodied existence.

One of the three options we noted for Barth's vision of after-life was the eternalising of man, an intriguing notion on at least two accounts. First it puts Barth amongst some unexpected company. We note that eternalising appears very close to the position of the process theologians in the tradition of Alfred North Whitehead and Charles Hartshorne,[4] a tradition with which Barth has little else in common. It could also place Barth close to Nietzche and his notion of the eternal recurrence of the same, an idea which could be interpreted as placing God in the unpleasant position of viewing everyone's past, which for His is disappointing in general, instead of enjoying His creatures in the present. Second there is a resonance between Barth's idea of eternalising and the notion of karma which is popular with Hick. Certainly the life of one who is eternalised is controlled by the life he led on earth, much as one's karma determines after-life for Hick. It is furthermore worth recalling that Berkouwer feels that the idea of eternalising in God results from the parallel which Barth draws between birth and death. The Bible speaks of eternal life, but Barth makes this secondary to the limitation he has imposed on his doctrine of man. Since man according to Barth can be no more, yet enjoys eternal life, the description of

future life which Barth offers is "eternalising," and certainly
Berkouwer would view this as eternalising in God rather than
with God. We concur with Berkouwer that the parallel which
Barth draws between birth and death does result in difficulties
for his conception of after-life. Yet for our perspective
Berkouwer still places too much emphasis upon continuity and
regards too little the finality of death, which Barth accurately
notes.[5] Furthermore if the parallel which Barth suggests
between birth and death be discarded, then there is no reason
to doubt that afterlife in and with God will be possible.

Nevertheless we noted Barth's reticence to describe after-
life due to unrestrained, conservative Christian portrayals of
after-life as well as the obvious fact that *Volume V* of the
Church Dogmatics never flowed from the pen of Barth. These
considerations, along with the fact that the earlier Barth
obviously held to an embodied, personal after-life, lead us to
conclude that Barth would favor a personal, autonomous resurrection life, but it is obviously a debatable point. What is
not debatable is that any personal, embodied after-life would
be at odds with Hick's disembodied ultimate state.

A CONVERGENCE OF HICK AND BARTH?

Due to the indefinite results which our study of after-life
in Barth yielded, we are unable to give a definite answer as to
whether Hick and Barth ultimately converge in their views of the
eschatological state. Nonetheless because Barth advocates a
view of the end of life which is parallel to the beginning of
life, the idea of personal autonomy after life may be abandoned,
this lending further support to Barth's notion of eternalising
in God. But this in turn could signify a convergence of opinion
between Barth and Hick. Personal identity and autonomy are
negligible in Hick as the individual is transcended. All centers
of consciousness contribute to the collective human self or
atman. There thus becomes evident a convergence of opinion of
Hick and Barth with regard to the final state of man.

Even if it is the second option for after-life which we
noted that Barth might have preferred, still the convergence
between Hick and Barth might be evident. If we ultimately
become identified with Christ, this might parallel the tran-
scending of the individual which Hick envisions in his eschatology. Thus the central affirmation of Hick and Barth would
again be convergent.

Hick would undoubtedly appreciate such convergence since
he has contended that the various religious traditions are
different paths to the same ultimate state, and this would tend
to confirm this contention. However it must also be noted that
the two options of Barth which allow for convergence were not
the preferred option in our understanding of Barth. The third
option, which advocates personal autonomy, seems preferable,
and it is one which would not be as easily understood to converge and/or agree with Hick.

We also recall that Barth derided the idea of life beginning all over again or the idea of going back to school after
life. Though this refers to the interim state rather than the
ultimate state, it is clear that Barth and Hick display vastly
different ideas concerning the interim after-life. The possible
convergence of Barth and Hick, then, seems unlikely, and
certainly the path to that ultimate state contrasts markedly.

APOCATASTASIS

Hick and Barth both tend to advocate apocatastasis or
universalism. With Hick this is obvious. Hick is the eternal
optimist, believing that man is bound to progress toward the
ultimate state. Hick in fact never acknowledges the possibility
of another eventuality. Barth, too, as we noted tends toward
universalism. In *Romans* Barth clearly suggested that all men
would be saved with his notion that the divine No is the prelude
and opposite side of God's Yes. Later Barth becomes more circumspect, writing that man may not have any claim against God for
universal reconciliation, but that does not mean that man may
not hope and pray for it.[6] Barth would not allow man to preempt
God either for or against universalism, though he is certainly
sympathetic to universal reconciliation, even the possibility
that all things will be eternalised in God. His criticism of
the arguments against universalism further represents a de facto
endorsement of apocatastasis, even if only be default.

A Personal Perspective

As was noted in our review of Barth and Hick, this ultimately is a two-staged question. The first aspect concerns the
interval between death and the final state, generally termed
the interim state, and the second the nature of the final state.

THE INTERIM STATE

With regard to the interval between death and the final
state we find Hick's stages unsatisfactory. Hick is unwilling
to trust God's grace, and ultimately therefore he envisions man
as earning his salvation. Hick is little removed from the notion
of purgatory, and the sorts of charges historically bandied
against purgatory seem appropriate in regard to Hick. Barth is
certainly the preferred alternative. The dialectic of death
and life which graces the thought of Barth may have prompted
Barth to be too restrained in his description at this point,
but we feel similarly reluctant to affirm too blessed of an
existence between life and the final state. We are not introduced into that final state immediately upon death. There is
an interim which seems best described in analogy to a very sound
sleep. At times when a person is in deep sleep we say that he
is "dead to the world." When one literally is dead to the
world, we envision it as the sleep of death.

We must note, however, that this does not mean that we
are cut off from God. From their experience of the exile in

Babylon the people of Israel learned that God remained faithful
to His covenant. The covenant relationship which existed
between man and God was not destroyed by the exile, and eventually this was applied as well to death. Among New Testament
writers death likewise does not destroy covenant relationship,
at least for those who have received the gift of "eternal life"
according to John or for those who are "in Christ" according to
Paul. As absence need not sever human relationship, death need
not for God. God maintains covenant relationship with us even
after we have died and our spirit has returned to God from
whence it came.

THE ESCHATOLOGICAL STATE

Rationale

We must next comment upon the final, ultimate, or eschatological state, which is commonly referred to as heaven or the
Kingdom of God. Several reasons lead us to believe that on the
basis of God's revelation there will be such a final state in
which men participate. The first of these is the nature of
the covenant relationship between God and man. When God establishes covenant relationship it is permanent and irrevocable.
God remains faithful to His word, even at times when man is
unfaithful. We also note that if there were no existence for
man after life, then God would be eternally frustrated in His
desire to enjoy covenant relationship with His creation man.
Second there is the matter of the death of Jesus. It was a dark
Friday when men nailed Jesus to the cross. Yet the New Testament writers understood that day quite differently as a result
of God's revelation. On the cross Jesus took upon himself the
curse which had become associated with death through human sin.
Though Jesus himself was without sin and though he enjoyed a
perfect covenant relationship with his Father in heaven, he
nevertheless bore the curse appropriate to sin and breach of
covenant upon the cross and thereby redeemed man from the curse.
Consequently the Friday of his death has at least since Luther
been termed "good Friday." Good Friday would be of negligible
benefit, however, if its sole benefit were the removal of the
curse form man. Though the death of Jesus seems to have enabled
the gift of the Holy Spirit in this life, if death remained
final, then the significance of Jesus' death would be limited
and restricted. Third the Easter event prompts our belief that
there is an ultimate state after life. It has been revealed
by God to man (n.b. the passive tense) that the resurrection of
Jesus is but "the firstfruits of those who have fallen asleep."
The resurrection of Jesus would become an insignificant display
of divine power if there were not a future for ordinary men
beyond death. Fourth and finally there is the work(s) of the
Holy Spirit. Though in Christ persons may be justified, by the
working of the Holy Spirit they become sanctified. Yet at
death this work of sanctification is never complete. The work
of the Holy Spirit would thus remain eternally incomplete if
there were no opportunity offered after life for its completion.

Description

　　The Italian poet and philosopher Danté Alighieri in his
Divine Comedy and the English author John Bunyan in his *Pilgrim's Progress* are representative of a long line of writers
who have attempted to detail for man what he may expect after
life. People want to know what lies beyond death, and certainly
this has contributed to the popularity of the works of Raymond
Moody and Elisabeth Kübler-Ross as well as necromancers throughout the ages. In our description of the ultimate state we will
offer three points of clarification and draw attention to a
basic presupposition.

　　Our presupposition is the belief that the interim state
will come to a definite conclusion. As Jesus was resurrected
from the dead, so we believe that God will resurrect all to
newness of life. As the presence of the spirit determines the
presence or absence of life in this life, so it is the Spirit
which will again enliven and transform all men at the resurrection. How the resurrection will occur we cannot detail. Not
even the New Testament writers, to many of whom Jesus had
appeared after the resurrection, make speculation in this regard.
It was in the second century that writing of such a nature begins
to appear. But we do believe on the basis of the revelation of
Jesus Christ that there will be a resurrection and all will be
involved.

　　The first description which we offer focuses upon Christ
as the basis for understanding the future. Indeed his resurrection appearances were the basis of faith. In them Christ
revealed Himself to the apostles. He was seen by the apostles.
He appeared to them. Yet always the initiative rests with
Christ. What they perceived in Him, or rather what was revealed
to them in Him, was envisioned for themselves as well. Their
own future was revealed in the resurrection of Christ. While
John writes in 1 John 3:2 that "we shall be like him," 2 Peter
1:4 is so bold as to suggest that we shall "become partakers
of the divine nature." Barth as we noted indicates that Christ
is the future for believers, though we questioned the degree of
individual autonomy which this might entail. For ourselves we
believe that there will be personal autonomy after the manner
of Jesus Christ. Still it must not be forgotten that Jesus
Christ exists in eternal covenant relationship with God. He is
one in purpose with God. Hence if we are to be like Christ we
will maintain as Christ did on earth and does in heaven a
perfect covenant relationship with God. His will and ours will
be identical.

　　The second description of heaven which we wish to note is
that the future will entail the completion of what God has
already initiated. This in turn relates to the work of the
three persons of the Trinity. First we note that that future
will entail the completion and perfection of the work of the
Holy Spirit. This work moves along two complementary lines--
the confession that Jesus is Lord and the upbuilding of the

Church. The Apostle Paul in particular views the present
πνευματικά (gifts of the Spirit) and καρπὸσ τοῦ πνεύματόσ
(fruit of the Spirit) as an αρραβῶν (pledge, first installment,
or deposit) or απαρχή (firstfruits). The implication is clear
that there is more forthcoming from the Spirit, though it is
difficult to ascertain what the future will be like when the
Spirit completes its work. Certainly αγάπη (love), the first
fruit of the Spirit, will be manifest, as will χαρά and ειρήνη
(joy and peace respectively), but we question whether there
will be any role for μακροθυμία (longsuffering). In any case
the work of the Spirit will be completed and perfected in the
Kingdom of God. Similarly the work of Jesus Christ will be
completed in the eschatological state, and we have drawn attention to this above. The work of the Father will also be brought
to a completion in heaven or the Kingdom of God. In the creation God elected a covenant partner for Himself. This goal
will be fulfilled in the future when as the body of Christ we
will be brought into eternal fellowship with God the Father.
The future thus will represent the perfection of the work of
the three persons of the Trinity.

The third point of clarification which we wish to make
in description of the eschatological state concerns the environment of the Kingdom of God. This is turn also involves three
points. First in the eschatological state man will be embodied
and ensouled. We hold along with Barth that the tomb of Jesus
was empty. Jesus was resurrected by God and appeared to the
apostles as the soul of a body and body of a soul. Certainly
the empty tomb tradition as well as the accounts of the resurrected Jesus' having eaten indicate that upon resurrection
Jesus was embodied. The eschatological Kingdom will not
involve ethereal spirits. Nonetheless we acknowledge that the
resurrected body will be quite different from our present body.
Indeed we expect that God will remove the aspect of mortality
from man by a permanent bestowal of the spirit, and this will
certainly alter our bodily character. According to Paul and
the New Testament writers the resurrected bodies will be transformed. It is also noteworthy that the Hebrew language has no
word for the idea of body.[7] The Hebrews would refer to the
individual parts or to the whole man in reference to a man.
Body is a more abstract idea which is derived from Greek.
Paul utilizes this more abstract notion, also terming it a
spiritual body as compared with our natural earthly bodies
(σῶμα πνευματικόν and σῶμα ψυχικόν respectively). We thus
believe that in the resurrection the body will undergo a most
radical transformation. The body will demonstrate continuity
with what lived in this world, but nevertheless the body will
be radically transformed as well. In either case individuals
will be embodied and ensouled.[8]

The second aspect of the environment of the eschatological
state is its communal character. In the Kingdom of God we will
not exist by ourselves. We will exist and associate with others.
Our image of heaven is not the hermit's cell but the Church as
the body of believers. Though philosophers have busied

themselves discussing whether we might be able to communicate
with one another via telepathy and/or extrasensory perception
(ESP) after life, these concepts become for us unnecessary
speculations which do not impinge directly upon our faith
because we believe that we will be resurrected embodied and
ensouled and therefore be able to speak and hear. Furthermore
we stress that our unity will be one of purpose, to worship
and serve God and to love one another, rather than a unity of
consciousness. Though in heaven life will be communal, it
will nonetheless be theocentric. The analogy of a chorus or
an orchestra suggests itself. Attention is focused upon the
director or conductor, who controls the goals and performance
of the chorus and orchestra members, though the individual
performers can still relate to one another.

These two aspects of the environment of the Kingdom of
God lend themselves to a third. The bodily and social nature
of after-life will be complemented with an appropriate environment. As God originally created the heavens, the earth, the
seas, and all that fills them as the external basis for covenant,
so we believe that God will provide an environment for His
renewed covenant relationship with man in the final state.
The New Testament suggests this when it speaks of a new heaven
and a new earth and the new Jerusalem which is to descend from
the heavens (cf. Revelation 21:1-2). Obviously the New Testament community believed that there would be an external basis
for covenant after life, and we would concur.

John Hick in his much debated concept of eschatological
verification raises the issue as to how one might know that he
has indeed really come to the Kingdom of God. Like Hick we
believe that there will be no doubt as to that reality. We
have given some general description of what we believe heaven
and earth will be like, but we recognize that transformation
or glorification may exceed our expectations. But certainly
we believe that when we come to the eschatological state we will
recognize it on the basis of the aspects which we have described.

Beyond these sorts of general tendencies in description we
feel unjustified to venture. In fact our description may be too
anthropomorphic in its projection of aspects of this life being
present in the eschatological state, but since this is the only
world with which we are familiar we utilize the terminology,
though being aware of its potential inadequacies. We are
compelled to use such categories for we know of no other world
and/or framework. Other individuals have suggested much, much
more concerning heaven, offering images of splendor for those
with God and often complementing these heavenly images with
graphic, horrid descriptions of hell. We prefer to leave our
description open, awaiting in faith the action of God to fulfill
and complete it.

APOCATASTASIS

It is becoming increasingly difficult to avoid advocating apocatastasis, the belief that all will eventually be saved. Hick and Barth both exemplify this. Hick's contacts with Eastern culture, Western religions, his basic optimism concerning the nature of man, and his understanding of the primary function of religious faith as the improvement of moral behavior have impelled him in this direction, while Barth's contact with the divine grace in Jesus Christ impels him to a similar conclusion. Nevertheless Barth refuses to presume that the grace of God will be extended to all, though it does appear that he assumes that it will be.

The prime deterrents to acceptance of apocatastasis are two. There is the problem of sin and evil and the place of faith in justification. The question is raised whether God will overlook the ills which attend and are prompted by individuals. For us it is not that God overlooks sin and evil but rather that in Christ He has overwhelmed them. The cross graphically demonstrates the horrid power of sin and evil, but it demonstrates the equally powerful and benevolent love of God. God has already wreaked His judgment upon sin and evil. Because God loved humankind while it was still sinful, we feel that God is likely to repeat the same sort of benevolent act at the future resurrection when everyone will be redeemed and saved and all will be established in covenant fellowship with God the Father and Christ the Son through the working of the Holy Spirit. To suggest that something less might happen would be to imply that man, his sin, and/or evil is more powerful than God and His love, a position we do not maintain. Or else it might be asserted that God is something other than love, thereby enabling God to condemn eternally at least some. But this again is something we do not believe. Our position places the decision whether man will eventually attain to the ultimate state of heaven, the Kingdom of God, or whatever it might be termed, upon God. We believe placing that decision upon man in whole or in part is to condemn man to an eternity of futile seeking and searching, which in fact would be a fair portrayal of hell. We believe that God's love will become so irresistible at some point, perhaps for some even after life here on earth, that they will come to faith in Jesus Christ as Lord. We recognize this as a point where criticism is often levied against Barth, but we feel better affirming the overwhelming triumph of God's grace rather than suggesting that man in some sense enables grace to be or become effective. We furthermore believe that if God did take time to create a realm called hell that it would be without residents. For us a blessed communion with God and others in heaven is one image of the ultimate state which could be nicely complemented by an image of an empty hell.

Footnotes

[1] Karl Barth, *Credo*, trans. Robert McAfee Brown (New York: Charles Scribner's Sons, 1962), p. 169.

[2] Ibid., p. 170.

[3] Karl Barth, *Church Dogmatics III/2*, trans. Harold Knight, G. W. Bromiley, J. K. S. Reid, and R. H. Fuller (Edinburgh: T. & T. Clark, 1960), p. 622.

[4] George M. Schurr, "Brunner and Barth on Life After Death," *Journal of Religious Thought* 24, no. 2 (1967-1968):105. This remarkable convergence is noted by Schurr as here in a footnote. Though it merits separate study, it is not germane to our study and will not be investigated here.

[5] G. C. Berkouwer, *Man: The Image of God*, trans. Dirk W. Jellema (Grand Rapids: William B. Eerdmans Publishing Co., 1962), pp. 234-278, esp. pp. 265-274.

[6] Karl Barth, *Church Dogmatics IV/3, part 1*, trans. G. W. Bromiley (Edinburgh: T. & T. Clark, 1961), pp. 477-478.

[7] *Theological Dictionary of the New Testament*, s.v. "σῶμα, σωματικόσ, σύσσωμοσ," by Eduard Schweizer, 6:1047.

[8] It is curious for us that some philosophers have suggested that disembodied existence involves difficulties. H. H. Price, whom Hick cites in his *Death and Eternal Life*, writes that man will require "at least a perceived physical environment after life or something which plays roughly the same role." (cf. H. H. Price, *Essays in the Philosophy of Religion* (Oxford: Clarendon Press, 1972), p. 99) Terence Penelhum likewise suggests that memory *and* body are both necessary to insure personal identity after life. (cf. Terence Penelhum, *Survival and Disembodied Existence* (New York: Humanities Press, 1970), p. 58) Among those who would advocate that after-life will be disembodied there is accordingly difficulty in describing disembodied existence. "Dream-worlds" are often given as possible conceptualizations. We find it remarkable that no one to our knowledge has thought to compare disembodied after-life to the life of a quadraplegic or someone suffering paralysis from a stroke. This is hardly a desired manner of life, and it would be desirable for someone who advocates disembodied after-life to clarify what differences if any there might be.

CHAPTER V

EPILOGUE

Man has since time immemorial posed for himself the three questions regarding the cause and significance of death, what transpires to the individual in death, and what happens after life which have served as the foci of our discussion. Some have responded to these questions with the suggestion that there is no meaning to death nor anything which transpires after life and that any positive responses to these issues represents wishful thinking. H. H. Price has accordingly noted that disbelievers in life after death may be wishful thinkers as well![1]

In his satire *Gulliver's Travels* Jonathan Swift writes that once or twice each generation a child is born with a red, circular spot on its forehead signifying that it would never die. Gulliver imagines these children to be the most fortunate, but as he comes to know them Gulliver realizes that they are in fact the most miserable and pitiable of creatures. They grow old and feeble, their bodies contract various diseases, their friends and contemporaries die, they accumulate grudges and grievances, they grow weary of the struggle of life, and they can never look forward to being released from the pain of living. Immortality, quite surprisingly for Gulliver, is not what he had imagined.

There are those who may be surprised with the results of this study of death and after-life for they might not have imagined that Christian theology would lead to the results which we have outlined. We noted that for both Barth and Hick death is not an accursed phenomenon, that death entails separation, and that man does not become nothing after life. Beyond that, however, we noted considerable differences between Barth and Hick. We have found ourselves siding more closely with the positions of Barth, though we are unable to endorse everything which Barth says, and we feel it is necessary at certain points to advance beyond the position of Barth. We also find much which meets our approval in Hick's earlier writings when he was functioning as a Christian apologete, but in his more recent writings as he is functioning as an apologete for a global theology we find much that is lacking, especially in regard to maintaining what we believe is essential to the revelation of God as it is proclaimed through Christ, the Word. In description of his own spiritual journey Hick compares dogmatic theology with the ballast of the ship of faith and problematic theology with the sails of that ship.[2] While Hick

has been driven by various historical and contemporary drifts
and breezes, we feel the ballast of Christ and Christian faith
keeps us on steady keel. Yet Hick may challenge someone to
improve upon his efforts, or perhaps Hick could attempt such an
improvement himself for he still hopefully has some years yet
in which to essay such an undertaking.

Our study of death and after-life thus comes to a conclusion. We began by questioning whether it was appropriate to
associate death with the Grim Reaper, and we conclude that it
is not. Rather in death as in life we focus upon the revelation
of God as Father, Son, and Holy Spirit and believe that we can
enjoy a blessed communion with God in this life, in death, and
after-life.

Footnotes

[1]H. H. Price, *Essays in the Philosophy of Religion* (Oxford: Clarendon Press, 1972), p. 98.

[2]John Hick, *God Has Many Names* (Philadelphia: Westminster Press, 1980, 1982), p. 13.

SAMENVATTING

De toegenomen gemiddelde levensduur in de twintigste eeuw is in de laatste jaren grotendeels verantwoordelijk voor de verminderde belangstelling die gericht is op de dood en het hiernamaals. Er zijn echter tekenen die er op wijzen dat deze periode van tijdelijke kalmte een einde neemt. Het is onvermijdelijk dat mensen sterven en we zijn gedwongen de realiteit van de dood vroeger of later onder ogen te zien. Studies binnen de gedragswetenschappen hebben de aandacht gericht op de dood, in het bijzonder de studies van Elizabeth Kübler-Ross en Raymond Moody Jr, die zich concentreren op ervaringen van mensen die op de rand van de dood gestaan hebben. Vanuit de medische en juridische beroepensfeer worden ook met een steeds hogere frekwentie vragen gesteld die betrekking hebben op de dood. Bovendien is er de menselijke drang om te speuren naar zin en waarde en het streven van de mens om zijn geloof te verduidelijken, hetgeen leidt tot de noodzaak om dieper na te denken over de dood. —

Dit proefschrift gaat in op de drie eeuwig terugkerende vragen ten aanzien van de dood: wat is de oorzaak en betekenis van de dood; wat gebeurt er met het individu in de dood, en wat gebeurt er na het leven. De reacties van Karl Barth en John Hick, twee vooraanstaande theologen uit de twintigste eeuw, worden in deze dissertatie uitvoerig uiteengezet en vergeleken. De keuze van deze twee schrijvers is ingegeven door verscheidene factoren. Ten eerste verschaft het feit, dat deze twee zo van elkaar verschillen een goede basis om vergelijkingen te maken en contrasten te schetsen. Ten tweede nodigen zowel Barth als Hick tot een vergelijking uit. Dit geldt in het bijzonder voor Hick die probeert een globale theologie betreffende de dood te ontwikkelen. Tenslotte kunnen we vaststellen dat deze twee mensen in grote lijnen als representatief gezien kunnen worden voor de twee fundamentale manieren waarop deze drie vragen en speciaal op de laatste twee gereageerd wordt binnen de christelijke traditie in het algemeen en de hervormde traditie in het bijzonder. —

In onze samenvatting presenteren we eerst zowel de reactie van Barth als die van Hick op de drie kwesties alvorens daar een vergelijking tussen de twee aan toe te voegen en onze eigen reactie erop naar voren te brengen. —

Onze studie van Barth begint met de baanbrekende tweede editie van *Der Römerbrief,* om zich vervolgens te concentreren op *Die Auferstehung der Toten, Credo en Die Kirchliche Dogmatik.* Hoewel wij er ons van bewust zijn dat ons onderzoek ten aanzien van *Der Römerbrief* niet geheel legitiem is, vinden we daar zowel orthodoxe als neo-orthodoxe reacties ten aanzien van de drie voornoemde vragen. Hoewel Barth het heeft over het paradijs en de predestinatie, en zelfs de term "de eerbiedwaardige leer van de predestinatie" bezigt en schrijft dat de dood zijn intrede deed door toedoen van de zonde, is het nietttemin duidelijk dat Barth zich begeeft buiten de orthodoxe traditie van het Christendom. Dit komt bijzonder duidelijk tot uiting in zijn uitleg van de dubbele predestinatie waarbij het goddelijke Neen slechts een voorspel vormt op het goddelijke Ja. Gods verwerping gaat vooraf aan zijn uitverkiezing. De alverzoening treedt op dit punt duidelijk naar voren in Barth's denkbeelden. Voorts houdt dit in, dat de dood, als Gods verwerping, slechts een voorloper is van Zijn uitverkiezing. Hoewel de dood een negatief verschijnsel blijft, is hij, gezien in het perspectief van het geloof, een noodzakelijke stap in de richting van een positief gebeuren. Geen enkel aspect van de mens is echter onsterfelijk. De mens mag dan onsterfelijkheid verwerven, maar dat vindt slechts plaats bij de wederopstanding, als door Gods toedoen de mens, die in dit leven sterfelijk is en onderhevig is aan het verderf, onsterfelijk en onverderfelijk zal worden in het Koninkrijk van God. —

In *Die Auferstehung der Toten,* Barth's studie van 1 Corinthiërs 1 en in het bijzonder hoofdstuk 15, tracht Paulus, volgens Barth, de nadruk te leggen op de heerlijkheid van God. Hoewel de Corinthiërs er erg bedreven in waren om het eeuwige in het eindige te ontdekken, weerlegt Paulus dit door de tegenstelling van goddelijke openbaring en menselijke logica te benadrukken. Hij beklemtoont ook dat de wederopstanding en het Koninkrijk van God realiteiten zijn van de toekomst en niet van het heden. De dood is de vijand, in feite de allerlaatste vijand, en de zonde is de prikkel van de dood. In *Die Auferstehung der Toten* voert Barth weinig positiefs aan met betrekking tot de dood. —

In *Credo* biedt Barth evenmin een positieve evaluatie van de dood. —

In *Die Kirchliche Dogmatik* gaat Barth het uitvoerigst in op het vraagstuk van de oorzaak en betekenis van de dood. Barth erkent dat de mens in de tijd leeft op een manier die strijdig is met God en met zijn geschapen natuur. Dientengevolge vertegenwoordigt de dood het oordeel van God ten aanzien van de zonde. Maar omdat Barth niet gelooft dat een onbegrensde tijd de mens een werkelijke vervulling van zijn tijd garandeert, stelt Barth vast dat de dood buiten het kader van de zonde ligt, zoals Christus dit getoond heeft in zijn tijd, als iets dat natuurlijk is en in overeenstemming met de wil en het plan van God. Barth noemt dan ook datgene wat in de dood onnatuurlijk is en onder de vloek ligt en voortvloeit uit de zonde, de 'tweede dood'. Vervolgens merkt Barth op dat Christus door zijn dood deze vloek van de mens weggenomen heeft en de dood gereduceerd heeft tot slechts het teken van het oordeel van God.—

Het boek *Death and Eternal Life* is de voornaamste bron voor ons onderzoek van John Hick, hoewel ook *Faith and Knowledge* en *Evil and the God of Love* en bovendien enkele artikelen van Hick die op het onderwerp betrekking hebben, onze aandacht opeisen. Hick kent aan de dood een meer positieve waarde toe dan Barth. Hij ziet de dood als iets natuurlijks, een deel van de door God ingestelde orde, terwijl hij vaststelt dat ieder idee betreffende een tijd dat sterfelijkheid onnatuurlijk was in het geheel van de menselijke ervaring, een "drastische compartimentalisatie van de geest" is. In het verlengde van deze gedachtengang gelooft Hick dat het enige negatieve aspect van de dood is de onderbreking van de progressie van de mens naar zijn vervulling. —

Er is een duidelijk onderscheid tussen de antwoorden die Barth en Hick geven op onze tweede vraag: wat gebeurt er met het individu in de dood. Hoewel we de lezer opmerkzaam willen maken op een verrassend 'tussenspel' in het *Credo*, waar Barth de dood betitelt als de scheiding van lichaam en ziel, duidt Barth verder de mens in zijn geschriften aan als een totaliteit en/of eenheid van lichaam en ziel, wat we een psychosomatische eenheid zouden kunnen noemen. Wij interpreteren *Credo* dan ook in het verlengde hiervan. Aangezien noch de ziel noch het lichaam onsterfelijk is en evenmin los van elkaar kunnen bestaan, drukt de dood de desintegratie van beide uit. In *Die Kirchliche Dogmatik* maakt Barth duidelijk dat het de geest is, het principe van de schepping van het leven ingegeven door God, die de aan- of afwezigheid van het leven bepaalt. In de dood wordt de geest door God onttrokken aan de eenheid van lichaam en ziel die het leven juist aan diezelfde geest te danken had. In tegenstelling hiermede ziet Hick de dood als de scheiding tussen lichaam en ziel, wat de traditionele terminologie voor de dood is. Maar voor Hick betekent de ziel niet zozeer een onsterfelijke substantie maar meer de zedelijke en geestelijke persoonlijkheid van het individu. De ziel verhuist volgens Hick naar een ander rijk terwijl het lichaam tot ontbinding overgaat. —

Wat na het leven gebeurt is de meest gecompliceerde van de drie vragen die we in deze studie opwerpen. Bij Barth brengt wat er na dit leven gebeurt, twee thema's met zich mee; het eerste thema heeft betrekking op de interimperiode tussen de dood en de opstandig en het tweede op het leven na de opstanding. Barth suggereert konsekwent dat de mens, zowel lichaam als ziel, afglijdt naar een toestand waarin hij niet bestaat gedurende de interimperiode, terwijl zijn geest terugkeert naar God. Voorafgaand de *Kirchliche Dogmatik* schrijft Barth dat de mens als lichaam en ziel wederom tot leven gewekt zal worden door God bij de opstanding. Maar in de *Kirchliche Dogmatik* is het de vraag, of Barth enige ruimte laat voor een opstandingsleven. Het lijkt inderdaad niet onterecht om Barth een christelijke 'mortalist' te noemen. Nochtans stellen we vast dat de idee waardoor Barth in dit opzicht in *Die Kirchliche Dogmatik* beheerst wordt, de term 'vereeuwiging' is. Wij geven een schets van twee mogelijke interpretaties van deze idee; vereeuwiging *in* God en vereeuwiging *met* God, die van elkaar verschillen door de mate van autonomie die zij toekennen aan de mens. Hoewel wij inzien dat andere interpretaties van Barth betreffende de laatste fase van de mens mogelijk zijn en hoewel wij ook erkennen dat alle drie interpretaties die wij bieden theoretisch mogelijk zijn, hebben wij toch het vermoeden dat Barth een voorstander geweest zou zijn van de vereeuwiging mèt God, als hij in de gelegenheid was geweest zijn inzichten gedetailleerd uiteen te zetten in het vijfde deel van de *Kirchliche Dogmatik* dat hij op stapel had staan. Opmerkelijk is ook het feit dat de rol van de tijdsdimentie uitgespeeld zal zijn als Christus terugkeert voor wat Barth noemt de 'derde keer'. —

John Hick betoogt dat de mens, of liever zijn ziel, gereïncarneerd wordt en opnieuw sterft na andere levens geleid te hebben volgens een proces dat verloopt via reeksen stadia, hetgeen veel overeenkomst vertoont met de sporten van een ladder. Hick suggereert dat elk van deze stadia belichaamd zal worden door middel van 'copie'-lichaam totdat de ziel tenslotte de uiteindelijke fase bereikt, waarin zij onbelichaamd zal zijn. Hick stelt zich voor dat dit een pluralistische fase is waarin de grenzen van het ego echter doorbroken worden. Het zal ook een tijdloze fase zijn omdat de tijd zijn betekenis verloren zal hebben.

Wij stellen bovendien vast dat zowel Hick als Barth meer neigen naar universalisme (alverzoening) of apokatastasis, Hick expliciet en Bart impliciet. —

De methoden, die Barth en Hick gebruiken vragen eerst onze aandacht, eer wij toekomen aan de vergelijking van hun standpunten ten aanzien van onze drie vragen. Hier valt het ons op dat zowel Barth als Hick de prioriteit van het geloof benadrukken. Maar Barth blijft zich gedurende zijn gehele loopbaan concentreren op de genade en het Woord van God en trekt zijn conclusies op die basis. Hick daarentegen probeert, hoewel hij zijn loopbaan begon als christelijk apologeet, een wereldwijde theologie van de dood te ontwikkelen door de fundamentele overtuigingen op dit punt binnen allerlei religieuze tradities op te sporen en vervolgens daaruit de passende conclusies te trekken op een meer inductieve basis. Hick maakt ook gebruik van de studies van verscheidene niet-theologische disciplines om de verstandelijke twijfels ten aanzien van zijn speciale conclusies weg te nemen. Wij geven de voorkeur aan de methode van Barth die zich concentreert op de christologie. In de interpretatie die Hick geeft van de twintigste-eeuwse christelijke theologen, merken we verscheidene omissies en onnauwkeurigheden op; wij vermoeden dan ook dat Hick soortgelijke fouten heeft begaan bij het interpreteren van niet-christelijke tradities. Niettemin heeft Hick, in het bijzonder in zijn vroegere rol van christelijk apologeet, met geloof en vertrouwen de uitdaging aanvaard van de logische positivisten, gebruik makend van zijn concept van eschatologische verificatie. —

Terwijl Hick en Barth beiden geloven dat de dood oorspronkelijk door God verordineerd is als een integraal deel van de natuurlijke orde, heeft Hick niets wezenlijk negatiefs te melden over de betekenis van de dood, terwijl Barth daarentegen schrijft dat, hoewel er enige gunstige aspecten aan de dood zitten, de dood waarmee de mens in feit geconfronteerd wordt, het teken is van het goddelijk oordeel over de mens en zijn zonde. Barth onderkent de zonde als een indrukwekkende macht, maar Hick beschouwt de zonde veel meer op een onschuldige en naïeve manier. Hoewel wij meer sympathie hebben voor de ideeën van Barth op dit punt, heeft Barth zelf de plaats van de vloek in de verbondstheologie over het hoofd gezien. Vandaar dat, hoewel hij opmerkt dat Christus de tweede dood overwint, zijn interpretatie geen ruimte biedt voor het feit dat de vloek van de dood en de opheffing daarvan door Christus centraal staan in de boodschap van het evangelie. Dat punt stellen we aan de orde bij de beantwoording van de eerste vraag in onze studie. —

Hick en Barth beseffen beiden dat de dood van het individu een scheiding met zich meebrengt. Terwijl voor Barth de geest weggenomen wordt door God, geldt voor Hick dat de ziel van het lichaam gescheiden wordt in de dood. Als wij op deze kwestie ingaan accepteren wij weer de leiding van Barth. Maar in dit gedeelte gaan we verder dan Barth, door ook commentaar te geven op de verkeerde uitleg die op populaire wijze gegeven wordt door Elizabeth Kübler-Ross en Raymond Moody Jr teneinde verschijnselen te verklaren die samenhangen met ervaringen op de rand van de dood. Deze twee hebben de ervaringen van vele anderen die op de rand van de dood gestaan hebben onderdrukt en/of weggelaten en hebben hun gegevens niet vergeleken met die van andere terreinen waarop onderzoek gepleegd is en waarbij soortgelijke verschijnselen naar voren gekomen zijn, maar waarbij geen resultaat wordt geponeerd dat zweemt naar een onsterfelijke ziel of een ontlichaamde geest. —

Met betrekking tot ons derde punt waarbij ingegaan wordt op wat er gebeurt na dit leven, zijn we weer de mening toegedaan dat Barth de beste weg aangeeft. Hick suggereert een weg die, hoewel logisch, niet voldoende ruimte laat aan de goddelijke genade. Wij hebben de neiging het bestaan van werelden met een vagevuur niet te accepteren. Ons inziens zal na een interim-periode waarin noch de mens noch enig deel van de mens leven bezit, bij de opstanding, het eind der tijden, en/of de uiteindelijke terugkeer van Christus, de mens opnieuw geest toegevoegd krijgen aan zijn getransformeerde lichaam en ziel, en hij zal in verbondsgemeenschap leven met God en zijn naasten. Voorts lijkt het ons het beste ons voor te stellen dat allen betrokken zijn in de eschatologische stand van zaken, waar immers Barth en Hick er beiden universalistische ideeën op na houden — hoewel er bij Barth toch wel sprake is van enige terughoudendheid. —

BIBLIOGRAPHY: SOURCES CONSULTED

Primary Works of Barth:

Barth, Karl. *Anselm: Fides Quaerens Intellectum*. Translated by Ian W. Robertson. London: SCM Press, Ltd., 1960.

_____. *Christ and Adam: Man and Humanity in Romans 5*. Translated by T. A. Smail. Edinburgh: Scottish Journal of Theology Occasional Papers No. 5, 1956.

_____. *The Christian Life: Church Dogmatics IV/4 Lecture Fragments*. Translated by Geoffrey W. Bromiley. Grand Rapids: William B. Eerdmans Publishing Company, 1981.

_____. *Church Dogmatics*. Edited by G. W. Bromiley and T. F. Torrance (1956-1975). Edinburgh: T. & T. Clark.
I, 1, *The Doctrine of the Word of God*, (1932), 2d ed. ET 1975.
I, 2, *The Doctrine of the Word of God*, (1938), ET 1956.
II, 1, *The Doctrine of God*, (1940), ET 1957.
II, 2, *The Doctrine of God*, (1942), ET 1957.
III, 1-4, *The Doctrine of Creation*, (1945-1951), ET Part 1 (1958), 2 (1960), 3 (1961), 4 (1961).
IV, 1-4 (fragment), *The Doctrine of Reconciliation*, (1953-1968), ET Part 1 (1956), 2 (1958), 3i (1963), 3ii (1965), 4 fragment (1969).

_____. *Credo*. Translated by Robert McAfee Brown. New York: Charles Scribner's Sons, 1962.

_____. *Dogmatics in Outline*. Translated by G. T. Thomson. London: SCM Press, Ltd., 1966.

_____. *The Epistle to the Romans*, 6th ed. Translated by Edwyn C. Hoskyns. New York: Oxford University Press, 1933; reprint ed. 1976.

_____. *Evangelical Theology: An Introduction*. Garden City, NY: Anchor Books, 1963.

_____. *The Heidelberg Catechism for Today*. Translated by Shirley C. Guthrie, Jr. Richmond: John Know Press, 1964.

_____. *How I Changed My Mind*. Edinburgh: Saint Andrew Press, 1969.

_____. *The Humanity of God*. Translated by John Newton
Thomas and Thomas Wieser. Atlanta: John Knox Press,
1960.

_____. *Protestant Theology in the Nineteenth Century: Its
Background and History*. Translated by Brain Cozens and
John Bowden. London: SCM Press, Ltd., 1972.

_____. *The Resurrection of the Dead*. Translated by H. J.
Stenning. New York: Fleming H. Revell Company, 1933;
reprint ed., Arno Books, 1976.

_____. *The Word of God and the Word of Man*. Translated by
Douglas Horton. New York: Harper Torchbooks, 1957.

Primary Works of Hick:

Hick, John. *Death and Eternal Life*. London: William Collins
Sons & Co., Ltd., 1976.

_____. "Eschatological Verification Reconsidered." *Religious
Studies* 13 (1977):189-202.

_____. *Evil and the God of Love*. Great Britain: Macmillan
and Co., Ltd., 1966; paperback ed., London: William
Collins Sons & Co., Ltd., 1977.

_____. *Faith and Knowledge*. 2d ed. Ithica: Cornell
University Press, 1966; paperback ed., London: William
Collins Sons & Co., Ltd., 1974.

_____. *God Has Many Names*. Philadelphia: Westminster
Press, 1980, 1982.

_____. "Learning from Other Faiths: IX. The Christian View
of Other Faiths." *The Expository Times* 84 (1972-1973):
36-39.

Hick, John, ed. *The Myth of God Incarnate*. London: SCM Press,
Ltd., 1977.

Hick, John. "On Conflicting Religious Truth-Claims." *Religious
Studies* 19 (1983):485-491.

_____. "On Grading Religions." *Religious Studies* 17 (1981):
451-467.

_____. *Philosophy of Religion*. 2d ed. Englewood Cliffs, NJ:
Prentice-Hall Inc., 1973.

_____. "Pluralism and the Reality of the Transcendent." *The
Christian Century* Vol. 98, No. 2 (1981):45-48. This article
is reprinted in Wall, James M., ed. *Theologians in Transition*. New York: Crossroad Publishing Company, 1981.

_____. "The Problem of Evil in the First and Last Things."
Journal of Theological Studies New Series Vol. 19 (1968):
597-602.

_____. "Theology and Verification." *Theology Today* 17
(April, 1960-January, 1961):12-31.

_____. "The Theology of Religious Pluralism." *Theology*
Vol. LXXXVI, No. 713 (September, 1983):335-340.

_____. "Towards a Philosophy of Religious Pluralism." *Neue
Zeitschrift fur Theologie und Religionsphilosophie* 22 Band
1980 Heft 2:131-149.

Secondary Sources:

Aldwinkle, Russell. *Death in the Secular City: Life After
    Death in Contemporary Theology and Philosophy.* Grand
    Rapids: William B. Eerdmans Publishing Co., 1972.

Althaus, Paul. *Die Letzten Dinge: Lehrbuch der Eschatologie.*
    10 Auflage. Germany: Gütersloher Verlaghaus, 1933.

Anderson, J. Kerby. *Life, Death and Beyond.* Grand Rapids:
    Zondervan Publishing House, 1980.

Audi, Robert. "Eschatological Verification and Personal
    Identity." *International Journal for the Philosophy of
    Religion* 7 (1976):391-408.

Badham, Paul. *Christian Beliefs about Life after Death.* New
    York: Barnes & Noble, Harper & Row Publishers, Inc., 1976.

Becker, Ernest. *The Denial of Death.* New York: Free Press,
    Macmillan Publishing Co., Inc., 1973.

Berkhof, Hendrikus. *Christ and the Powers.* Translated by John
    H. Yoder. Scottdale, PA: Herald Press, 1962, reprint ed.
    1977.

_____. *Christ the Meaning of History.* Translated by Lambertus
    Buurman. Richmond: John Knox Press, 1966.

_____. *The Christian Faith: An Introduction to the Study of
    the Faith.* Translated by Sierd Woudstra. Grand Rapids:
    William B. Eerdmans Publishing Company, 1979.

_____. *The Doctrine of the Holy Spirit.* Richmond: John
    Knox Press, 1964.

_____. "Drie Problemen bij de Interpretatie van de jonge
    Barth," *Nederlands Theologisch Tijdschrift* 34 (1980):294-306.

_____. *Well-Founded Hope.* Richmond: John Knox Press, 1969.

Berkouwer, G. C. *Man: The Image of God*. Translated by Dirk
    W. Jellema. Grand Rapids: William B. Eerdmans Publishing
    Co., 1962.

_____. *The Return of Christ*. Translated by James Van
    Oosterom. Edited by Marlin J. Van Elderen. Grand Rapids:
    William B. Eerdmans Publishing Co., 1972.

_____. *The Triumph of Grace in the Theology of Karl Barth:
    An Introduction and Critical Appraisal*. Translated by
    Harry R. Boer. Grand Rapids: Wm. B. Eerdmans Publishing
    Company, 1956.

Bettis, Joseph D. "Is Karl Barth a Universalist?" *Scottish
    Journal of Theology* 20 (1967):423-436.

Bloesch, Donald G. *Jesus Is Victor! Karl Barth's Doctrine of
    Salvation*. Nashville: Abingdon Press, 1976.

Busch, Eberhard. *Karl Barth: His Life from Letters and Auto-
    biographical Texts*. Translated by John Bowden. Philadel-
    phia: Fortress Press, 1975.

Carey, John J. "Hans Küng and Karl Barth: One Flesh or One
    Spirit?" *Journal of Ecumenical Studies* 10 (1973):1-16.

Crawford, Robert. "The Theological Method of Karl Barth."
    Scottish Journal of Theology 25 (1972):320-326.

Deegan, Dan L. "The Christological Determinant in Barth's
    Doctrine of Creation." *Scottish Journal of Theology* 14
    (1961):119-135.

Edwards, David L. *The Last Things Now*. London: SCM Press, Ltd.,
    1969.

Enright, D. J. *The Oxford Book of Death*. New York: Oxford
    University Press, 1983.

Fangmeier, Jürgen, and Stoevesandt, Hinrich, eds. *Karl Barth
    Letters 1961-1968*. Translated by Geoffrey W. Bromiley.
    Grand Rapids: William B. Eerdmans Publishing Co., 1981.

Feifel, Herman, ed. *The Meaning of Death*. New York: McGraw-
    Hill Book Company, 1959.

Forrester, Duncan B. "Professor Hick and the Universe of Faiths."
    Scottish Journal of Theology 29 (1976):65-72.

Gallup, George, Jr., and Proctor, William. *Adventures in Immor-
    tality*. New York: McGraw-Hill Book Company, 1982.

Godsey, John D., ed. *Karl Barth's Table Talk*. Richmond: John
    Knox Press, 1962.

Gollwitzer, Helmut. *Karl Barth: Church Dogmatics. A Selection with Introduction.* Translated and edited by G. W. Bromiley. Edinburgh: T. & T. Clark, 1961.

Hampe, Johann Christoph. *To Die Is Gain: The Experience of One's Own Death.* Translated by Margaret Kohl. London: Darton, Longmann, & Todd, 1979.

Hartshorne, Charles. "John Hick on Logical and Ontological Necessity." *Religious Studies* 13 (1977):155-165.

Hartwell, Herbert. *The Theology of Karl Barth: An Introduction.* Philadelphia: Westminster Press, 1964.

Hellwig, Monika K. *What Are They Saying about Death and Christian Hope?* New York: Paulist Press, 1978.

Hoekema, Anthony A. *The Bible and the Future.* Grand Rapids: William B. Eerdmans Publishing Co., 1979.

Jüngel, Eberhard. *Death: The Riddle and the Mystery.* Translated by Iaian and Ute Nicol. Philadelphia: Westminster Press, 1971.

Kastenbaum, Robert, ed. *The Literature of Death and Dying.* New York: Arno Press, 1977.

Kavka, Gregory S. "Eschatological Falsification." *Religious Studies* 12 (1976):201-205.

Kelsey, Morton T. *Afterlife: The Other Side of Dying.* New York: Crossroad Publishing Company, 1979.

Kreeft, Peter J. *Everything You Ever Wanted to Know about Heaven but Never Dreamed of Asking.* San Francisco: Harper & Row Publishers, 1982.

Kübler-Ross, Elisabeth. *Death: The Final Stage of Growth.* Englewood Cliffs, NJ: Prentice-Hall, Inc., 1975.

_____. *On Death and Dying.* New York: Macmillan Company, 1969.

_____. *Questions and Answers on Death and Dying.* New York: Collier Books, Macmillan Publishing Co., Inc., 1974.

Küng, Hans. *Eternal Life? Life After Death as a Medical, Philosophical, and Theological Problem.* Translated by Edward Quinn. Garden City, NY: Doubleday & Company, Inc., 1984.

Ladd, George Eldon. *I Believe in the Resurrection of Jesus.* Grand Rapids: William B. Eerdmans Publishing Co., 1975.

Lewis, C. S. *A Grief Observed.* London: Faber and Faber, 1961.

Lipner, Julius. "Christians and the Uniqueness of Christ." *Scottish Journal of Theology* 28 (1975):359-368.

_____. "Truth-Claims and Inter-Religious Dialogue." *Religious Studies* 12 (1976):217-230.

Londis, James J. "God, Probability and John Hick." *Religious Studies* 16 (1980):457-463.

Mills, Liston O., ed. *Perspectives on Death*. Nashville: Abingdon Press, 1969.

Moody, Raymond A., Jr. *Life After Life*. New York: Bantam Books, Inc., (Mockingbird Books), 1976 (1975).

_____. *Reflections on Life After Life*. New York: Bantam Books, Inc., 1977.

Nielsen, Kai. "Eschatological Verification." *Canadian Journal of Theology* 9 (1963):271-281.

_____. "Truth-Conditions and Necessary Existence." *Scottish Journal of Theology* 27 (1974):257-267.

Olding, A. "Resurrection Bodies and Resurrection Worlds." *Mind* (1970):581-585.

Parker, T. H. L. *Karl Barth*. Grand Rapids: William B. Eerdmans Publishing Company, 1970.

Pelikan, Jaroslav. *The Shape of Death: Life, Death, and Immortality in the Early Fathers*. Nashville: Abingdon Press, 1961.

Penelhum, Terence. *Survival and Disembodied Existence*. New York: Humanities Press, 1970.

Perkins, Pheme. *Resurrection: New Testament Witness and Contemporary Reflection*. Garden City, NY: Doubleday & Company, Inc., 1984.

Price, H. H. *Essays in the Philosophy of Religion*. Oxford: Clarendon Press, 1972.

Puccetti, Roland. "The Loving God--Some Observations on John Hick's Evil and the God of Love." *Religious Studies* 2 (1966):255-268.

Reichenback, Bruce R. "Price, Hick, and Disembodied Existence." *Religious Studies* 15 (1979):317-325.

Robinson, John A. T. *In the End God*. London: Collins, Fontana Books, 1968.

Schurr, George M. "Brunner and Barth on Life After Death." *Journal of Religious Thought* 24 No. 2 (1967-1968):95-110.

Steinfels, Peter, and Veatch, Robert M., eds. *Death Inside Out: The Hastings Center Report*. New York: Harper & Row Publishers, 1974.

Stendahl, Krister, ed. *Immortality and Resurrection: Four Essays by Oscar Cullmann, Harry A. Wolfson, Werner Jaeger, and Henry J. Cadbury*. New York: Macmillan Company, 1965.

Thielicke, Helmut. *Death and Life*. Translated by Edward H. Schroeder. Philadelphia: Fortress Press, 1970.

_____. *Living With Death*. Translated by Geoffrey W. Bromiley. Grand Rapids: William B. Eerdmans Publishing Co., 1983.

Tolstoy, Leo. *The Death of Ivan Ilych and Other Stories*. New York: New American Library, 1960.

Tooley, Michael. "John Hick and the Concept of Eschatological Verification." *Religious Studies* 12 (1976):177-199.

Torrance, Thomas F. *Space, Time, and Resurrection*. Grand Rapids: William B. Eerdmans Publishing Co., 1976.

Trethowan, Illtyd. "Dr. Hick and the Problem of Evil." *Journal of Theological Studies* New Series Vol. 18 (1967):407-416.

Veitch, J. A. "Revelation and Religion in the Theology of Karl Barth." *Scottish Journal of Theology* 24 (1971):1-22.

Whitehouse, W. A. *Creation, Science, and Theology: Essays in Reponse to Karl Barth*. Edited by Ann Loades. Grand Rapids: William B. Eerdmans Publishing Company, 1981.

Wilckens, Ulrich. *Resurrection: Biblical Testimony to the Resurrection An Historical Examination and Explanation*. Translated by A. M. Stewart. Edinburgh: Saint Andrew Press, 1977.

INDEX

Names:

Subjects:

Bible Passages:

KEITH RANDALL SCHMITT

CURRICULUM VITAE

Keith Randall Schmitt was born on July 12, 1950, in Waterloo, Iowa, U. S. A. Reared in the rural, farm community of Dike, Iowa, his post-high school education includes the study of philosophy at Central College in Pella, Iowa, where he was awarded the Bachelor of Arts degree (*magna cum laude*) in 1972; the study of theology at New Brunswick Theological Seminary in New Brunswick, New Jersey, where in 1974 he was awarded the Master of Divinity degree (*magna cum laude*); and the continued study of theology at the State University of Leiden in the Netherlands where he completed the *doctoraal-examen* in 1977.

He is an ordained minister in the Reformed Church in America and has served as assistant pastor of the American Protestant Church of The Hague, Netherlands (1974-1975) and since 1979 as pastor of Trinity Reformed Church in North Plainfield, New Jersey. He has served as president of the Association of Religious Organizations of Plainfield, New Jersey, and currently serves as president of the Classis of Newark, chairman of the Commission on Ecumenical Life and Mission of the Particular Synod of the Mid-Atlantics, and as a member of the General Program Council of the Reformed Church in America. He is also a member of the Faith and Order Commission of the New Jersey Council of Churches and has lectured at New Brunswick Theological Seminary

Married to Janet Cole Schmitt since 1974, he is the father of two daughters, Amanda and Stephanie, and a son, Perry.

IMP/15
45г